AQA Spanish Teacher's Book

GCSE

Jean-Claude Gilles
John Halksworth
Ana Kolkowska
Libby Mitchell
Fiona Wilson

Nelson Thornes

Text © Jean-Claude Gilles, John Halksworth, Ana Kolkowska,
Libby Mitchell, Fiona Wilson 2009
Original illustrations © Nelson Thornes Ltd 2009

The right of Jean-Claude Gilles, John Halksworth, Ana Kolkowska,
Libby Mitchell and Fiona Wilson to be identified as authors of this work
has been asserted by them in accordance with the Copyright, Designs
and Patents Act 1988.

All rights reserved. No part of this publication may be reproduced or
transmitted in any form or by any means, electronic or mechanical,
including photocopy, recording or any information storage and
retrieval system, without permission in writing from the publisher or
under licence from the Copyright Licensing Agency Limited, of Saffron
House, 6–10 Kirby Street, London, EC1N 8TS.

Any person who commits any unauthorised act in relation to this
publication may be liable to criminal prosecution and civil claims for
damages.

Published in 2009 by:
Nelson Thornes Ltd
Delta Place
27 Bath Road
CHELTENHAM
GL53 7TH
United Kingdom

09 10 11 12 13 / 10 9 8 7 6 5 4 3 2 1

A catalogue record for this book is available from the British Library

ISBN 978 1 4085 0431 4

Cover photograph Photolibrary/Digital Vision

p13, 39, 85 iStockphoto.com
p63, Fotolia.com

Page make-up by GreenGate Publishing, Tonbridge, Kent

Printed and bound in Croatia by Zrinski

Contents

Introduction	4
Course components	4
AQA GCSE Spanish Student Book and kerboodle!	4
Controlled Assessment	5
Teacher's Book	5
Practice for Assessment: Listening and reading	5
Schemes of Work	6
Teaching Notes	10
Key Stage 3 Revision: Numbers, ages and days of the week; Months, dates and time; Weather and the seasons; Classroom equipment, colours; All numbers, dates; Parts of the body, frequently-used words	10

Context 1 – Lifestyle — 13

Overview and kerboodle! resources		13
Key Stage 3 Revision:	Family, pets; Food, drink and adverbs	15
Topic 1	Health	16
Topic 2	Relationships and choices	25

Context 2 – Leisure — 39

Overview and kerboodle! resources		39
Key Stage 3 Revision:	Sports and other leisure activities, fashion and clothes; Places in town, transport and compass points	41
Topic 1	Free time and the media	42
Topic 2	Holidays	54

Context 3 – Home and environment — 63

Overview and kerboodle! resources		63
Key Stage 3 Revision:	Rooms in the house, things in the house; House types and locations; Normal routine; Helping at home	65
Topic 1	Home and local area	66
Topic 2	Environment	77

Context 4 – Work and education — 85

Overview and kerboodle! resources		85
Key Stage 3 Revision:	School subjects, school buildings; Jobs and careers	87
Topic 1	School / college and future plans	88
Topic 2	Current and future jobs	95

Controlled Assessment	107
Controlled Assessment FAQs	110

Introduction

Welcome to the new AQA GCSE course material for Spanish. The Nelson Thornes approach that you have chosen will allow your students to maximise their potential, leading to improved exam performance.

Written by a team of AQA Examiners, experienced teachers and writers of Key Stage 4 materials, this is the only GCSE Spanish course to have been officially endorsed by AQA. The content is tailored precisely to the learning objectives of the specification so that it directly meets the needs of learners preparing for the AQA Spanish GCSE assessment.

The course provides an accessible, engaging and integrated learning package through its unique blend of print-based and online *kerboodle!* resources.

Course components

A fully blended print and electronic resource provides:

- A Student Book for classroom-based teaching and homework.
- A corresponding Teacher's Book.
- Extensive online electronic support through *kerboodle!* including:
  - interactive reading, listening, grammar and video-based activities (with feedback)
  - differentiated support and extension activities and worksheets for all four skills areas
  - assessment preparation and practice
  - audio and video resources.
- Audio CDs.

AQA GCSE Spanish Student Book and *kerboodle!*

The Student Book is arranged in a sequence approved by AQA which matches precisely the structure of the GCSE specification.

- The Student Book begins with a section dedicated to Key Stage 3 revision to get students up to speed before beginning the GCSE specification.
- The content is then split into four sections, one for each Context of the specification.
- Each Context is split into two Topics – each beginning with further Key Stage 3 revision material.
- The Topics are divided into sub-topics which fit the Purposes of the specification.

At the beginning of each Context you will find the sub-topics, grammar and communication strategies listed, so you can see precisely how the content you are teaching matches the GCSE specification and be sure you are covering everything your students need to know for their exams.

The features in the Student Book include:

Objetivos – listed at the start of each teaching spread, reflecting the requirements of the new GCSE.

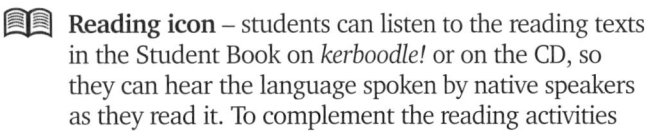

Reading icon – students can listen to the reading texts in the Student Book on *kerboodle!* or on the CD, so they can hear the language spoken by native speakers as they read it. To complement the reading activities in the Student Book, interactive reading activities are also available on *kerboodle!* along with Extension Reading worksheets (and answers) to stretch abler candidates.

Listening icon – audio material for listening (and audio for reading) activities is online and also on CD. To complement the listening activities in the Student Book, interactive listening activities are available on *kerboodle!* along with Extension Listening worksheets (and answers) to stretch abler candidates.

Video icon – videos can be found online to support the Student Book video-based activities; further interactive activities exploiting the video are also available on *kerboodle!*

Speaking icon – speaking activities in the Student Book are supported and developed by worksheets on *kerboodle!*

Further practice in Speaking skills is available through the Nelson Thornes Audio Role Play and Audio Record Tools, also available on *kerboodle!*

- Working with the audio role plays, students can listen to a conversation between two native speakers, and then they have the opportunity to replace one speaker so they can record their own responses and play them back.
- The Audio Record Tool offers students the opportunity to record free conversation, by themselves or in groups.

Writing icon – writing activities in the Student Book are supported and developed by worksheets on *kerboodle!*

> **Language structure boxes** – show students how to construct key sentences designed to help carry out the Speaking and Writing tasks.

Estrategia – outlines different strategies students can employ to help effective communication. The strategy box includes the icon of the skill it supports: Listening, Reading, Speaking or Writing.

Strategy icon – when this appears next to an activity, students should use the strategy box on that page to help them complete the task.

Consejo – provides handy hints which students can use to help with language learning.

Gramática – provides a summary of the main grammar point practised on the spread. Further grammar points are also referenced here, and students should go to the pages listed to find activities to practise these.

G **Grammar icon** – identifies activities designed to help students practise the grammar point. You will also find interactive grammar practice on *kerboodle!*

V **Vocabulary** – this indicates a vocabulary learning activity. The essential vocabulary used within each Topic is listed on Vocabulary pages. Here students can learn key words for each Topic. They can also go to *kerboodle!* to hear how the words should sound. Some words are in light grey. This is to indicate that students do not need to learn them for Listening and Reading exams, but they may find them useful for Speaking and Writing Controlled Assessments.

Audio files of the Spanish vowel sounds, patterns of letters and the Spanish alphabet are also available on *kerboodle!* to aid pronunciation.

AQA Examiner's tip – these provide hints from AQA examiners to help students with their study and prepare for their exams.

Resumen – a summary quiz at the end of each Context tests key language and grammar learnt in that Context. This is also available as a multiple-choice quiz, with feedback, on *kerboodle!*

¿Lo sabes? – an anecdotal insight into facts/figures relating to the Context.

Controlled Assessment

Our course book provides sample Controlled Assessment tasks in both Speaking and Writing for each of the four Contexts in the new specification: *Lifestyle; Leisure; Home and environment; Work and education*. Also provided are cross-Context Controlled Assessment task types that cover the entire topic range of the AQA GCSE.

Each of these tasks is accompanied by detailed guidance notes in the form of Examiner's Tips to take students through the process of developing a suitable response, outlining what points they could address in their answers, and key points to take into consideration.

Note that the Controlled Assessment tasks in the Student Book are designed as a teaching resource and not as an assessment tool. They include levels of support and guidance which are not permissible in tasks used for assessment purposes.

These tasks cannot, therefore, be submitted to AQA. For any tasks which you adapt from the tasks in the Student Book or which you devise for your students, the level of guidance and support must comply with the guidelines in the specification and in AQA's *Controlled Assessment Handbook*.

Students can go to *kerboodle!* to review sample answers for each of the tasks. These take the form of 'On Your Marks' activities, enabling students to assess the sample answers (identifying good aspects of the answers and how they could improve them). Students can then compare their analysis with the Examiner's Observations.

Teacher's Book

The Teacher's Book follows the same order of presentation as the Student Book, with four main sections – one for each Context of the specification. The Teacher's Book provides guidance notes on how to work with each of the activities in the Student Book, and presents these in the same order as they appear in the Student Book, except for Controlled Assessment which is a separate section at the back of this book (see notes below).

In addition, the Teacher's Book provides:

- Starter and Plenary activity ideas for each teaching spread of the Student Book
- The transcripts for all listening and video activities in the Student Book
- Answers for all the activities in the Student Book
- Schemes of Work (also available on *kerboodle!*)
- Cross-reference tables to show at a glance the electronic materials available on *kerboodle!* for each spread of the Student Book.

The Teacher's Book contains a section dedicated to Controlled Assessment for the new GCSE specification.

This provides a brief overview of the purpose of Controlled Assessment, with guidance on how to work with the Controlled Assessment tasks provided in this course in the classroom for practice opportunity. The Topic and Context coverage we have incorporated in these tasks is also outlined in this section.

Detailed notes on Task Setting, Task Taking and Task Marking are then presented for each Speaking and Writing Controlled Assessment. For Speaking Controlled Assessment, Task Marking is related back to the GCSE Assessment Criteria to provide further guidance on implementing this to your students' submitted work.

The final section lists Frequently Asked Questions, and their answers, which are likely to arise from students encountering Controlled Assessment for the first time.

Practice for Assessment: Listening and reading

We have provided a set of Practice Assessment question worksheets on *kerboodle!* These are written in the style of the AQA exam to provide practice of the type of questions candidates will encounter in the Listening and Reading papers.

For each of the four Contexts of the specification, there are both Foundation and Higher Practice Assessment questions for Listening and for Reading skills.

All audio and transcripts for the Listening Practice Assessment questions are located on *kerboodle!*

All audio files for the reading texts and listening activities that feature in the Student Book are available free of charge on CD upon purchase of a *kerboodle!* user licence.

AQA GCSE Spanish — Schemes of Work

Key Stage 3 Revision (Student Book pages 9–14)

Numbers, ages and days of the week; Months, dates and time; Weather and the seasons; Classroom equipment, colours; All numbers, dates; Parts of the body, frequently-used words

Context 1 – Lifestyle

Key Stage 3 Revision (Student Book pages 16–17)

Family, pets; Food, drink and adverbs

Specification Topic: Health

Specification Purpose: Healthy and unhealthy lifestyles and their consequences

Teaching spread	Student Book pages	Main grammar point	Subsidiary grammar point	Communication strategy
1.1 La dieta	18–19	Agreement of adjectives	The verb *ser*	Identifying key words when reading and listening
1.2 El bienestar	20–21	Use of verbs with the infinitive	Phrases to use with *tener*	Learning vocabulary
1.3 El tabaco	22–23	Regular -*ar* verbs in the present tense	Question formation	Giving opinions
1.4 El alcohol y las drogas	24–25	Comparative adjectives	Formation of -*er* and -*ir* verbs in the present tense	Asking and answering questions in written work

Further support: Reading and listening (Student Book pages 26–27); Grammar practice (Student Book pages 28–29); Vocabulary (Student Book pages 30–31)

Specification Topic: Relationships and choices

Specification Purpose: Relationship with family and friends; Future plans regarding: marriage / partnership; Social issues and equality

Teaching spread	Student Book pages	Main grammar point	Subsidiary grammar point	Communication strategy
1.5 Las descripciones personales	32–33	Possessive adjectives	Subject pronouns	Words which have the same or a similar form in both Spanish and English (false friends)
1.6 La situación familiar	34–35	*estar* + past participle	*desde hace* + present tense	Using verbal context to work out the meaning of new words
1.7 Las relaciones personales (Includes video)	36–37	Reflexive verbs	Conjunctions	Extending phrases in speaking and writing tasks
1.8 Los planes del futuro	38–39	*ir* + *a* + the infinitive	The conditional tense	Fluency in conversation
1.9 La igualdad para todos	40–41	Reflexive constructions	Negative forms	Checking pronunciation
1.10 La pobreza	42–43	*hay que, tener que*	*lo* + adjective	Ignoring words which are not needed for successful completion of the task

Further support: Reading and listening (Student Book pages 44–45); Grammar practice (Student Book pages 46–47); Vocabulary (Student Book pages 48–49)

Controlled Assessment – Speaking (Student Book pages 50–51)		La vida sana
Controlled Assessment – Writing (Student Book pages 52–53)		Mi familia, mis amigos y yo

Context 2 – Leisure

Key Stage 3 Revision (Student Book pages 56–57)

Sports and other leisure activities, fashion and clothes; Places in town, transport and compass points

Specification Topic: Free time and the media

Specification Purpose: Free-time activities; Shopping, money, fashion and trends; Advantages and disadvantages of new technology

Teaching spread	Student Book pages	Main grammar point	Subsidiary grammar point	Communication strategy
2.1 El tiempo libre en casa	58–59	The preterite tense of regular verbs	The use of infinitives	Improving fluency by learning complete phrases
2.2 Fuera de casa	60–61	Using irregular preterites: *ir, ser*	Time and place expressions	Using time expressions to recognise whether a statement is in the past or present tense
2.3 ¿En qué gastas tu dinero?	62–63	Direct object pronouns	Gerunds	Colloquial expressions
2.4 ¿Te gusta estar de moda? (Includes video)	64–65	Demonstrative pronouns	Indefinite adjectives	Expressing preference
2.5 Los jóvenes y la tecnología	66–67	Indirect object pronouns	Comparative and superlative adverbs	Justifying opinions

Further support: Reading and listening (Student Book pages 68–69); Grammar practice (Student Book pages 70–71); Vocabulary (Student Book pages 72–73)

Specification Topic: Holidays

Specification Purpose: Plans, preferences, experiences; What to see and getting around

2.6 Las vacaciones	74–75	Irregular preterite verbs	The passive voice	Showing ability in the language
2.7 ¿Adónde vas?	76–77	The immediate future	Disjunctive pronouns	Common prefixes between Spanish and English
2.8 He ido a la fiesta	78–79	The perfect tense	Interrogative pronouns	Using time phrases in written work
2.9 ¡Vamos de viaje!	80–81	Imperative verb forms	How to say 'Let's ...'	High numbers and 24-hour time

Further support: Reading and listening (Student Book pages 82–83); Grammar practice (Student Book pages 84–85); Vocabulary (Student Book pages 86–87)

Controlled Assessment – Speaking (Student Book pages 88–89)		Las vacaciones
Controlled Assessment – Writing (Student Book pages 90–91)		El tiempo libre

Context 3 – Home and environment

Key Stage 3 Revision (Student Book pages 94–95; 96–97)

Rooms in the house, things in the house; House types and locations;
Normal routine; Helping at home

Specification Topic: Home and local area

Specification Purpose: Special occasions celebrated in the home; Home, town, neighbourhood and region, where it is and what it is like

Teaching spread	Student Book pages	Main grammar point	Subsidiary grammar point	Communication strategy
3.1 De fiesta	98–99	The imperfect tense	When to use the imperfect and preterite tenses	Making use of social and cultural contexts to work out meaning
3.2 ¿Cómo es tu casa?	100–101	Possessive pronouns	Interrogative adjectives	Using quantifiers and intensifiers
3.3 ¿Cómo es tu barrio?	102–103	Relative pronouns	Using *hay* and *había*	Using common patterns within Spanish
3.4 Mi región	104–105	Describing past weather conditions	The imperfect tense	Recognising percentages, common fractions and temperatures

Further support: Reading and listening (Student Book pages 106–107); Grammar practice (Student Book pages 108–109); Vocabulary (Student Book pages 110–111)

Specification Topic: Environment

Specification Purpose: Current problems facing the planet; Being environmentally friendly within the home and local area

Teaching spread	Student Book pages	Main grammar point	Subsidiary grammar point	Communication strategy
3.5 La contaminació (Includes video)	112–113	*por* and *para*	The perfect tense	Learning complete phrases to promote fluency
3.6 El futuro del planeta	114–115	The future tense	Avoiding the passive	Using acquired knowledge of Spanish to express ideas
3.7 Cómo cuidar el medio ambiente	116–117	Verbs of obligation	Indefinite pronouns	Introducing variety to enhance work

Further support: Reading and listening (Student Book pages 118–119); Grammar practice (Student Book pages 120–121); Vocabulary (Student Book pages 122–123)

Controlled Assessment – Speaking (Student Book pages 124–125)	El medio ambiente
Controlled Assessment – Writing (Student Book pages 126–127)	Donde vivo

Context 4 – Work and education

Key Stage 3 Revision (Student Book pages 130–131)
School subjects, school buildings; Jobs and careers

Specification Topic: School / college and future plans
Specification Purpose: What school / college is like; Pressures and problems

Teaching spread	Student Book pages	Main grammar point	Subsidiary grammar point	Communication strategy
4.1 Bienvenidos al colegio	132–133	Impersonal verbs	Demonstrative adjectives	Developing answers to questions
4.2 Colegios británicos y españoles	134–135	Using different tenses	Comparative adjectives	Identifying different tenses
4.3 ¡Cuánto estrés!	136–137	*desde hacía* and the imperfect tense	The subjunctive in exclamatory phrases	Providing all the information requested
4.4 ¿Qué piensas de tu colegio?	138–139	The conditional tense	Adjectival agreement	Looking for clues to help understanding

Further support: Reading and listening (Student Book pages 140–141); Grammar practice (Student Book pages 142–143); Vocabulary (Student Book pages 144–145)

Specification Topic: Current and future jobs
Specification Purpose: Looking for and getting a job; Advantages and disadvantages of different jobs

Teaching spread	Student Book pages	Main grammar point	Subsidiary grammar point	Communication strategy
4.5 El trabajo a tiempo parcial	146–147	The pluperfect tense	Use of *cuyo*	Including different tenses in speaking and writing
4.6 Buscando trabajo (Includes video)	148–149	Asking questions using the preterite tense	Use of *usted / ustedes*	Making use of context to work out meaning
4.7 Poniéndose en contacto	150–151	Using *quisiera*	Possessive adjectives	Using knowledge of grammatical categories
4.8 Después de los exámenes	152–153	Imperatives	Question formation using prepositions	Avoiding repetition of phrases and vocabulary
4.9 Comparando empleos diferentes	154–155	Irregular adverbs	Comparative and superlative adverbs	Checking grammar in written work

Further support: Reading and listening (Student Book pages 156–157); Grammar practice (Student Book pages 158–159); Vocabulary (Student Book pages 160–161)

Controlled Assessment – Speaking (Student Book pages 162–163)	Las prácticas laborales
Controlled Assessment – Writing (Student Book pages 164–165)	Mi colegio
Controlled Assessment FAQs – Speaking (Student Book page 167)	
Controlled Assessment FAQs – Writing (Student Book page 169)	
Cross-Context Controlled Assessment – Speaking (Student Book page 170)	Mi vida
Cross-Context Controlled Assessment – Writing (Student Book page 171)	¡Los jóvenes no somos así!

Page 9

Revision
Numbers, ages and days of the week

kerboodle! • Audio files for core reading texts

1 📖 🎧 Match up each person with the correct photo.

Revision of understanding numbers in written form, supported by the adjacent *Vocabulario*.

Answers: **1** F,   **2** B,   **3** C,   **4** D

2 📖 💬 Read out the following telephone numbers in Spanish.

Revision of pronouncing numbers, supported by the adjacent *Vocabulario*, the Pronunciation guidance box and the example.

3 ✏️ Put the days of the week into the correct order, starting with Monday.

Revision of the days of the week.

4 ✏️ Design a programme for a week of activities for a Spanish exchange visit, writing the days (and activities if you can) in Spanish.

Consolidation of the days of the week; you could prepare students by doing a whole-class English–Spanish matching task or picture prompting for the activities so that they can produce the complete poster in Spanish.

Page 10

Revision
Months, dates and time

kerboodle! • Audio files for core reading texts

1 📖 🎧 Read the information in the table above and answer the following questions.

Revision of the months in the context of special occasions, supported by the *Vocabulario*. For question 1 you could ask students to give the date as well as the occasion, where it is stated.

Answers:

1 1 January: New Year's Day, 14 February: Valentine's Day, a Sunday in March: Mother's Day, 1 April: April Fool's Day, 1 May: May Bank Holiday (Labour Day), June: Father's Day, 5 November: Guy Fawkes (Bonfire Night), 25 December: Christmas Day.

2 school holidays

3 September and October

2 ✏️ Write a list of birthdays that are important to you. You can write the numbers in figures.

You could set a minimum or approximate number of dates that students should write; they can model their sentences on the examples.

> A summary of how to tell the time in Spanish, to support activity 3. This includes how to say 'at' a time using the 24-hour clock, which you may want to spend some time on before students try the activity.

Gramática

3 ✏️ Match up each time mentioned with the correct clock face.

Revision of the 12-hour and 24-hour clock, supported by the *Gramática* box. Some of the clock faces (A, B, G) are not used, so you could ask students to tell you the times they show, in 12-hour clock format (A *Son las ocho y media*, B *Son las nueve menos cuarto*, G *Son las cinco menos diez*).

To consolidate the 24-hour clock you could ask students to make 'announcements' of the arrival or departure of trains at each of the times shown (as per the wording for question 5). It could be made more fun by prompting with Spanish place names if you have a map on display.

Answers: **1** E,   **2** D,   **3** H,   **4** F,   **5** I,   **6** C

Page 11

Revision
Weather and the seasons

kerboodle! • Audio files for core reading texts

1a 📖 🎧 Match up each picture with the correct expression in the box.

Revision of weather descriptions in the present tense (including present continuous: see *Gramática* box below).

Answers:

A 7,   B 4,   C 10,   D 8,   E 9,
F 1 or 5,   G 6,   H 2,   I 5,   J 3

1b 📖 🎧 Read sentences a–d and answer questions 1–4 that follow, in English.

Consolidation of understanding of weather phrases in the context of saying what you would like to do, are doing or are going to do, so that tenses get some receptive practice too.

Answers:

1 It's raining.   2 It's foggy.
3 It's snowing.   4 There's a storm.

Revision 11

2 ✏️ Look at the pictures. For each one, write a sentence in the present continuous tense describing the weather and what is happening.

Suggested answers:

1 Estoy / Está comiendo un helado porque hace calor. / Hace calor así que estoy / está comiendo un helado.
2 Estoy / Está tomando el sol porque hace sol. / Hace sol así que estoy / está tomando el sol.
3 Estoy / Está comprando un paraguas porque está lloviendo. / Está lloviendo así que estoy / está comprando un paraguas.
4 Estoy / Está jugando al tenis porque hace buen tiempo. / Hace buen tiempo así que estoy / está jugando al tenis.
5 Estamos / Están haciendo un muñeco de nieve porque está nevando. / Está nevando / Nieva así que estamos / están haciendo un muñeco de nieve.

> **Gramática**
> A summary of how to form the present continuous tense and when to use it. Students should revise the different parts of the verb *estar* and then practise forming the gerund of the key verbs *comer, tomar, comprar, jugar* and *hacer* before doing activity 2.

3 💬 Working in pairs, look at the table below. Partner A asks a question about the information in it and Partner B gives the answer. Then swap roles.

Page 12

Revision

Classroom equipment, colours

kerboodle! • Audio files for core reading texts

1a ✏️ Copy the sentences and fill in the gaps with *el, la, los* or *las*.

Revision of noun gender and definite articles, supported by the *Gramática* box.

Answers: **1** la, **2** las, **3** el, **4** los

> **Gramática**
> A reminder of definite and indefinite articles and their agreement with the number and gender of their noun, to support activities 1 and 2.

1b ✏️ Match up the Spanish sentences 1–4 in Activity 1a with their English translations below.

Answers: **1** d, **2** b, **3** a, **4** c

---

2 📖 🎧 Match up each sentence with the correct picture.

You could ask students to read the sentences aloud and to translate them into English either before or after they attempt the matching process. Note that there is one spare picture.

Answers: **1** D, **2** B, **3** C

> **Gramática**
> A reminder of how to use colour adjectives in Spanish, to support activity 3.

3 ✏️ Look at the pictures. Which box, A or B, does each item 1–8 appear in?

Students simply write A or B to indicate which box contains each item – the colours must be correct as well as the items.

Answers: **1** B, **2** A, **3** B, **4** A, **5** A, **6** B, **7** B, **8** B

Page 13

Revision

All numbers, dates

kerboodle! • Audio files for core reading texts

1 ✏️ 💬 Work in pairs. Partner A writes down six numbers and reads them out. Partner B writes them down. Check the numbers together, then swap roles.

Make it clear that the numbers should be written down as figures! Demonstrate it with the whole class first. Students should use the *Vocabulario* box for preparation but as they do the activity itself, the partner reading the number out should have access to the list, but the partner writing the figures should not.

> **Gramática**
> A summary of how to write out numbers in Spanish, including higher numbers, to be used in conjunction with the *Vocabulario* to support activities 2–4.

2 📖 🎧 Match up the dates.

Practice in recognising dates when written out in Spanish. The *Vocabulario* and the *Gramática* support this activity. More practice could be carried out using a Spanish diary or calendar as a prompt.

Answers: **1** c,   **2** a,   **3** b

> **Gramática**
> A brief reminder of how dates are written in Spanish, which students can refer to for help with activities 2–4.

3 📖 🎧 Read the bubbles and answer the questions in English.

Students now read three speech bubbles referring to dates in the context of special occasions.

Answers:

1a 8 July		**1b** 7 July
2a 2 August		**2b** 1 August
3a 3 September		**3b** 29 August

4 ✏️ Look at the following pictures and dates. Use the words under each picture to write a description of what happens on each date.

You could expand this form of practice by using photos (e.g. of flowers, a sporting activity, a place which students are likely to be able to name (e.g. *el cine*) and a Spanish calendar or diary, to show pairs of prompts in response to which they must produce a sentence saying what happens on a given date.

Suggested answers:

El ocho de abril abre el restaurante nuevo con una cena especial.

El diecisiete de agosto voy a ir de vacaciones en avión a Mallorca.

Page 14

Revision

Parts of the body, frequently-used words

kerboodle! • Audio files for core reading texts

> **Gramática**
> A summary of what imperatives look like in Spanish, to support the activities on this page.

1a 📖 🎧 Read the instructions and match up each set with the correct picture.

Revision of the language for parts of the body, supported by the *Vocabulario*. Make sure also that students remember the words for 'left' and 'right' before they start to decipher the instructions. They will also need to understand the imperatives, supported by the *Gramática* box.

Answers: **1** C,   **2** B,   **3** A

1b ✏️ 💬 Work in pairs. Write down some instructions, using words from the box below. Take turns to give and carry out the instructions. Make up some longer instructions using the joining words in the box.

The language structure box allows students to invent their own instructions without needing to remember or work out the verb forms, though abler students may be able to add some more instructions of their own (sticking to positive ones only to avoid the subjunctive trap!).

1 Lifestyle

Health
Healthy and unhealthy lifestyles and their consequences

Reading and listening

KS3 Revision
Family, pets; Food, drink, adverbs

Online materials
- Audio files for core reading texts

1.1 La dieta
- Making adjectives agree
- Picking out the key words when reading and listening

- Audio file for core reading text
- Audio file and transcript for listening activity 2
- Reading activity: *La dieta*
- Grammar activity Using adjectives, nouns and simple verbs
- Writing worksheet
- Foundation reading worksheet
- Extension reading worksheet

1.2 El bienestar
- Using verbs with the infinitive
- Testing yourself on the meanings of words

- Audio file for core reading text
- Audio file and transcript for listening activity 4
- Listening activity and transcript: *La vida sana*
- Grammar activity: Using key verbs with the infinitive
- Speaking worksheet
- Extension reading worksheet
- Foundation listening worksheet
- Audio file and transcript for foundation listening activity

1.3 El tabaco
- Using regular -*ar* verbs in the present tense
- Giving opinions

- Audio file for core reading text
- Audio file and transcript for listening activity 4
- Listening activity and transcript: *La prohibición del tabaco*
- Grammar activity: Practising the endings for regular -*ar* verbs
- Writing worksheet
- Extension listening worksheet
- Audio file and transcript for extension listening activity
- Audio role play activity

1.4 El alcohol y las drogas
- Making comparisons
- Asking and answering questions in written work

- Audio file for core reading text
- Audio file and transcript for listening activity 3
- Reading activity: *El alcohol y las drogas*
- Grammar activity: Practising comparatives
- Speaking worksheet
- Extension listening worksheet
- Audio file and transcript for extension listening activity

Health

- Audio file for core reading text
- Audio file and transcript for listening activity 3

Grammar

Health
- *Ser* – to be
- Adjectives
- *Tener* – to have
- How to form questions with verbs
- Regular -*er* verbs
- Regular -*ir* verbs

Vocabulary

Health
- MP3 files for each vocabulary list

Relationships and choices

Relationships with family and friends

1.5	**Las descripciones personales** ■ Saying 'my, your, his / her, our, their' ■ Avoiding being caught out by false friends	• Audio file for core reading text • Audio file and transcript for listening activity 3 • Reading activity: *Las descripciones personales* • Grammar activity: Using possessive adjectives • Writing worksheet • Extension reading worksheet • Foundation reading worksheet
1.6	**La situación familiar** ■ Using *estar* + past participle ■ Working out the meaning of new words from the context	• Audio file for core reading text • Audio file and transcript for listening activity 3 • Listening activity and transcript: *La situación familiar* • Grammar activity: Practising the endings for the verb *estar* • Speaking worksheet • Extension reading worksheet
1.7	**Las relaciones personales** ■ Using reflexive verbs ■ Extending phrases in speaking and writing tasks	• Audio file for core reading text • Video and transcript for listening activity 2 • Listening activity to accompany video • Grammar activity: Using reflexive verbs • Speaking worksheet • Extension listening worksheet • Audio file and transcript for extension listening activit

Future plans regarding marriage / partnership

1.8	**Los planes del futuro** ■ Talking about what you are going to do ■ Keeping your conversation going	• Audio file for core reading text • Audio file and transcript for listening activity 2 • Reading activity: *Los planes del futuro* • Grammar activity: Using the verb *ir* to form the immediate future tense • Writing worksheet • Extension listening worksheet • Audio file and transcript for extension listening activit • Foundation listening worksheet • Audio file and transcript for foundation listening worksheet • Audio role play activity

Social issues and equality

1.9	**La igualdad para todos** ■ Using reflexive phrases like *se puede* ■ Checking pronunciation	• Audio file for core reading text • Audio file and transcript for listening activity 3 • Reading activity: *La igualdad para todos* • Grammar activity: Using reflexive phrases • Speaking worksheet • Extension listening worksheet • Audio file and transcript for extension listening activit
1.10	**La pobreza** ■ Saying what you have to do or must do ■ Ignoring words You don't need to understand	• Audio file for core reading text • Audio file and transcript for listening activity 3 • Listening activity and transcript: *La pobreza* • Grammar activity: Using the verbs *tener que*; *deber* an *hay que* • Writing worksheet • Extension reading worksheet

Reading and listening

Relationships and choices	• Audio file for core reading text • Audio file and transcript for listening activity 2

Grammar

Relationships and choices	
■ Subject pronouns ■ *desde hace* ■ Linking words	■ Saying 'would like' ■ Forming the negative ■ *lo* + adjective

Vocabulary

Relationships and choices	• MP3 files for each vocabulary list

Summative assessment

Lifestyle	• Interactive multiple-choice quiz

The opening page for Context 1, Lifestyle, provides a quick-reference overview of how the teaching spreads, grammar and strategies within this Context in the Student Book map to the Topics and Purposes of Context 1 in the GCSE specification. Also included here is an overview of the online resources available for each of these spreads in the Student Book.

Context 1 Lifestyle 15

Page 16

Revision

Family, pets

kerboodle! • Audio files for core reading texts

1a ✏️ Look at the family tree and fill in each gap a–f with the name of the correct family member.

The vocabulary needed is all available in the *Vocabulario* on the page but students could attempt the task initially without reference to this list (i.e. with it covered up).

Answers:

a abuelo	b madre	c tío
d hermanastro	e prima	f primo

1b ✏️ 💬 Work in pairs. You both make up an imaginary family and write a description of it following this example.

Students carry out a spoken pairwork as described on the page, and / or produce a written sentence. If you think it is necessary for some students, indicate which words they could replace in the example: depending on the students' ability, they could replace names only, or the family member nouns, and could be asked to add a given number of additional members.

2a 📖 🎧 Read the poems and work out which three unusual pets are mentioned.

Students need to use the process of elimination by recognising the usual animal nouns (most are in the *Vocabulario* on this page) and working out that the three odd ones out are *un delfín*, *una pantera*, and *una leona*. It would be good practice of students' skills in recognising cognates to work out what these animals must be.

Answers: un delfín, una pantera, una leona

2b ✏️ Write a description of some real or imaginary pets, including colours, size and character. You could write it as a poem.

Less able students could be supported by being supplied with a couple of the poems from page 16, with the articles, nouns and adjectival phrases blanked out. With or without this support, remind students that it is important to include the indefinite article using the correct gender with each noun that they choose. Ask higher-ability students to include at least one animal that is not on the page, by researching one of their own, using a dictionary for support.

2c 💬 Read out your description and get a partner to draw it.

This could be a timed exercise, with pairs swapping roles. Alternatively it could be a useful reading exercise, with students exchanging their written descriptions and drawing the animal(s) they are given. A third student could then 'mark' the drawing, awarding a point for each correct characteristic.

Page 17

Revision

Food, drink and adverbs

kerboodle! • Audio files for core reading texts

1 📖 🎧 Read what Lucía, Eduardo and Margarita say they <u>like</u> to eat and choose the letters of the correct pictures from the box below. Then find what they <u>don't like</u> to eat.

Students should write the three speakers' names and make a list of the correct letters for each one. Make sure they have understood that they are to note only the items that the speakers say they like, not all the items they mention. Then follow up by asking students to tell you the letters of the items each speaker says they do *not* like.

Answers:
  Lucía likes: C, H, J
  Margarita likes: G, I
  Eduardo likes: B, F, M
  Lucía dislikes: D, L
  Margarita dislikes: A
  Eduardo dislikes: K, N

> **Gramática**
> A reminder of how to use *gustar* (with *me* only, but singular and plural forms). Students will need to refer to this reminder to help them with activity 2.

2 ✏️ Write two lists, saying what you do and don't like to eat and drink.

Students should try to include other food and drink that they already know, and they should include *el, la, los* or *las* with each one. You could set a time limit and / or ask students to work in groups to give this a competitive edge. Abler students could use *me encanta(n)* as well as *me gusta(n)*.

> **Gramática**
> A reminder of how adverbs work in Spanish. Students will need to refer to this reminder and to the lists of verbs and adverbs to help them with activity 3.

3 ✏️ Make up some sentences of your own containing adverbs. Use the suggestions in the grammar box and the list of verbs and adverbs below.

Tell students to describe their mealtime routines, pointing out that the vocabulary they need for meals is in the *Vocabulario* on the page. Give students a couple of examples to start them off, highlighting the adverb in each one, e.g.

Tomo el desayuno **rápidamente**.

Normalmente bebo té.

Pages 18–19

1.1 La dieta

Healthy and unhealthy lifestyles and their consequences

Subject	Discussing different types of diet
G 1	Making adjectives agree
G 2	Learning more parts of the verb *ser* (to be)
	Picking out the key words when reading and listening

kerboodle!
- Audio file for core reading text
- Audio file and transcript for listening activity 2
- Reading activity: *La dieta*
- Grammar activity: Using adjectives, nouns and simple verbs
- Writing worksheet
- Foundation reading worksheet
- Extension reading worksheet

Starter activity

Students could write a list in two columns of all the healthy food and unhealthy food they can remember, using these texts (perhaps displayed on the board), visuals or plastic food. They could work in pairs or teams and get a point for each correct answer.

Core reading text

Four young people describe their diets. As well as key language for describing healthy and unhealthy diets, the text includes many examples of the main *Gramática* points: adjective agreement and the use of *mucho*, both as an adverb and as an adjective agreeing with its noun. The positive and negative adjectives in the text such as *sana, ideal, bueno*, are the focus of the *Estrategia* on the spread.

If you wish you could also use examples from the text to present / practise the secondary *Gramática* point, (present tense) forms of the verb *ser*.

The reading text is also available online as an audio file.

Estrategia

The *Estrategia* focuses on picking out key words, in particular positive and negative adjectives. This should help students to identify healthy and unhealthy diets as described in the core text for reading activities 1a and 1b, and the audio for listening activity 2.
After doing listening activity 2, students could listen again to the audio for examples of the use of *poco* and *demasiado*. Tell them to pay close attention to Juan and José and see if they can identify the examples for you and explain the meaning.

1a Match up each photo with the correct speech bubble. Write the name of the person and 1, 2, 3 or 4.

Students read the texts and match them up with the correct photo. This is to understand the gist of the texts.

Answers: Javier: 3, Luisa: 4, Elena: 1, Antonio: 2

1b Write the name of the person who …

Students have to read the texts in more detail and decide which person fits the description. For some students it may be helpful to go over the meanings of the key structures and vocabulary in the *Gramática* and language boxes first.

Answers:

1 Antonio 2 Javier 3 Elena 4 Luisa
5 Antonio 6 Elena 7 Antonio

2 *Transcript:*

Ana: Me encanta la comida rápida y voy mucho a las pizzerías y hamburgueserías con mis amigos.

Carolina: Mi dieta es sana porque como mucha fruta y verduras – cinco porciones al día. No tomo comida basura.

Juan: Tomo mucha comida italiana y china. Sé que tiene mucho azúcar y mucha grasa y es poco sana, pero no me gustan nada las verduras ni la ensalada ni la fruta. ¡Qué asco!

María: Normalmente como un poco de todo. Tomo pescado, verduras … bueno, cosas sanas, ¿no? Y también me gusta comer patatas fritas, perritos calientes, dulces, que es normal para los jóvenes.

José: Sé que una dieta equilibrada es importante, pero preparar platos sanos como legumbres, pollo y carne es difícil y lleva demasiado tiempo. Soy estudiante y para mí la comida rápida es barata y fácil.

2 Listen to some people talking about their diet. Decide if they eat a healthy diet, an unhealthy diet or both. Write notes in English to back up your answer.

Students have to decide if the diet they hear described is healthy, unhealthy or both. They should read the *Estrategia* box first in order to help them pick out the key words. Afterwards they could read the transcript and underline the positive and negative clues in the texts.

Answers:

1	Carolina	H	Eats (5 portions of) fruit and veg **or** Doesn't eat junk food
2	Juan	U	Eats a lot of (Chinese / Italian) food with sugar and fat **or** Doesn't like fruit, salad or veg
3	María	H + U	Eats fish / veg **and** chips / hot dogs / sweets
4	José	U	Eats fast food **or** no time to prepare veg / chicken / meat / healthy food

Context 1 Lifestyle 17

The *Gramática* presents the basic rules for making adjectives agree. Before they study it, ask students to find noun–adjective pairs in the core reading text on page 18 and to try to work out how the noun's gender and number affects the adjectives. Activity 3 practises the rules. Since *ser* is being used here with adjectives, the secondary *Gramática* point is to consolidate parts of this verb.

3 **G** Copy the sentences and fill in the gaps with the appropriate adjective and ending from the list below.

Students should read the *Gramática* box first, then copy and complete the sentences with the most appropriate word from the list.

Answers:

1 sano	**2** ideales	**3** delicioso
4 malas	**5** picantes	**6** típica

The *Consejo* explains that *mucho* must agree when used with a noun. Ask students to give you examples from the core reading text. They could do this in four groups A, B, C, D, each group focusing on one of the 'bubbles'. This should then be applied as they work on activity 4.

4 Work in pairs. Take turns to be A and B. It is healthy-eating week at school.

Students need to know all of the food items in the pictures before starting this speaking task.

They work in pairs taking turns to be A and B, changing the words underlined to fit the pictures. They can award up to 10 points for being healthy. As an extension activity they could add reasons as to why the food is healthy or unhealthy, using the phrases in the language structure box and giving their opinion.

Plenary activity

To reinforce the vocabulary and structures either in pairs or two class teams, students could play an 'I went shopping' game, using different starting phrases. When one student / team runs out of ideas, the other student / team wins.

e.g. Team / Student A: '*Mi dieta es muy sana porque … como fruta*'

Team / Student B: '*Mi dieta es muy sana porque … como fruta y como pescado*'

Team / Student A: '*Mi dieta es muy sana porque … como fruta, como pescado y bebo agua*', etc.

Other starting phrases could be:

'*Mi dieta es un desastre porque …*'

'*Como verduras porque …*'

'*No me gusta la comida rápida porque …*'

Pages 20–21

1.2 El bienestar

Healthy and unhealthy lifestyles and their consequences

Subject	Discussing well-being and what can prevent it
G 1	Using verbs with the infinitive
G 2	Learning the verb *tener* (to have) and phrases to use it with
	Testing yourself on meanings of words

kerboodle!
- Audio file for core reading text
- Audio file and transcript for listening activity 4
- Listening activity and transcript: *La vida sana*
- Grammar activity: Using key verbs with the infinitive
- Speaking worksheet
- Extension reading worksheet
- Foundation listening worksheet
- Audio file and transcript for foundation listening activity

Starter activity

Ask students to predict which healthy or unhealthy activities might be mentioned in the texts before looking at them. This could be done in Spanish or English. They could do it in pairs or teams and write them on A3 paper. Students could then skim read the texts to find out if their predictions were right and get a point for each correct answer.

1 **V** Choose which statement you agree with most and write down **a**, **b** or **c**.

Students choose the option they most agree with: a, b or c. They could refer to the vocabulary list on pages 30–31. The activity provides a lead-in to the core reading text as well as an introduction to the *Gramática* point, using verbs with the infinitive.

Core reading text

Three young people describe their attitudes and habits concerning healthy or unhealthy lifestyles, particularly diet and exercise; each has a *Conclusión* commenting on what they say. The three texts representing healthy (Gabriela), unhealthy (Marta) and mixed (Juan) attitudes tie in with the a, b, c, scoring system in activity 1. They also contain many examples of the *Gramática* point, using verbs with the infinitive, including *tener que*.

The *Estrategia* on testing the meanings of words could be applied to the text, working on cognates and near-cognates such as *mantenerse*, *odio*, *activo*.

The reading text is also available online as an audio file.

2a Read the article and decide if the following statements are true (T), false (F) or not mentioned (?).

Students read the descriptions and comments about the three people's lifestyles and decide if the statements are true, false or not mentioned. They could use the language structure box and the vocabulary list on pages 30–31 to help. The activity requires close reading and some inference, which will require students to grasp fully the meaning of the verb + infinitive structures in the texts.

Answers: 1 T,   2 T,   3 F,   4 ?,   5 T

2b What three pieces of advice are given to Marta and Juan?

Students now focus on the *Conclusión* commentaries which follow Marta and Juan's statements, and have to list three pieces of advice given to each of them. This involves understanding *tener que* structures.

Answers:

Marta: any three of the following: eat more healthily, sleep more, do more exercise (with friends), drink fewer fizzy drinks, change her habits now / immediately.

Juan: any three of the following: do more to be fit, do more active activities (as part of daily routine), eat fruit, eat vegetables, make an effort.

> **Gramática**
> You could use activities 3a and 3b, before working on the *Gramática*, to consolidate recognition and understanding of structures using verbs with the infinitive. Then ask students to come up with more possible infinitive endings for the verbs listed in the *Gramática*, before they do activity 3c which brings it all together.
> The secondary grammar point, using *tener*, can be drawn out using examples from the reading text or the listening transcript (particularly the last text which contains three different uses of *tener*).

3a Make a list of all the infinitives used in the magazine article.

Students have to identify the infinitives used in the reading texts.

Answers: comer, beber, mantenerme, dormir, estar, llevar, hacer, salir, jugar, morir, tener, cambiar, fumar, estudiar, practicar, motivarme

3b Match up these key Spanish verbs with their English equivalent.

The activity tests students' understanding of verbs that are frequently used with infinitives.

Answers: 1 d,   2 c,   3 b,   4 e,   5 a

3c Translate these sentences into Spanish.

Students have to use the key verbs from 3b and the infinitives from 3a in order to translate the sentences into Spanish. They could refer to the *Gramática* box for help. The main verbs and infinitives could be displayed on an interactive whiteboard or the students could make cards / pieces of paper with Spanish on one side and English on the other in order to match them up.

Answers:

1 Detesto / Odio comer fruta, pero me gusta beber agua.
2 Es importante dormir bien y estar en forma.
3 Tengo que hacer más deporte.
4 Se puede evitar malos hábitos.

4 Transcript:

1
Male speaker 1:   Aquí tienen al médico Miguel para escuchar sus problemas.
Female speaker 1:   Buenos días, Doctor Miguel. Soy adicta al chocolate. Me gusta muchísimo y ahora es como una obsesión.
Male speaker 1:   Sí, sí. Para algunas personas es muy adictivo. Pues mira. La solución no es difícil: no tienes que comprar chocolate y así no puedes comerlo.

2
Male speaker 2:   ¡Hola, Miguel! Para mí el problema es el tabaco. No quiero fumar, pero mi amigo fuma.
Male speaker 1:   Sí, es difícil. Es necesario hablar con tu amigo y decir 'si tú quieres fumar, es tu decisión, pero no me gusta el tabaco.'

3
Female speaker 2:   Miguel, no puedo dormir. Me gusta acostarme temprano, pero luego es imposible dormir.
Male speaker 1:   ¿Te gusta beber café?
Female speaker 2:   Sí, mucho.
Male speaker 1:   El café es muy malo porque es un estimulante. Es importante evitar el café por la tarde.

4
Female speaker 3:   Tengo dolor de cabeza todo el tiempo. Me siento realmente enferma.
Male speaker 1:   ¿Tienes sueño también?
Female speaker 3:   Sí, pero dormir no es un problema. Me gusta dormir ocho horas cada noche.
Male speaker 1:   Bueno. Tienes que beber más agua. Es necesario beber ocho vasos cada día.

> **Estrategia**
> Practical hints on how to use similarities between Spanish and English words to work out the meanings of words, and how to memorise and test yourself on key words.
> This should help students to pinpoint the information they need to answer the questions in activities 4a and 4b.

4a People call *el médico Miguel* on his radio show. What are they worried about? Choose one option from this list for each of the four people.

In this first listening activity, students concentrate on identifying which problem each person is worried about. Tell students to listen carefully to the first sentence in each conversation.

Answers: 1 diet,   2 smoking,   3 sleeping,   4 feeling ill

Context 1 Lifestyle 19

4b Listen again. What advice does Miguel give to each person?

Students now focus on the doctor's advice to each person. As in activity 4a, the language contains examples of either a verb + infinitive structure or a use of *tener* which students need to understand in order to answer the questions.

Answers:
1. doesn't have to buy chocolate
2. needs to talk to friend, tell friend he doesn't like smoking
3. has to avoid drinking coffee in the afternoon / evening
4. has to drink more water / needs to drink 8 glasses of water a day

5a Pick a team: the 'Superfits' or the 'Sofa Slobs'.

Students have to prepare a description of what they do as a 'superfit' person or a 'sofa slob', say something positive about themselves and something negative about their opponent. This is also preparation for the speaking activity 5b. It could be done as a whole-class exercise if it is felt the students need more support, using the key verbs and infinitives from the grammar activities. Also refer to the *Consejo* box to help with forming the second person of the verb. The students could then choose which arguments they wish to use.

The Writing worksheet also provides more support and ideas.

> **Consejo**
> A reminder of the typical -s ending of second person singular verb forms. There are many examples of these in the core reading text which you could ask students to point out or list, and they could practise quick question-and-answer exchanges in pairs, using and adapting structures from the *Gramática* or the *Consejo* boxes.

5b Use your lists to argue with the other team and prove that your lifestyle is the best. You can do this in pairs or groups.

Students now use the ideas they have written in activity 5a to conduct a debate between the two teams.

Plenary activity

Give students a list of infinitives e.g. *comer; beber; hacer; practicar; evitar*. They have three minutes to make as many sentences as possible with them using the key verbs they have learnt in this unit. They could also translate them into English.

Pages 22–23

1.3 El tabaco

Healthy and unhealthy lifestyles and their consequences

Subject	Discussing who smokes and the consequences
G 1	Using regular -*ar* verbs in the present tense
G 2	Learning more about how to ask questions
	Giving opinions

kerboodle!
- Audio file for core reading text
- Audio file and transcript for listening activity 4
- Listening activity and transcript: *La prohibición del tabaco*
- Grammar activity: Practising the endings for regular -*ar* verbs
- Writing worksheet
- Extension listening worksheet
- Audio file and transcript for extension listening worksheet
- Audio role play activity

1 V Look at the two texts and write down all the words you can find that relate directly to smoking.

As a starter vocabulary-building activity, students should skim read the texts to find the key words.

To make further use of the text and revise use of verb + infinitive from the previous spread, ask questions about where you can / can't smoke, according to the text *La Ley Anti-tabaco*, e.g. *Soy fumador(a) y estoy en España. ¿Puedo fumar en un bar? ¿Puedo fumar en un colegio?* etc.

Answers: el tabaco, fumadores, fuman, fumadoras, fumar, fumador, no fumador

2 Read the two texts again and answer the following questions in English.

Students reread the texts in more detail to identify specific facts and figures.

Answers:
1. 8–10 million
2. They die (from smoking)
3. Number of women smokers has doubled in last 25 years / 31.3% of women smoke / 30% of pregnant women smoke / at the age of 13 more girls smoke than boys (any 2 facts)
4. workplaces / public places / bars and restaurants more than 100 m^2

Core reading text

A short article about levels of smoking in Spain and restrictions on smoking in public leads into three young people's opinions about smoking. The text includes several forms of *fumar* in the present tense, reflecting the *Gramática*, as well as a couple of examples of the *Estrategia* opinion phrases.

You could ask students to build on their '*tabaco*' vocabulary list started in activity 1 by skimming the text for more key language to do with smoking and writing these down.

The reading text is also available online as an audio file.

3 📖 🎧 Match up each person with the correct statement. Write A (Ana), J (Javier) or N (Nuria).

The questions focus students' attention on the main points of the speakers' opinions.

Answers:

1 A (Ana)
2 N (Nuria)
3 J (Javier)
4 N (Nuria)
5 J (Javier)

4 🎧 *Transcript:*

1

| Male speaker 1: | Recordamos a nuestros clientes que éste es un restaurante para no fumadores y aquí está prohibido fumar. |

2

| Female speaker 1: | ¿Fumas?… ¿Dónde? … ¿Hay otras personas cerca?… Entonces, son víctimas del fumar pasivo que también es muy peligroso. Si quieres fumar … tienes que ser responsable. |

3

| Male speaker 2: | ¡Estás embarazada! ¡Enhorabuena! Pero si fumas es importante cambiar tus hábitos. El tabaco también afecta a la salud de tu bebé. |

4

| Female speaker 2: | El 31 de mayo es el día del No Fumador. ¿Quieres dejar de fumar? Para más información, puedes visitar la farmacia o contactarnos en www.díasintabaco.es |

4 🎧 Listen to announcements 1–4. Match up each one with one of the summaries below.

To help students correctly match each description with the correct part of the audio, you could display the following key words (from the transcript) in jumbled order, make sure students understand them, and ask them to predict which description will relate to each word: *restaurante, prohibido, pasivo, peligroso, embarazada, bebe, dejar de.*

Answers: **1** f, **2** d, **3** a, **4** c

> Introduce the grammar point (Using regular -*ar* verbs in the present tense) by asking students to find for you in the texts on page 22 the Spanish for 'I smoke', 'my dad smokes', 'we smoke' and 'they smoke', before presenting the whole paradigm as in the *Gramática*. Run though the paradigm of another regular -*ar* verb, ideally a familiar one such as *hablar*, to consolidate the endings, before students practise the forms in activity 5.
> The secondary grammar point, learning more about how to ask questions, ties in with the content of speaking activity 6 and the *Consejo*.
>
> **Gramática**

5 **G** Choose the appropriate verb form in each sentence.

Practice of the *Gramática* main point, Using regular -*ar* verbs in the present tense. Make sure students also know the meanings of *fumar, afectar, causar, necesitar, evitar* and *hablar*.

Answers:

1 No **fumo** porque no me gusta el olor.
2 ¿**Fumas**? – yo no.
3 El tabaco **afecta** a muchas personas.
4 Los cigarrillos **causan** cáncer.
5 **Necesitamos** una prohibición total.
6 ¿**Evitáis** todos los cigarrillos? ¡Muy bien!

> 💬 Phrases for expressing positive and negative opinions which students will need to carry out for speaking activity 6. Practise these before they attempt the activity so that they are familiar with how to use them (e.g. how to continue *Estoy a favor / en contra de* with an infinitive).
>
> **Estrategia**

> A tip on simple ways to form questions, which students can practise with *gustar* and a range of infinitives or nouns so that they can see the usefulness of the construction and apply it in speaking activity 6.
>
> **Consejo**

6 💬 🌐 You are conducting a survey with sixth-form students from your Spanish-speaking link school. Interview your partner about smoking.

Use the *Estrategia* for practice of giving opinions before doing this activity.

Students work in pairs, taking it in turns to be A and B. They should change the parts underlined, using the language structure box and the vocabulary on page 23 to help.

Higher-ability students could add extra details and opinions.

The Speaking worksheet provides further support and practice.

Plenary activity

Each student prepares a statement about smoking. Individuals read their statement out to the rest of the class, who have to decide if it is true or false. Encourage them to use different persons of the verb. You could give them the verb they have to use, e.g.

fumo > 'no fumo'
fuma > 'mi hermano fuma / Sarah fuma'
fumar > 'se puede fumar en clase'
fuman > '20 millones de españoles fuman'.

Pages 24–25

1.4 El alcohol y las drogas

Healthy and unhealthy lifestyles and their consequences

Subject	Talking about drugs and alcohol
Ⓖ 1	Making comparisons
Ⓖ 2	Learning how to form -er and -ir verbs in the present tense.
🗣	Asking and answering questions in written work

kerboodle!
- Audio file for core reading text
- Audio file and transcript for listening activity 3
- Reading activity: *El alcohol y las drogas*
- Grammar activity: Practising comparatives
- Speaking worksheet
- Extension listening worksheet
- Audio file and transcript for extension listening activity

Starter activity

Display a Spanish–English vocabulary matching task e.g. on a whiteboard, to introduce 10 or so key terms that students will need when reading the core text. Some of the pairs could usefully introduce the comparative structures that are the focus of the *Gramática*. For example (pairs given in correct order here, to be jumbled when you use them):

botellones	binge drinking
borracho	drunk
más caro	more expensive
el alcoholismo	alcoholism
paga mejor que	it pays better than
drogadicto	drug addict
el alcohol barato	cheap alcohol
hay más dinero	there's more money
más crimen	more crime
la droga blanda	soft drugs

Ask students to come out and draw link lines between the pairs they can match up. They could use the vocabulary list on pages 30–31 to look up new words.

1a 📖 💬 Work in pairs. Take turns to read the following statements from a web debate. Decide if you agree or not.

Give students the phrases *Sí, estoy de acuerdo* and *No, no estoy de acuerdo* so that they can express their agreement / disagreement in Spanish. Abler students could be given a wider range of agreement / disagreement expressions to use as they choose.

Core reading text

Two blogs expressing people's concerns about alcohol and drug-related problems. The blogs contain some quite difficult vocabulary but explain to students that they do not need to understand every word in order to understand the main points of the text and to show their understanding by doing activity 1b. They could use the vocabulary list on pages 30–31 to help, but this does not include every word in the text! You could go through the first text with the students before they attempt the questions. The text could be displayed on an electronic whiteboard in order to highlight key words and structures.

From the text, students should be able to work out the Spanish for 'more ... than' as a basis for working on the comparatives in the *Gramática*.

If you wish you could also use examples from the blogs to practise the secondary *Gramática* point, present tense forms of *-er* and *-ir* verbs.

In the context of the *Estrategia* on this spread (Asking and answering questions in written work) you could draw students' attention to examples of how Felipe and Graciela use questions and answers in their blogs to make a point (¿Por qué ...? ... Porque ... etc.)

The reading text is also available online as an audio file.

1b 📖 🎧 Read the blogs and decide if the following statements are true (T), false (F) or not mentioned in the text (?).

You could have the text displayed on an electronic whiteboard with key words and structures highlighted, while students do the true / false comprehension activity, which tests their understanding of main facts and opinions given in the text but also their grasp of the use of *más (... que)*.

Answers:

Felipe: **1** T, **2** ?, **3** F   Graciela: **4** F, **5** T

> **Gramática**
> Introduce the *Gramática* point, Making comparisons, by displaying a short list of items e.g. *la cerveza, el vino, la vodka, los cigarrillos, la cocaína*, and discussing with students which are more / less dangerous / unhealthy. To add the harder structures with *tan / tanto/a(s) ... como*, you could display an invented bar price list and compare the prices of drinks.
> The secondary grammar point, -er and -ir verb present tense forms, can be drawn out using examples from the blogs if you wish.

2 Ⓖ Copy the sentences and fill in the gaps with *más, menos, mejor, peor, tan, tanto(s)* or *tanta(s)*.

Students will need some whole-class practice based on the *Gramática*, before doing the activity: remind them to think about agreement as well as meaning, perhaps running through the first two questions with the whole class before they work on the rest of the activity individually or in pairs.

Answers:

| 1 más | 2 menos | 3 tantos |
| 4 mejor | 5 tan | 6 peor |

3 🎧 Transcript:

a

Female speaker 1: Bueno, en mi opinión hay más problemas con el alcohol ahora. A muchas personas les gusta beber y emborracharse. No saben controlarse.

b

Male speaker 1: Sí, pero me preocupan más las drogas. Un borracho causa menos problemas que un drogadicto. Un drogadicto puede entrar en tu casa, robar tus cosas y ser violento.

c

Female speaker 1: Los drogadictos son víctimas también. Necesitan ayuda.

Male speaker 1: ¿La rehabilitación? Muchos drogadictos no se interesan por la rehabilitación. Les gusta drogarse. Los programas de ayuda son inútiles. La cárcel es mejor para ellos.

d

Female speaker 1: Pero hay drogas en la cárcel: canabis, éxtasis, incluso cocaína. El problema es que todas las drogas son demasiado baratas en España y no es difícil obtenerlas.

---

3 🎧 You are going to hear four parts (a–d) of a TV debate about drugs and alcohol. Match up each part with one of the summaries 1–6.

Before students listen to the television debate, work with them to make a short list of key terms they will need to recognise. Encourage them to:

- remember vocabulary from earlier in the spread such as *drogadicto, alcohol, crimen*
- work out cognates such as *rehabilitación*
- make links between adjectives and verbs, e.g. *borracho – emborracharse; drogas – drogarse.*

Finally they could look at the transcript and translate key words and structures.

Answers: **a** 2, **b** 4, **c** 1, **d** 6

> ✏️ Following on from the *Consejo* on page 23, more guidance on question forming, with a reminder that word order does not need to change in Spanish. Show students how they can apply this in activity 4, with examples from the language structure box.
>
> *Estrategia*

> The structure *es* + adjective + infinitive is presented here, which could be incorporated into the 'opinions' element of the debate activity 4.
>
> *Consejo*

4 ✏️ 💬 🌐 You are taking part in a web debate about alcohol and drugs with some Spanish-speaking young people.

Students prepare for and take part in a web debate, covering the four bullet points. They should use the language structure box, the *Consejo* and *Estrategia* on 'Asking and answering questions' for help. They could also refer back to the *Estrategia* on page 23 (Giving opinions) and the vocabulary list on pages 30–31. Another source of useful language is Felipe's blog in the core reading text as well as the Speaking worksheet.

Plenary activity

Either in pairs or in teams, one student begins a comparative statement about how serious / dangerous / addictive a particular activity is. The other student or team has to finish off the sentence with another appropriate noun. For example:

A: *La sidra es menos peligrosa que …* B: *la cocaína.*

This could be kicked off by a vocabulary-gathering session – students call out nouns (with their definite articles!) which you write up for use as prompts. Students will probably need to prepare their statements in advance.

Pages 26–27

Reading and listening

📖🎧 Health

kerboodle!
- Audio files for core reading texts
- Audio file and transcript for listening activity 2

Core reading text

Sofía and Roberto's blogs describe the food regime at the health boot camp and their feelings about the programme. As an initial preparation, divide the class into two groups and ask each group in turn to give you a food word from the text in Spanish, and its English translation.

The reading text is also available online as an audio file.

1a 📖 🎧 Sofía, from Mexico and Roberto, from the Canary Islands are taking part in a worldwide reality TV show *Campamento de salud* (Health boot camp). Read the menu and the blogs on the website.

On this initial reading of the texts, you could simply ask students the general question, who finds the health boot camp more difficult, Roberto or Sofía? (= Sofía). Depending on your students' ability, ask them to explain their answer, in Spanish or English.

1b 📖 Look at the menu and name two things that Sofía and Roberto are eating today.

There are four items mentioned on the menu: vegetable soup, fish, salad and baked apples. Students are required to identify only two (which they should give you in English).

1c Which foods does Roberto say he likes? Write down the letters of three food items.

Students should identify the items by writing or telling you the correct letters. Emphasise that they are to identify the things he says he likes, not everything that he mentions. You could check the students' vocabulary by asking them simply to name the pictures, before they do the activity.

Answers: C, F, B

> The box provides reference to some help that will support students for activity 2a.
>
> *Gramática*

2a Read the following questions and choose the correct name. Write S (Sofía), R (Roberto) or S + R (Sofía and Roberto).

Students need to read the texts closely for this information. You could help them by pointing out key words (display the text and highlight key phrases if you wish) such as *adicción*, *hábito malo*, etc. They should also refer to the *Gramática* and the Examiner's tips for help.

Answers: 1 R, 2 R, 3 S, 4 R, 5 S, 6 R

2b Read the following questions and choose the correct option, a, b or c for each.

This is important practice of the skills of inference when reading, looking out for key words to distinguish attitudes and feelings. Students should refer to the Examiner's tips for help.

Answers: 1 b, 2 c

3a *Transcript:*
1 Tomo tostadas para el desayuno.
2 Bebo mucha agua.
3 Practico deporte todos los días.
4 Quiero dormir ocho horas cada noche.
5 Bebo demasiado alcohol: vino y cerveza. Pero no fumo.

3a Sofía is talking about a typical day at the health camp. Answer the following questions in English.

A printable version of this transcript is also available online, along with the audio file.

Answers:
1 toast
2 water
3 plays sport
4 8 (hours a night)
5 drinks too much alcohol (wine and beer)

3b *Transcript:*

1 Ana
Es horroroso aquí. No quiero hacer tanto ejercicio. Estoy muy cansada. Prefiero relajarme más.

2 Benjamín
Me gusta mucho estar en el campamento porque tengo que comer cosas sanas y no hay comida basura.

3 Luisa
Quiero dejar de fumar y por eso el campamento es fenomenal para mí. Las otras personas no fuman, no hay cigarrillos y es más fácil resistir la tentación. Lo único es que no puedo dormir por la noche, que me molesta bastante.

4 José
El campamento es muy útil porque quiero llevar una vida más sana y normalmente no como bien y no estoy en forma. Aquí se puede hacer mucho ejercicio, que es importante, y no es muy difícil.

3b What opinion do these other Spanish speakers have of the camp? Write P (positive), N (negative) or P + N (positive and negative).

Two young men and two young women describe their impressions of the health camp. Students write down the speakers' names (or just numbers 1–4), as given with their photos on the page, before they listen, and then write the appropriate letter(s) P, N or P + N, for each one, as they listen.

A printable version of this transcript is also available online, along with the audio file.

Answers:
1 Ana N   2 Benjamín P
3 Luisa P + N   4 José P

Pages 28–29

Grammar practice

G Health

> **Ser – to be**
>
> The paradigm of the present tense of *ser*, to support activities 1a and 1b.
>
> *Gramática*

1a Translate the following sentences into English.

Answers:
1 I am English.   2 My diet is healthy.
3 Are you Spanish?   4 Hot dogs are horrible.
5 We're vegetarian(s).   6 My friends are funny.
7 You are very intelligent.

Adjectives

A table of regular adjective endings, to support activity 1b.

1b Now use this box of adjectives to make up your own sentences using different parts of the verb *ser*.

Answers: Students' own answers.

Tener – to have

A list of common expressions with *tener*, to support activities 2a and 2b.

2a Make up conversations for pictures 1 and 2 using the example below. Replace the underlined words with an appropriate expression from the box of *tener* phrases.

Answers:

Picture 1: A: ¿Tienes sueño?
　　　　　B: No, no tengo sueño.
　　　　　C: Sí, tiene sueño.
Picture 2: A: ¿Tienes miedo?
　　　　　B: No, no tengo miedo.
　　　　　C: Sí, tiene miedo.

2b Now write the dialogues in the plural.

The example shows how the example conversation in activity 2a would appear in plural form, so that students can see how they should change the other two conversations.

Answers:

Picture 1: A: ¿Tenéis sueño?
　　　　　B: No, no tenemos sueño.
　　　　　C: Sí, tienen sueño.
Picture 2: A: ¿Tenéis miedo?
　　　　　B: No, no tenemos miedo.
　　　　　C: Sí, tienen miedo.

How to form questions with verbs

A summary of how to form questions with verbs, to support activities 3a and 3b.

3a Write appropriate questions for the following answers.

Make sure students understand which verb form is appropriate for the question, according to the verb form in the answer, by running through the first couple of questions with them. Remind them also that in Spanish you can turn a statement into a question without altering the word order.

Answers:

1. ¿Fumas?
2. ¿Habláis español?
3. ¿Los cigarrillos son adictivos?
4. ¿El tabaco produce cáncer?
5. ¿Comes comida basura?
6. ¿El tabaco afecta a muchas personas?
7. ¿Te gusta fumar?
8. ¿Es importante evitar el tabaco?

3b Now make up a survey about health. Make up your own questions.

You may want to suggest a particular number of questions, or provide question word prompts, according to the ability of the students.

Regular -er and -ir verbs

The final two grammar boxes on the spread provide a reminder of the present tense forms of *-er* and *-ir* verbs, to support activities 4a and 4b.

4a Copy out the following emails and fill in the gaps with the correct part of the regular *-er* and *-ir* verbs in brackets.

It may be worth reminding students about the common pitfall that you need the *nosotros* form of the verb for e.g. *mi familia y yo*, *mis amigos y yo*, etc.

Answers:

First email:　como, bebo, come, beben, comprende, comemos, comes, bebes

Second email:　vivo, viven, escribimos, recibo, escribe, vives, recibes

4b Make up some simple sentences of your own using regular *-er* and *-ir* verbs, writing both the Spanish and English. Now work in pairs. Partner A gives the English version and Partner B translates into Spanish. Partner A checks his / her original Spanish sentence.

You may wish to suggest a specific number of sentences, depending on students' ability. Abler students could write an email modelled on one of the emails in activity 4a.

Context 1 Lifestyle 25

Pages 30–31

Vocabulary

Health

- MP3 files for each vocabulary list

The essential vocabulary used within Topic 1, Context 1 is presented on this vocabulary spread.

Here, students can learn the key words for the topic area *Health*. You may also want to direct students to the online audio files of these vocabulary lists, so they can hear how the words are pronounced by a native speaker.

Some words are in light grey on the vocabulary spreads in the Student Book. This indicates items that are not included in the GCSE specification vocabulary list, so students do not need to learn these items for Listening and Reading assessment. However, you may wish students to use them in Speaking and Writing Controlled Assessments.

Pages 32–33

1.5 Las descripciones personales

Relationships with family and friends

Subject	Describing physical appearance and personality
G 1	Saying 'my, your, his / her, our, their'
G 2	Learning more about subject pronouns (*yo / tú / él / ella*, etc).
	Avoiding being caught out by false friends
kerboodle	• Audio file for core reading text • Audio file and transcript for listening activity 3 • Reading activity: *Las descripciones personales* • Grammar activity: Using possessive adjectives • Writing worksheet • Extension reading worksheet • Foundation reading worksheet

1 V Write down as many words related to someone's physical appearance and personality as you can remember.

Students could do this from memory to start with and then develop this preliminary work as follows:

There are a lot of adjectives in the reading text. A group of students could look at one of the texts and share the job of looking up the meanings on the vocabulary list on pages 48–49. They could read, then show the Spanish word and give the other groups three possible meanings in English to guess. This could introduce the idea of a 'false friend'.

Core reading text

Four young people introduce themselves in web page extracts. The texts provide a range of examples of personal description phrases and possessive adjectives in relation to family members (in line with the focus of the *Gramática*). All the 'false friends' given in the *Estrategia* also appear in the texts.

The reading text is also available online as an audio file.

Estrategia: The guidelines given here help students to avoid 'false friends', pointing out examples from the core text, which should help them with the details in the text that they need to pick out for activities 2a and 2b.

2a Read the web page and answer the following.

Students need to pay close attention to the detail of the text and to be on the alert for the 'false friends' explained in the *Estrategia*. They could use the language structure box to help. Make sure they understand that Esteban starts with a false description as a joke.

Answers:

1 Eduardo C; Juanita B; Esteban E; Sofía A
2 Students' own answers backed up by similar descriptions from one of the texts.

2b Summarise in English the information Sofía gives about her family. Mention at least eight things.

The summary requires students to read Sofía's text on page 32 in detail; as shown in the Answers, below, there are 15 details given in the text, so they should be able to find eight. It would be worth picking out the first couple with them as a whole-class exercise so that they realise the details can be picked up one by one.

Answers:

Any eight points from among the following:
she has two parents
mother is called Lourdes
father is called Juan Luis
she has one brother
brother is called Francisco

Francisco …
– is tall
– is thin
– is very naughty
she has one sister
sister is called Cristina

Cristina …
– is quite short
– is very cheerful
they have a dog
dog is called Rodrigo

Rodrigo is …
– a bit fat
– very funny

3a 🎧 *Transcript:*

1 Tengo los ojos azules.
2 Mi pelo es rubio.
3 Soy alta y delgada.
4 En mi familia somos seis en total. Tengo dos hermanas y un hermano.
5 Como hermanas somos muy distintas. Mi hermana mayor es tímida, yo soy habladora y mi hermana menor es simpática.

3a 🎧 Listen to Nuria talking about herself and her family. Copy the sentences and fill in the gaps.

A simple detail-comprehension activity, applying students' newly consolidated vocabulary about personal descriptions in a listening context.

Answers:

1 blue   2 blond   3 tall and thin
4 two   5 talkative / chatty

3b 🎧 *Transcript:*

Normalmente hay problemas entre hermanos y hermanas porque son muy diferentes. Pero mi hermano es simpático y gracioso. Tenemos mucho en común y es como un amigo.
Bueno, ¡adiós por ahora! Mañana puedo hablar más. Me gusta más hablar que escribir porque es más fácil y soy bastante vaga.

3b 🎧 Answer the following questions in English.

Nuria gives more information, and students now have to pick out information from a more flowing audio item and deduce information as well as identifying stated facts.

Answers:

1 Yes. He is nice / He is funny / they have a lot in common / he is like a friend. (any two details)
2 (Talking) is easier than writing / she is lazy.

> Introduce the grammar point, Possessive adjectives, using activity 4a. You could practise the use of the most difficult one, *su / sus*, by quizzing students for information on Sofía's family, for example: *¿Cómo se llaman sus padres? ¿Cómo se llama su perro? ¿Cómo son sus hermanos?* You could then prompt students to reply to simple questions about their family, to practise responding to *tu / tus* with *mi / mis*. This should prepare them for making the correct selections in activity 4b.
>
> *Gramática*

4a Ⓖ Find examples of different forms of 'my', 'your' and 'our' in the web page.

Having looked at the *Gramática*, students now concentrate on finding examples in context. Point out that they should search in Sofía's text in detail.

Make sure the students understand the singular and plural forms and also the masculine and feminine forms for *nuestro / vuestro*. Also stress that the possessive adjective agrees with the noun that comes after it e.g. *su hermano* = their brother.

Refer to the reminder in the *Consejo* about *su / sus*.

Answers:

Eduardo: **mi** deporte favorito; **tu** deporte favorito
Juanita: **vuestros** pasatiempos; **vuestras** ambiciones
Esteban: **vuestro** novio
Sofía: **mis** padres; **mi** hermano; **mi** hermana; **mis** amigas; **nuestro** pasatiempo; **tu** pasatiempo; **tus** amigos

4b Ⓖ Select the appropriate form of the possessive adjective in the following sentences.

Students now apply what they have learned from the *Gramática* and the examples they worked on in 4a, to supply the correct missing possessive adjectives.

Answers: 1 Mi,   2 tus,   3 Nuestro,   4 vuestros

> A reminder to use *tener* and not *ser* to state someone's age. Students should bear this in mind for activity 5.
>
> *Consejo*

5 💬 Imagine you are taking part in a speed-dating event. Talk for 30–60 seconds about yourself and your family.

Students are prompted to give personal details (name, age), their physical and personality characteristics, information about their family and friends, any other relevant information – encourage them, for example to say what they like doing, to practise key verb + infinitive constructions from earlier in the chapter. Some may wish to use cue cards with key words on them as they do the activity.

(See notes on the suggested plenary activity below: for the purposes of this idea, the profile notes students write should be anonymous.)

Plenary activity

As a round-up activity you could make use of the profile notes which students wrote in preparation for activity 5. Collect in and then randomly redistribute the notes. Ask a student to read out the notes, followed by the question *¿Quién soy?* – the rest of the class have to guess who wrote the notes.

Alternatively, write names of famous people on the board or show photos. In pairs or teams, students describe a person for the other student(s) to guess.

Context 1 Lifestyle

Pages 34–35

1.6 La situación familiar

Relationships with family and friends

Subject	Describing different family situations
G 1	Using *estar* + past participle
G 2	Learning how to use *desde hace* + present tense to say how long you have been doing something
🌐	Working out the meaning of new words from the context

kerboodle!
- Audio file for core reading text
- Audio file and transcript for listening activity 3
- Listening activity and transcript: *La situación familiar*
- Grammar activity: Practising the endings for the verb *estar*
- Speaking worksheet
- Extension reading worksheet

1 🗣 Work in pairs. Partner A chooses one of the people from the photos below and describes them to Partner B, without saying their name. Partner B has to guess who it is. Then swap roles.

This builds on work done on the previous spread (personal descriptions using *ser*), as a lead-in to the main new focus of this spread – making other statements about people's situations using *estar*.

Core reading text

The texts are profiles of characters from a Latin American soap opera *La Calle de Intriga*, giving details of their situation in the story. There is a good number of new vocabulary items and the *Estrategia* will help students to work on their meanings. The texts also demonstrate the use of *estar* to make statements about non-permanent characteristics, particularly when used with the past participle – the main grammar points of the spread (*Gramática* and *Consejo*). There are also examples of the secondary grammar point *desde hace* + present tense.

The reading text is also available online as an audio file.

> 📖 Students should refer to this guidance on working out the meaning of new words, before they attempt the reading activities 2a and 2b. Students could find other clues in the text to work out meanings of: e.g. *madre soltera, trata* (Mariela y Yolanda); *gemelas, niñera* (La familia Menéndez); *padrastro, soltero, hermanastros* (Hugo text); *celoso, espiar* (Ramón text).
>
> *Estrategia*

2a 📖 🎧 🌐 Read the article and write the name of the person who …

To answer the questions students need to pay attention to phrases using *estar* with a past participle or adjective, and to the detail of the time frame of each statement.

For working out the meaning of new vocabulary they can refer to the *Estrategia* to help as well as the vocabulary list on pages 48–49 and the language structure box. The text could be displayed on an electronic whiteboard in order to highlight key words and phrases.

Answers:

1 Lucía   2 Yolanda   3 Hugo
4 Ramón   5 Hugo   6 Mariela

2b 📖 🎧 🌐 Answer the following questions in English.

For this activity students need to read the article again to work out broader facts about the characters from the text.

Answers:

1 Her marriage is boring and loveless / she wants more adventures in life
2 She is in love with Hugo
3 The (new) nanny (for the Menéndez family)
4 Hugo: likes sleeping / doesn't want to work / isn't worried about anything.

3 🎧 *Transcript:* _____

Víctor

Paulina: Buenos días. Soy Paulina.
Víctor: Buenos días. Me llamo Víctor. Vivo aquí desde hace treinta años.
Paulina: ¡Treinta años! Y, ¿está casado?
Víctor: Antes, sí. Ahora soy viudo. Mi mujer está muerta.
Paulina: Lo siento. ¿Tiene hijos?
Víctor: Sí. Tengo un hijo y tres nietos.
Paulina: ¡Qué bien! Me gustan mucho los niños.

Rosa

Paulina: ¡Hola! Soy Paulina.
Rosa: ¡Hola! Soy Rosa.
Paulina: ¿Vives en esta calle?
Rosa: Sí, pero sólo desde hace cinco meses.
Paulina: ¡Ah! Entonces eres la novia de Paco.
Rosa: ¿Novia? Estamos casados. Soy su mujer. Y tenemos dos hijas. ¿Cómo conoces a Paco?
Paulina: Bueno … somos … amigos. A veces le veo en el bar o la discoteca. Pero, tranquila, no pasa nada.

Juan

Juan: ¡Hola! Me llamo Juan.
Paulina: ¡Hola! Soy Paulina. Vivo con la familia Menéndez.
Juan: Yo vivo en la casa número diez.
Paulina: ¿Desde hace mucho tiempo?
Juan: Tres años.
Paulina: ¿Vives solo?
Juan: Sí, soy soltero. No tengo novia ni niños. Estoy libre. Totalmente.
Paulina: Bueno, bueno …

3a 🎧 Listen to the conversations Paulina has with three people (Victor, Rosa and Juan) she meets on the street. Note down their marital status, the number of children they have and how long they have lived in the street.

The vocabulary content of the questions is familiar from the reading work already done on the spread, but students may need to listen a few times to pick up all the details. They could prepare a table (as shown in the Answers, below) to make it easier to note their answers. Note that they will need to recognise the construction *desde hace* + present tense (the secondary point in the *Gramática*).

Answers:

Name	Marital Status (married / divorced / separated / single)	Children	How long lived in street
Victor	widowed	1 son; 3 grandchildren	30 years
Rosa	married	2 daughters	5 months
Juan	single	none	3 years

3b 🎧 Listen again and answer the following questions.

Now students have to listen carefully for the speakers' attitudes as well as the factual content. Afterwards students could look at the transcript again for the 'soap opera' undertones in each conversation.

Answers:

1 She likes children / she is friends with Paco (sees him in bars / nightclubs) / she lives with the Menéndez family
2 (b) suspicious
3 (c) flirtatious

> **Gramática**
> Introduce the use of *estar* with a past participle or adjective to describe someone's situation, by asking a couple of questions about the characters from *La Calle de Intriga* to model what students are required to produce in activity 4a. The *Consejo* reinforces the *Gramática* on usage of *estar*, so you may wish to point this out also before students apply the *Gramática* guidelines to activity 4.
> The secondary point, *desde hace* + present tense, is seen in a few instances in the reading text and is also heard in the audio, so it's important that students understand how it works.

4a 🅖 💬 Work in pairs. Partner B pretends to be one of the characters from the article on page 34. Partner A has to work out who it is by asking questions using *estar*. Partner B answers in full sentences. Then swap roles.

As suggested above, model this with a couple of questions to show students how to form the questions. Ask students to produce a couple of example questions, so that you can weed out any that require *ser*. You may wish also to write ¿Estás …? on the board to remind them as they work through the activity.

4b 🅖 💬 Now describe a character or pair of characters to the rest of the class for them to guess.

This will almost certainly involve students in using both *ser* and *estar*. Make sure they study the *Consejo* on which verb to use when.

> **Consejo**
> The information reinforces the *Gramática* and provides support for the productive activities 4 and 5, to help students use *estar* and *ser* correctly.

5 ✏️ Write your own description of a real or imaginary family or group of people. You could make up your own soap-opera characters.

As with activity 4b, this writing task will require students to make choices between *ser* and *estar*. Make sure they study the *Consejo*. You could also ask them to use two colours to highlight the two verbs in a copy of the audio transcript, to reinforce understanding of which verb to use when. Higher-ability candidates should be encouraged to add extra details and opinions to their descriptions. They could write about whether they: are married / single / divorced; have any children; are happy / worried / have problems; work / are retired / unemployed; how long they have lived together / in the area; their personalities.

Plenary activity

Students or the teacher should prepare a set of phrases using part of the verb *estar* + past participle / adjective, e.g. *estoy contento; estamos enamorados*. These phrases should be distributed to students.

Students play a version of charades. According to the phrase they have received, they should:

– indicate the person, for example pointing to themselves (for an *estoy* … phrase, or at someone else (for an *estás* … phrase)

– act out past participle / adjective (*enamorado / contento*, etc.)

Other students have to guess correctly which phrase the performer is trying to depict.

Pages 36–37

1.7 Las relaciones personales

Relationships with family and friends

Subject	Discussing relationships with family and friends
G 1	Using reflexive verbs
G 2	Learning more about conjunctions and how to link phrases together
🗣	Extending phrases in speaking and writing tasks

kerboodle!
- Audio file for core reading text
- Video and transcript for activity 2
- Listening activity to accompany video
- Grammar activity: Using reflexive verbs
- Speaking worksheet
- Extension listening worksheet
- Audio file and transcript for extension listening activity

Starter activity

Ask students to skim read the emails to find a) any relationship words in Spanish e.g. *pareja, novio, amigo* and b) any words or phrases that describe a positive and / or negative relationship e.g. *feliz, cariñoso, comprensivo, nos llevamos muy bien, se enfada*.

Alternatively these words could be copied so that the students have to divide them into positive or negative descriptions about relationships.

Core reading text

Three emails in which young people describe relationships and related issues in their home life. There are several examples of present tense reflexive verbs as explained in the *Gramática*. Longer sentences are included to help familiarise students with the use of conjunctions (the secondary grammar point and supported by the *Estrategia*).

The reading text is also available online as an audio file.

1 📖 🎧 Read the emails and answer the following questions in English.

To answer these questions, the students have to read the texts in detail (having skim read them previously for the Starter activity) to pick up on the nature and quality of the relationships described, justifying their impressions with reasons found in the text.

Answers:

1

	Relationship
María and Antonio	Boyfriend / girlfriend
Antonio and Enrique	Friends
Borja and Teresa	Brother / sister
Luis and Elena	Boyfriend / girlfriend

2 a María: changes of mood
  b Borja: arguments between family members
  c Luis: different opinions about marriage

3 No; two reasons are: he is not a positive influence on Antonio; after seeing Enrique, Antonio is impatient / gets angry / changes personality.
4 No; any two of the following reasons: she criticises teenagers a lot / she is a bit intolerant / she causes arguments with Teresa (sister).
5 No; reason: she thinks marriage causes problems.

2 🎥 *Transcript:*

Entrevistadora:	Buenas noches a todos. Aquí tenemos a Javier … su madre María José, su padre Manolo … y su novia Elisa. [*María is crying*]. Bien, María. ¿Qué te pasa? ¿Cuál es el problema?
María José:	La relación entre Javier y yo es muy mala. No nos llevamos bien desde hace mucho tiempo.
Entrevistadora:	¿Hay muchas discusiones?
María José:	No, no. Cuando llega del instituto, va a su dormitorio o sale con amigos o con su novia. No quiere hablar conmigo. No hay comunicación entre nosotros. Nada. Creo que me detesta y no comprendo por qué. Me siento muy triste.
Entrevistadora:	Y Javier, ¿por qué no te relacionas bien con tu madre?
Javier:	Porque siempre me critica. No le gusta mi pelo, mi ropa, mis piercings, mi novia …
María José:	Claro, tu aspecto físico es horrible. Y francamente me llevo mal con Elisa porque es una chica mal educada y antipática.
Javier:	Cuando Elisa viene a casa, tú eres la antipática. Mira, mamá, ya no tengo 10 años. No soy tu hijo pequeño y no puedes controlar mi vida. Tienes que respetar mis opiniones.
Entrevistadora:	Y, Manolo. ¿Cómo es tu relación con Javier?
Javier:	Ni buena ni mala. La relación casi no existe. Mi padre está siempre en la oficina.
María José:	¡Javier! Por favor … [*upset, crying*]
Manolo:	Es verdad. Trabajo mucho … demasiado … y me siento mal porque tengo que ayudar más con las relaciones entre Javier y María José.
Entrevistadora:	Pues, estás aquí ahora. No es demasiado tarde. Puedes ser una influencia muy positiva. Y, finalmente, Elisa, ¿qué opinas de estos problemas?
Elisa:	No me gusta cuando hay problemas entre miembros de la familia. Es importante relacionarse bien con todo el mundo. Por eso estoy contenta de que por fin haya una oportunidad para hablar y buscar una solución juntos.
Entrevistadora:	¡Bien dicho! Y después de los anuncios vamos a continuar con esta charla …

2 Watch the video clip and answer the following questions.

The video clip is split up into sections which correspond with the questions. Students could, however, watch the whole clip first to get an overall impression of the situation and pick up on non-verbal clues, without worrying about the details, before they rewatch and attempt activity 2.

Answers:

1 c
2 hair / clothes / piercings / girlfriend (any 3)
3 a
4 b
5 b

Gramática

Students need to study this reminder of present tense reflexive verb forms before they try activity 3. You could introduce the point by running through reflexive forms with the more familiar verb *llamarse*, which students should feel confident using, especially since they have been working with it in the previous two spreads in the context of language for presenting family members. (See also the *Consejo*.)

The secondary grammar point (using conjunctions to link phrases into extended sentences) supports speaking activity 4 and writing activity 5.

3 Copy the sentences and fill in the gaps with the correct reflexive pronoun: *me / te / se / nos / os*.

Students should work on the *Gramática* and *Consejo* first to ensure they understand how reflexive verbs work. They should also know the meanings of the verbs: *llevarse, pelearse, quejarse, marcharse* and *ponerse*. You could work through some examples of these verbs in present tense form, modelling the use of the reflexive pronoun until students can give you the correct one, prompted by the verb form displayed on the board with a gap for the pronoun.

Answers:

1 me
2 se
3 nos
4 te
5 os
6 se

Estrategia

You can work with students to find how this strategy – using conjunctions to extend sentences by linking phrases together – can be seen in the reading texts. The video script, by contrast, is composed mainly of very short sentences so with abler students you might like to give them a copy of the transcript for them to see if they can use conjunctions to link some of these shorter sentences into longer ones. Also, ask students to make up as many different sentences as they can using these words:

mi	horrible	me	llevo
	gusta	hermano	
es	con	cómico	bien
	no		porque

The main practice opportunities for this strategy, however, are speaking activity 4 and particularly writing activity 5.

4 Work in pairs. Take turns to practise saying the different parts of these verbs. Throw a dice.

Students work in pairs. One student chooses the infinitive of the reflexive verb and the other student throws the dice and has to say the correct part of the verb according to the number on the dice (1= first person singular; 2= second person singular, etc.). To reinforce the meaning the students could translate the verb into English. As an extension activity the students could then make up whole sentences including the reflexive verb.

5 Make up your own email to a problem page. Try to extend your sentences using words such as: *pero, también, y, por eso, porque*.

To write their email describing a problem with relationships, students should use the vocabulary list on pages 48–49, the language structure box and the linking words as explained in the *Estrategia* to extend their sentences. They could be encouraged to refer to examples in the reading texts for model phrases.

Students should also be encouraged to look back at the *Estrategia* and language structure boxes on previous pages in order to use previously learnt structures with different vocabulary. A model email could include:

- what problem(s) there is / are
- who with
- what you think / feel about the problem and why
- what you want and why
- extra descriptions and details.

Consejo

This tip supports and adds to the *Gramática* on reflexive verbs.

Plenary activity

Students could listen to the recorded version of María's, Borja's and Luis's emails and identify a) the reflexive verbs b) the linking words, with half the class responsible for a) and the other half for b).

This could be done in various ways: writing on mini-whiteboards; writing on the board; standing up when they hear the word(s).

Pages 38–39

1.8 Los planes del futuro

Future plans regarding marriage / partnership	
Subject	Discussing future plans about marriage / partnership and children
G 1	Talking about what you are going to do
G 2	Learning how to say what people **would** like / **would** be, etc.
	Keeping your conversation going

kerboodle!
- Audio file for core reading text
- Audio file and transcript for listening activity 2
- Reading activity: *Los planes del futuro*
- Grammar activity: Using the verb *ir* to form the immediate future tense
- Writing worksheet
- Extension listening worksheet
- Audio file and transcript for extension listening activity
- Foundation listening worksheet
- Audio file and transcript for foundation listening worksheet
- Audio role play activity

Starter activity

Students could discuss or write down in English what they might be doing in the future at the ages of 25, 35 and 65. They could then scan the reading texts to see if they can recognise any words that link with their own plans.

Core reading text

Three young people describe their hopes and plans for their future family life, specifically their immediate plans and how they see themselves aged 65. The text naturally includes numerous examples of references to the future using *ir + a + infinitive*, which will be referred to in activity 1; this structure is the focus of the *Gramática*. The several phrases containing *me gustaría* can be drawn out if wished as examples of the secondary grammar point.

The reading text is also available online as an audio file.

1 Students at your Spanish-speaking link school imagine what their life will be like when they are 25, 35 and 65 years old. Read what they have to say about their future plans. Who …

Students read the texts in some detail and match the correct person to their summary. Point out that they will find the future references *ir a* reflected in the 'going to' questions, and they could use the vocabulary list on pages 48–49 and the language structure box to help. Each article could be displayed on an electronic whiteboard to highlight key words and future time frames.

Answers:
1 Raúl
2 Chelo
3 Roberto
4 Chelo
5 Roberto
6 Chelo
7 Roberto
8 Raúl

2 *Transcript:*

Guillermo:	Bueno … francamente no quiero tener niños.
Salomé:	Me gustaría mucho tener novio y, y … casarme, pero es difícil encontrar a tu pareja ideal.
Carolina:	Pues, voy a casarme en agosto … emmm … y … sé que voy a ser feliz. No quiero vivir con mi novio. Primero quiero estar casada.
Bernardo:	La verdad es que si estás casado … es, es … un compromiso importante. Como persona, no … no soy muy responsable y mi novia sabe que, vamos, que no voy a ser un buen marido.
Ana:	Mi mejor amiga no quiere tener niños porque, porque … le gustaaaaa, le gusta su independencia y … tiene unos sobrinos horrorosos. Pero en mi opinión, tener un hijo sería algo maravilloso y tener a tu bebé en brazos por primera vez seríaaa … sería … el mejor momento de tu vida.

2 🎧 Listen to the extracts from a radio talk show about marriage, partners and children. Choose the correct option for each.

Students listen to five extracts from a radio talk show about marriage, partners and children and do a multiple-choice comprehension exercise identifying what the speakers say they are going to do / would like to do about marriage and children. Refer to the *Estrategia* and ask students to tell you what they notice about how the speakers are giving themselves time to think by repeating, pausing and drawing out their words.

Answers: **1** b, **2** a, **3** b, **4** b, **5** a

> **Gramática**
>
> You could concentrate initially on first person singular forms of *ir a* + infinitive, as this comes up frequently in the reading and audio texts, but then ask students to find one more example of the construction in the reading (*¿qué vamos a hacer Rosario y yo?*) and prompt students to predict the rest of the paradigm from their knowledge of *ir*. Emphasise the importance of including *a*. You could display a gapped paradigm which students come forward to complete, in which the *a* is in red. This will help to prepare them for speaking activity 4 as well as for the grammar activity 3 which tests the *ir* verb forms.
>
> The secondary grammar point is not tested in activity 3 but students will need to be able to produce *me gustaría* in activity 4, so as preparation for that activity, make sure they have fully understood how this construction works, for example via a whole-class 'Who says what?' exercise based on the audio transcript.

3 Ⓖ Choose the appropriate verb form for the person named in brackets and copy out the correct sentences.

Students should look at the *Gramática* to find out all of the parts of the verb *ir* and then copy out the sentences, choosing the correct part of the verb. They could practise the verb forms of *ir* with a dice, taking turns to throw the dice and saying the correct part of the verb according to the number on the dice (1= first person singular; 2 = second person singular, etc.).

Answers:

1 **Voy** a casarme el año próximo.
2 Mi hermana **va** a trabajar en Australia.
3 Oye, Cristina, ¿**vas** a tener niños en el futuro?
4 Mi novio y yo **vamos** a ir a la universidad.
5 ¿**Vais** a casaros por la iglesia?
6 Mis padres **van** a visitar a mi abuelo en Argentina.

> **Estrategia**
>
> Ask the students to read the *Estrategia*, then listen again to the audio for activity 2, and pick out specific examples of how the speakers are using drawn-out words, hesitation, and repetition to give themselves time to think and formulate what they want to say; e.g. *bueno*, *vamos*, *emm* not 'umm'; elongate the vowel sound at the end, e.g. *me gustaaa* … Get them to do a fluency activity: they must use these techniques, talking non-stop for 30 seconds about their future plans, using at least two examples of *ir a* and *me gustaría*. They should then apply this technique to help them in speaking activity 4.

4 💬 🌐 Predict what you will be doing at the ages of 25, 35 and 65. Work in pairs asking and answering the following questions. Use the language structure box to help you.

Students work in pairs and take turns to ask and answer questions about future plans. They should refer to the language structure box and the vocabulary list on pages 48–49 to help. They should also try to use the suggestions in the *Estrategia* and remember that it is acceptable to repeat or draw out words occasionally when they need time to think about what they want to say.

> **Consejo**
>
> A note on the simple future forms *habrá* and *será*, to make sure students understand how these relate to *haber* (specifically, *hay*) and *ser* (specifically, *es*).

Plenary activity

Students could volunteer to be on the 'hot spot' on a chair at the front of the class.

- Either they could keep talking about their future plans for as long as possible without hesitating too much and the student who talks for longest, wins.
- Or students could ask them the questions in activity 4.
- Alternatively, students could all talk about their future plans at the same time and the one who is left still talking, wins.

Context 1 Lifestyle 33

1.9 La igualdad para todos

Pages 40–41

Social issues and equality

Subject	Discussing race and gender
G 1	Using reflexive phrases like *se puede*
G 2	Making a phrase negative
	Checking pronunciation

kerboodle!
- Audio file for core reading text
- Audio file and transcript for listening activity 3
- Reading activity: *La igualdad para todos*
- Grammar activity: Using reflexive phrases
- Speaking worksheet
- Extension listening worksheet
- Audio file and transcript for extension listening activity

Starter activity

Students could try to remember the main differences between Spanish and English pronunciation, e.g. j; ci; z. Look at pages 194–195 to revise the pronunciation rules. Remind students that stress rules are simple in Spanish and that accents are there to help them with the exceptions.

> *Estrategia*
> This follows on from the starter activity. You could make pronunciation practice more fun by playing the audio and pausing the recording every so often; students have to predict the pronunciation of the next word or two, and then listen to compare their expectation with what they hear.
> Students should then try their best to concentrate on good pronunciation in speaking activity 5.

1 Work in pairs. Partner A reads out one word from list A below, working out the correct pronunciation. Partner B guesses the meaning. Then swap roles.

Students work in pairs and take it in turns to read out the words relating to Equal Opportunities with the correct pronunciation. They should read the *Estrategia* for further help.

They could then listen to the recorded version of the following reading text to check if they got the pronunciation correct.

Core reading text

A short online item about Women's Night in Bogotá (men must stay in, only women may go out) and its significance, followed by two comments from bloggers Marcelo and Pilar.

Encourage students to work out, in particular, the meaning of phrases using the reflexive forms *se celebra*, *se pueden considerar*, etc. as this is the structure they will be studying in this spread's *Gramática*. They should be able to find five examples in the text.

The reading text is also available online as an audio file.

2 Read the blogs about Women's Night in Bogotá and decide whether the following statements are true (T), false (F) or not mentioned (?).

Students should use the vocabulary list on pages 48–49 and the language structure box to help. Each blog could be displayed on an electronic whiteboard to highlight key words and phrases. The answers to the questions test comprehension of the opinions in the text, more than understanding of individual words; emphasise to students that when reading they need to look at whole phrases / sentences, not just word by word, because word order is different in Spanish, and constructions are not word-for-word equivalents of English. Use the reflexive phrases to draw out this point.

Answers: 1 F, 2 F, 3 T, 4 ?, 5 T, 6 F, 7 ?

3 *Transcript:*

1
Male speaker 1: En Argentina tienen la primera presidenta. Ahora en España también hay más oportunidades para las mujeres en el gobierno.

2
Male speaker 2: Cada año hay demasiadas víctimas de la violencia doméstica.

3
Female speaker 1: Claro, la discriminación contra las mujeres existe todavía pero tenemos la Ley de Igualdad que es positiva. Creo que ahora la discriminación contra los homosexuales es más seria.

4
Male speaker 3: No comprendo el racismo que hay contra los inmigrantes. En Europa se necesitan inmigrantes para hacer muchos trabajos importantes.

5
Female speaker 2: Se habla de la 'tolerancia' hacia los gitanos y los extranjeros, pero no estoy de acuerdo. Se debe comprender y aceptar a las personas diferentes, no sólo ser tolerante.

6
Female speaker 3: Para cambiar las actitudes se debe educar a la gente sobre las desigualdades que hay en la sociedad.

3 Listen to the opinions about gender and race issues (1–6). Which of the following options A–F does each statement refer to?

Students listen to six different people's opinions about gender and race issues and match up each opinion with the correct summary. There are some unfamiliar words not covered in the reading texts, but students should try to listen to the gist of what they hear, pick out key words and recognise some cognates.

Answers: 1 F, 2 C, 3 D, 4 E, 5 A, 6 B

Pages 42–43

1.10 La pobreza

Social issues and equality

Subject	Discussing and understanding issues relating to poverty
G 1	Saying what you have to do or must do
G 2	Learning more about how to use *lo* + adjective
	Ignoring words you don't need to understand

kerboodle!
- Audio file for core reading text
- Audio file and transcript for listening activity 3
- Listening activity and transcript: *La pobreza*
- Grammar activity: Using the verbs *tener que*, *deber* and *hay que*
- Writing worksheet
- Extension reading worksheet

Starter activity

Ask students to do a spider diagram (in English or Spanish) with '*Perú*' in the middle and arrows going out with words they associate with Peru. Can they identify Peru and find Lima on a map of South America?

Core reading text

For the last spread of the Context, the reading text is a relatively lengthy article on *pueblos jóvenes* in Lima. For this reason the first activity is a skim-reading vocabulary task. The *Estrategia* also gives support to boost students' confidence when tackling longer passages. They can also use the vocabulary list on pages 48–49 as a source of help.

You could improvise a vocabulary matching task – 10 or so English words on the left, Spanish words jumbled on the right, and ask students to draw link lines between the pairs – to (re)familiarise them with some of the key words in the passage such as: *la ciudad, el pueblo, el barrio, la población, el campo, la enfermedad, el tratamiento, la carretera, la salud*.

There are multiple examples in the text of the structures explained in the *Gramática* (see below for ideas on how to make use of these).

The reading text is also available online as an audio file.

1 📖 **V** Skim read the following article and pick out as many words as you can that relate directly to poverty, building houses and illness.

You may want to ask different groups of students to look for different things or scan a text each.

Possible answers:

Poverty: un pueblo joven; (un barrio) pobre; las casas son básicas; no hay agua corriente ni electricidad; las condiciones de vida no son muy sanitarias; los padres … no pueden pagar el tratamiento; la pobreza; los pobres; rico; riqueza.

Building houses: están hechas de cartón o de metal; construir las casas con piedra o ladrillos; un techo y ventanas de cristal; (participar juntos en obras como) la construcción de carreteras y alcantarillas.

Gramática

You could introduce the grammar point – Using reflexive phrases – by displaying the reading text, giving students five minutes to read it over again, then showing it again with the reflexive phrases blanked out. Can they tell you precisely what is missing? And / Or you could use the same process with the audio transcript, which would be a harder challenge, but could be supported by replaying the audio.

Check students' understanding of *Nunca voy a …* in the last sentence of the reading text (see secondary grammar point, ways to make a phrase negative).

4 **G** Put the following words in these phrases into the correct order.

Students should look at the *Gramática* to learn about how to use reflexive phrases before doing this activity and also refer to the examples in the language structure box. They could copy the individual words onto pieces of paper and reorder them. They should translate the sentences into English once they have found the correct order.

Answers:

1 Se necesita más tolerancia.
2 Se puede educar al público.
3 No se habla mucho de la violencia doméstica.
4 Se dice que hay racismo en España.

5 ✏️ 💬 Write a short speech in Spanish about how to tackle gender and race discrimination. You could look up different nouns and infinitives of verbs.

Students are instructed to mention specific points. They should use the language structure box and vocabulary list on pages 48–49 to help. They should also be encouraged to look up new nouns and infinitives of verbs, but be careful only to use the language structures they know and not make it too complicated.

This is a good opportunity for students to work in pairs or groups and for higher-ability students to use the linguistic structures they know creatively.

Consejo

These agreement / disagreement phrases are not new but it's important that students make use of them to express opinions in productive tasks like activity 5.

Plenary activity

Once students have written their speech, they could perform it in front of the class and students could vote for those with the best ideas.

Context 1 Lifestyle 35

Illness: las condiciones de vida no son muy sanitarias; no hay agua limpia; hay muchas enfermedades como el cólera; la diarrea causa la mayoría de las muertes entre los niños; los padres no comprenden … el tratamiento.

> **Estrategia**
> 📖 🎧 Students are reminded of useful techniques for reading and listening to longer texts.

2a 📖 🎧 🌐 Read the article and answer these questions. Try to work out the meanings of words you don't know before looking them up. Remember, you do not need to understand every word.

The students should read the first and last parts of the article: *Una visita a un pueblo joven* and *Los pobres y los ricos* where the answers to these multiple-choice questions are to be found. Refer them to the *Estrategia* which gives important support for coping with longer reading passages such as this article.

Answers: **1** a, **2** b, **3** c

2b 📖 🎧 🌐 Find three positive and three negative things the writer mentions about Peru and the 'pueblos jóvenes'. Note them down in English.

Students should now read the whole text in more detail, using the vocabulary list on pages 48–49 and the *Estrategia* box for help. Make sure they have noticed that they should note down the positive / negative things in English.

There is quite a lot of potentially new and challenging language in these texts and you may want to focus on individual texts separately, or divide the class so that half of the students look for the three positive things, the others for the three negative ones. Each part of the article could be displayed on an electronic whiteboard, so that as students give you their answers you can highlight the positive and negative phrases in the Spanish using two different colours.

Answers:

Positive things: any three of the following:
  Area is new / 'young'; going to be better in future; possibility for development
  People work together / participate in work for the community
  People build roads / drains; get / bring in clean water / electricity

Negative things: any three of the following:
  Poor area / area on outskirts of town / area
  Houses are very basic; have no water / electricity / drains
  Not very healthy living conditions / sanitary; no clean water, diseases (like cholera)
  Children die of diarrhoea / parents don't understand treatment / parents can't pay for treatment
  Difficult for poor people to get well paid jobs
  There is a lot of prejudice (against poor people)
  5% of population has 95% of wealth / is very rich / unjust situation

3 🎧 🌐 *Transcript:*

a
Male speaker 1: Estoy muy contento con mi nueva casa y con mi comunidad. Me gusta mucho.

b
Female speaker 1: No hay agua limpia aquí y es muy duro.

c
Male speaker 2: Trabajamos mucho para tener condiciones mejores. Ahora tenemos electricidad y es estupendo. Además la casa es muy linda. Lo malo es que hay mucho crimen en el pueblo joven.

d
Female speaker 2: Aquí los colegios son buenos y mis niños tienen más oportunidades para estudiar. Lo cierto es que cambiar de barrio nos ha traído muchos beneficios. Además la gente es muy simpática y te acoge en seguida.

3 🎧 🌐 Listen to the four people talking about where they live. Decide whether each person's comments are positive (P), negative (N), or both (P + N).

Students listen to four people talking about where they live and should try to pick out the key adjectives which indicate a positive or negative opinion. Refer them to the *Estrategia* for support in tackling this kind of gist understanding of listening passages.

After listening to the text, students could look at the transcript and highlight the key words and phrases.

Answers: **a** P, **b** N, **c** P + N, **d** P

> **Gramática**
> To introduce the main grammar point (Saying what you have to do or must do), you could display the reading text, highlight the *hay que*, *tener que* and *deber* phrases and challenge students to translate these, encouraging them to look at the context as well as the phrase itself. They should then be well prepared for grammar activity 4.
> If you wish to draw out the secondary grammar point (*lo* + adjective) there are plenty of examples of this in the text. You could highlight the first one (*Lo triste es que …* in line 5 of the second paragraph) and then ask students to highlight and translate the others. They should then be encouraged to build this structure into their work in activity 5.

4 🅖 Match up the two halves of these sentences, then translate them into English.

Work on the reading text and *Gramática* should have prepared students to manage this matching exercise.

Answers: **1** c, **2** d, **3** a, **4** b

Consejo

The tip reminds students to concentrate on using the language structures they know. Encourage them to jot down some ideas for activity 5 based on the *deber / tener que / hay que* structures they have been studying on this spread. With abler students you could also remind them to build in language learned during the course of this Context, such as reflexive constructions (see 1.9). You could remind them that they need to use *ser* to talk about long-term characteristics. Also remind students only to look up new nouns, adjectives, adverbs or infinitives of verbs in the dictionary (and make sure they know how to use them). Warn them never to use an electronic translator, as they don't work!

5 Work in pairs. Take turns to ask and answer these questions. Change the underlined parts and add extra details and opinions. Use the language structure box to help you.

Students should refer both to the language structure box and to the *Consejo*, which warns students about trying to say things that are too ambitious rather than using the language they know.

More able students could use the matched-up sentences from grammar activity 4 as models for some things they want to include in their answers.

Plenary activity

Students could work in pairs or teams. One student / team mentions a problem related to poverty in Spanish. The other student / team has to come up with a logical solution. Refer them back to the *Gramática* in 1.9 for some useful reflexive constructions. Model some expressions with nouns and infinitives (to try to avoid the trap of the subjunctive when talking about what people should do).

Student / Team A: *Hay enfermedades como el cólera (en los pueblos jóvenes).*

Student / Team B: *Se necesita agua limpia.*

Alternatively the teacher could prepare problems and solutions on pieces of card or paper, and the teams take it in turns to nominate students in teams A and B to try to match them up.

Pages 44–45

Reading and listening

Relationships and choices

- Audio file for core reading text
- Audio file and transcript for listening activity 2

Core reading text

The reading text is an extensive interview with María in which she gives information about herself, her family, her friends, and some social issues affecting a Moroccan friend, as an immigrant in Spain. It therefore goes over most of the topic ground of the Context, as well as including examples of key language structures from it.

The reading text is also available online as an audio file.

1a Read the interview. Which of María's relatives live in Spain? Complete the list in English by adding four more relatives.

Point out to students that they need not read the whole text word for word in order to do this kind of activity; they can simply look for the key words i.e. family member nouns, and then for each one, read around it to find out if that person lives in Spain or not. This is good practice of the skill of reading for specific information, as well as revision of key family member vocabulary. In this particular instance all the information they need for the question is in María's first answer.

Answers: (Brother), aunt and uncle, cousin and grandfather.

1b Match up each of María's friends with the correct description. Copy the grid and fill in the correct letter for each.

Make it clear to students that they will not need all the lettered answers, only one for each person.

Answers:

(Elisa)	(C)
Eduardo	E
Juanita	G
Laura	A
Yusuf	F

Gramática

This reminder of how the structures *desde hace* and *tener que* work will help students with their comprehension of the text for reading activity 1c.

1c Decide whether the following statements are true (T), false (F) or not mentioned (?).

Remind students that they may need to look at the data preceding the interview as well as the interview itself. They could predict key words to look for to find the answer to each question (e.g. *universidad* for question 2). They should study the *Gramática* for a reminder of the two language structures *desde hace* and *tener que* before they attempt this activity.

Answers: 1 T, 2 T, 3 ?, 4 T, 5 F, 6 T

2 *Transcript:*
1. Me gustaría tener muchos niños.
2. Después del instituto voy al extranjero para estudiar en la universidad.
3. Después de la universidad me gustaría encontrar un buen trabajo.
4. En el futuro me gustaría casarme. Mi marido ideal sería amable, generoso y muy guapo.
5. No voy a trabajar hasta los setenta años. Quiero jubilarme temprano.

Context 1 Lifestyle 37

2 🎧 Listen to the five young people talking about their future plans. Match up each person with the correct summary (A–G).

Students match up each statement with the correct speaker. Warn them that there are **two** statements that do not match any of the speakers. The Examiner's Tip offers support for this listening task.

A printable version of this transcript is also available online, along with the audio file.

Answers:

1 D, 2 G, 3 C, 4 A, 5 B

3 🎧 Transcript:

A	Entrevistador:	Háblame de tu familia en Guatemala.
	María:	La mía es una familia muy unida y nos relacionamos muy bien. Claro, es difícil estar tan lejos, pero nos escribimos y sé que me quieren mucho.
B	Entrevistador:	Y, hablando de amigos, ¿qué es un buen amigo para ti?
	María:	Un buen amigo está allí cuando lo pasas mal. Te puede ayudar y escuchar cuando tienes problemas.
C	Entrevistador:	Y ¿qué planes tienes para el futuro?
	María:	Bueno, después de la universidad voy a volver a Guatemala para hacerme profesora. Me gustaría mucho educar a los niños. Creo que es el trabajo más importante del mundo.
D	Entrevistador:	¿Por qué?
	María:	Mira, hay muchos pobres en Guatemala y con una buena educación van a tener más oportunidades como yo tengo ahora. Creo que debemos ayudar a otras personas en la vida.
	Entrevistador:	Gracias por la entrevista, María.

The interview adds more information to the profile of María in the reading text.

The Examiner's Tip offers support for this listening task, which requires close listening.

3 🎧 Listen to the interview with María and choose the correct answer from the options given.

A printable version of this transcript is also available online, along with the audio file.

Answers: 1 a, 2 b, 3 a, 4 a

Pages 46–47

Grammar practice

G Relationships and choices

Subject pronouns *Gramática*

A reminder of subject pronoun form and usage, to support activity 1.

1 ✏️ Copy the sentences and fill in the gaps with the correct subject pronoun.

Answers:

1 Yo, tú
2 Él, ella
3 Nosotros, vosotros
4 usted
5 ustedes

Desde hace *Gramática*

A note on how to use *desde hace* with the present tense, to support activity 2.

2 ✏️ Imagine that you are a character in a soap opera. Write about how long you have done the things in the box.

Answers: Students' own answers

Linking words *Gramática*

A list of linking words and phrases, to support activity 3.

3 📖 Copy the text and fill in the gaps with the most appropriate linking word(s) from the grammar box. There may be more than one option.

Answers: y, porque, pero (*or* sin embargo), además (*or* también), en cambio (*or* por otro lado), por eso, sin embargo (*or* claro (que)), entonces (*or* al final, por eso).

Saying 'would like' and 'would be' *Gramática*

Examples of *gustar* and *ser* in the conditional, to support activities 4a and 4b.

4a 📖 Choose the appropriate verb form in each sentence and write out the sentences correctly.

Answers: sería, Me gustaría, Te gustaría, les gustaría

4b ✏️ 💬 Imagine you are a celebrity. You have been asked to describe your ideal weekend break. Use the conditional tense of *gustar* or *ser* to talk about:

Students are given four prompts of things to talk about. When they have prepared their notes they could give this information to their partner or the rest of the class, who have to try to guess who they are.

Forming the negative

Gramática

A reminder of word order when using *no*, and a summary of how to use the other negative expressions *nunca / jamás, nadie, nada, ni … ni,* and *no … ningún*, to support activity 5.

5 Write the following sentences in the negative form.

Students are supplied with the glossed vocabulary items *siempre* and *todo* to ensure that they understand the questions prompting *nunca* and *nada*. Point out that there may be more than one way of writing the negative sentences – they should study the grammar box carefully to remind themselves of these alternatives.

Once they have completed the questions they could be asked to prepare some similar ones of their own, using vocabulary that they know.

Answers:

1. No es español.
2. No hay violencia en mi ciudad. (*or* Nunca hay violencia en mi ciudad. *or* No hay nunca violencia en mi ciudad.)
3. Nunca soy paciente. (*or* No soy nunca paciente.)
4. No tenemos ningunas oportunidades.
5. Mi amigo no tiene nada.
6. Las chicas no son ni inteligentes ni divertidas.

Lo + adjective

Gramática

A reminder of how to use *lo* with an adjective, to support activity 6.

6 Look at the diagram about Mexico. Write some sentences giving your reaction to the information, using the examples in the box below. Try to extend your sentences with more details.

This could be started off as a whole-class spoken activity to make sure students understand the construction and have some ideas as to how to add more detail to their sentences. Remind them of the linking words listed in the *Gramática* which accompanies activity 3.

Pages 48–49

Vocabulary

Relationships and choices

kerboodle!
- MP3 files for each vocabulary list

The essential vocabulary used within Topic 2, Context 1 is presented on this vocabulary spread.

Here students can learn the key words for the topic area *Relationships and choices*. You may also want to direct students to the online audio files of these vocabulary lists, so they can hear how the words are pronounced by a native speaker.

Some words are in light grey on the vocabulary spreads in the Student Book. This indicates items that are not included in the GCSE specification vocabulary list, so students do not need to learn these items for Listening and Reading assessment. However, you may wish students to use them in Speaking and Writing Controlled Assessments.

Pages 50–53

Controlled Assessment

Refer to the section on Controlled Assessment, pages 107–112 in this Teacher's Book.

Page 54

1 Context summary

kerboodle!
- Interactive multiple-choice quiz

The closing page for Context 1, Lifestyle, provides a multiple-choice quiz which tests the key language learnt in this Context.

A longer version of this quiz is also available online as an interactive, self-marking multiple-choice test.

Answers:

1. Student's own choice but the most logical is *buena*
2. Student's own choice
3. Student's own choice
4. Drugs are more dangerous than alcohol.
5. Mi amiga, Rosa, es muy amable, tiene el pelo rubio y no es muy baja.
6. casada
7. porque
8. Student's own choice
9. (suggested answer) cambiar
10. true

2 Leisure

Free time and the media

Free-time activities

Shopping, money, fashion and trends

Advantages and disadvantages of technology

Reading and listening

Grammar

Vocabulary

KS3 Revision:
Sports and other leisure activities, fashion and clothes; places in town, transport and compass points

Online materials
- Audio files for core reading texts

2.1 El tiempo libre en casa
- Using the preterite tense of regular verbs
- Improving fluency by learning complete phrases

- Audio file for core reading text
- Audio file and transcript for listening activity 3
- Reading activity: *El tiempo libre en casa*
- Grammar activity: Learning preterite verb endings for regular *-ar*, *-er* and *-ir* verbs
- Speaking worksheet
- Extension listening worksheet
- Audio file and transcript for extension listening activity

2.2 Fuera de casa
- Using irregular preterites *ir, ser*
- Using time expressions to recognise whether a statement is in the past tense or the present

- Audio file for core reading text
- Audio file and transcript for listening activity 4
- Listening activity and transcript: *¿Qué tal tu fin de semana?*
- Grammar activity: Using irregular preterites *ir, ser*
- Writing worksheet
- Extension listening worksheet
- Audio file and transcript for extension listening activity

2.3 ¿En qué gastas tu dinero?
- Using direct object pronouns
- Learning colloquial expressions

- Audio file for core reading text
- Audio file and transcript for listening activity 2
- Listening activity and transcript: *El dinero y tú*
- Grammar activity: Using direct object pronouns
- Speaking worksheet
- Extension reading worksheet
- Audio role play activity

2.4 ¿Te gusta estar de moda?
- Using demonstrative pronouns (*éste, ése, aquél*)
- Using a variety of words and phrases to express preferences

- Audio file for core reading text
- Video and transcript for activity 2
- Activity to accompany video
- Grammar activity: Using demonstrative pronouns
- Speaking worksheet
- Extension listening worksheet
- Audio file and transcript for extension listening activity

2.5 Los jóvenes y la tecnología
- Using indirect object pronouns
- Justifying your opinions and adding extra information

- Audio file for core reading text
- Audio file and transcript for listening activity 2
- Reading activity: *Las ventajas y desventajas de la nueva tecnología*
- Grammar activity: Using indirect object pronouns
- Writing worksheet
- Extension reading worksheet
- Foundation reading worksheet
- Foundation listening worksheet
- Audio file and transcript for foundation listening worksheet

Free time and the media
- Audio file for core reading text
- Audio file and transcript for listening activity 2
- Audio file and transcript for listening activity 3

Free time and the media
- Regular verbs with spelling changes in the preterite
- Time and place expressions
- Present participles, the gerund and infinitives
- Indefinite adjectives
- Comparative and superlative adverbs

Free time and the media
- MP3 files for each vocabulary list

Holidays
Plans, preferences, experiences

2.6 Las vacaciones
- Using irregular preterite verbs
- Showing off the language you know

  - Audio file for core reading text
  - Audio file and transcript for listening activity 2
  - Reading activity: *Las vacaciones de Lucía, Cristóbal y Eduardo*
  - Grammar activity: Using irregular preterite verbs
  - Writing worksheet
  - Extension listening worksheet
  - Audio file and transcript for extension listening activity

2.7 ¿Adónde vas?
- Using the immediate future
- Noting prefixes that are the same in Spanish and English

  - Audio file for core reading text
  - Audio file and transcript for listening activity 3
  - Listening activity and transcript: *Una visita de intercambio*
  - Grammar activity: Using the immediate future
  - Speaking worksheet
  - Extension reading worksheet
  - Audio role play activity

What to see and getting around

2.8 He ido a la fiesta
- Using the perfect tense to talk about what you have done recently
- Using time phrases in your written work

  - Audio file for core reading text
  - Audio file and transcript for listening activity 2
  - Reading activity: *Las Fallas de Valencia*
  - Grammar activity: Using the perfect tense
  - Speaking worksheet
  - Extension listening worksheet
  - Audio file and transcript for extension listening activity

2.9 ¡Vamos de viaje!
- Using imperative verb forms
- Using high numbers and 24-hour time

  - Audio file for core reading text
  - Audio file and transcript for listening activity 2
  - Listening activity and transcript: *De viaje*
  - Grammar activity: Using imperative verb forms
  - Speaking worksheet
  - Extension reading worksheet
  - Foundation reading worksheet
  - Foundation listening worksheet
  - Audio file and transcript for foundation listening worksheet

Reading and listening
Holidays
- Audio file for core reading text
- Audio file and transcript for listening activity 2

Grammar
Holidays
- Recognising the passive voice
- How to say 'for me', 'with me'
- Interrogatives
- The perfect tense
- Imperatives

Vocabulary
Holidays
- MP3 files for each vocabulary list

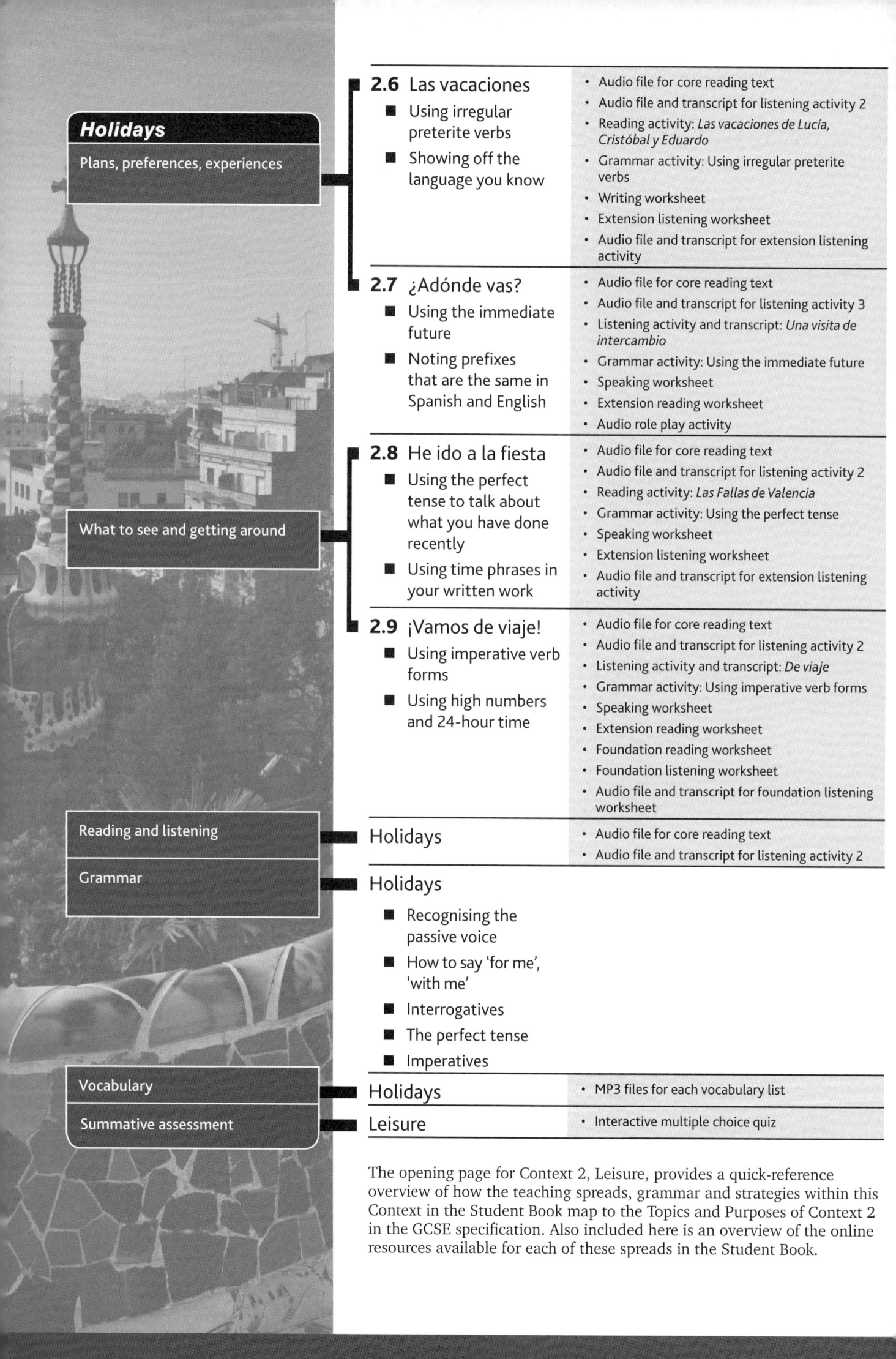

Summative assessment
Leisure
- Interactive multiple choice quiz

The opening page for Context 2, Leisure, provides a quick-reference overview of how the teaching spreads, grammar and strategies within this Context in the Student Book map to the Topics and Purposes of Context 2 in the GCSE specification. Also included here is an overview of the online resources available for each of these spreads in the Student Book.

Context 2 Leisure 41

Page 56

Revision

Sports and other leisure activities, fashion and clothes

kerboodle! • Audio files for core reading texts

Gramática

A reminder of how to use *por* and *para*. Students will need to refer to this reminder to help them with activity 1.

1 📖 🎧 Read Alfonso's blog and answer the following questions in Spanish.

The vocabulary needed is all available in the *Vocabulario* on the page but students could attempt the task initially without reference to this list (i.e. with it covered up).

Answers:

1 navega por Internet, toca y escucha música (longer answers also acceptable, provided they cover these essentials)
2 tenis
3 la batería, la flauta
4 una vez
5 con sus amigos

2a 📖 🎧 Read the conversation and answer the following questions in English.

Answers:

1 for going to school
2 if she's going to a party
3 comfortable shoes

2b 💬 Work in pairs. Partner A asks the questions in the conversation and Partner B gives their own answers. Then swap roles.

Students adapt the language in activity 2a to create their own dialogue; encourage them to invent facts, and not to feel that they have to stick to literal facts about themselves.

Page 57

Revision

Places in town, transport and compass points

kerboodle! • Audio files for core reading texts

Gramática

A summary of demonstrative adjective forms and uses. Students may need to refer to this to support their understanding of the reading text.

1 📖 🎧 Read the conversation. There is one error in each of the following sentences. Rewrite each sentence correctly.

Answers:

1 The town hall is **in the Plaza Mayor**.
2 The police station, Post Office and **library** are close to each other.
3 There **are some department stores**.
4 The town **does not have** an underground train system.

2a 📖 Read this description and draw a map showing the location of all the places mentioned.

Students draw a map to depict the details given in the short description.

2b ✏️ Write a description of an imaginary town. Locate four places according to their compass points.

Students should draw a simple map and may want to copy the compass points, as given in the *Vocabulario* on the page, next to their map, as a reference point for writing a description of where places are. The map need not show a diagram of streets – it can be very simple with just lines and labels to show what is to the north, south, etc. You may want to demonstrate the process with the whole class, marking just two or three places on your map, before students begin.

2c 💬 Work in pairs. Partner A reads their description and Partner B draws a map to show the places mentioned. Then swap roles.

Partner A must read their description of their town without showing their map to Partner B. Partner B attempts to draw the map according to what they hear, and then compares the result with Partner A's original map. They then swap tasks.

Pages 58–59

2.1 El tiempo libre en casa

Free-time activities

Subject	Talking about leisure activities at home
G 1	Using the preterite tense of regular verbs
G 2	Learning about the use of infinitives
🔊	Improving fluency by learning complete phrases

kerboodle!
- Audio file for core reading text
- Audio file and transcript for listening activity 3
- Reading activity: *El tiempo libre en casa*
- Grammar activity: Learning preterite verb endings for regular *-ar*, *-er* and *-ir* verbs
- Speaking worksheet
- Extension listening worksheet
- Audio file and transcript for extension listening activity

Starter activity

Brainstorm vocabulary for what you usually do at the weekend – time expressions, leisure activities, daily routine, etc: *el sábado / el domingo / los fines de semana, me levanto / me acuesto, temprano / tarde, veo la tele / juego en mi videoconsola / toco la guitarra / escucho música*, etc.

Core reading text

An extract from the diary of a Spanish teenager, Gabriela, describing a leisure day at home and then at her friend's house. Encourage students to note examples of *-ar*, *-er* and *-ir* verbs in the preterite, and use of different persons – i.e. first person singular, third person singular, first person plural, etc.; there are several in the text. They could note also vocabulary related to leisure, and time expressions.

The reading text is also available online as an audio file.

1a 📖 🎧 Read Gabriela's diary, then put the pictures into the correct order.

To make sure that students recognise which verbs relate to which pictures, and to keep the focus on the preterite tense, make statements such as '*Gabriela jugó al ping-pong con su hermano*' in response to which, students have to tell you the letter of the appropriate picture. They will then be well prepared for the reordering process of the activity.

Answers: C, E, D, A, B (students may interpret D as 'receiving a message', in which case the correct order is C, E, A, D, B)

1b 📖 🎧 Choose the correct infinitive to complete each phrase and then match up each phrase with the correct picture (A–E).

This activity reminds students that Spanish uses *ver*, not *mirar*, for 'watch' e.g. TV, film, and that there are two verbs for 'to play' – one for music, one for sports and games.

Answers:

1 **jugar** al ping-pong = A 2 **tocar** la batería = C
3 **ver** una película = B 4 **escuchar** música = E
5 **recibir / enviar** mensajes = D

1c 📖 🎧 From reading the diary page, what do you know about Gabriela, her family, her personality and what she does in her free time?

Make sure students know that they should reply in English and give as much detail as they can. If you want to allocate smaller tasks, display (or distribute) the three headings Gabriela's family, Gabriela's personality, what Gabriela does in her free time and students then concentrate on one heading.

Answers: (This information could be allocated to the headings if you decide to follow that route.)

Gabriela lives with her mum and dad, her brother and her little sister. She is quite patient and likes to stay out of family arguments. She looks after her little sister. She's sociable and she has quite a lot of friends. She has a friend called Alba. She prefers action films to comedies and romantic films. In her free time she listens to music, she reads the news on the internet, sends emails, talks to her friends on the phone, plays table tennis and video games with her brother and spends time with her friend, Alba.

> **Gramática**
> The paradigms of regular preterite verb forms for *-ar*, *-ir* and *-er* verbs, which students will need as support for activities 2–4.
> The secondary grammar point encourages students to pick up on more uses of infinitives (such as *Me invitó a ver una película*, in the reading text).

2 G Copy the sentences and fill in the gaps with the correct verb.

This activity tests only regular forms. Abler students may benefit from being given some spelling-change first person preterite forms of very common verbs (e.g. *empecé*, *jugué*, *toqué*) and asked to form sentences with these.

Answers:

1 me desperté 2 recibiste 3 lavó 4 tocaron

Context 2 Leisure 43

3 🎧 *Transcript:*

1

Marián:	Hola, Alberto. ¿Qué tal tu fin de semana?
Alberto:	Pues muy bien. El sábado por la mañana me desperté bastante tarde. Luego, después de comer, lavé los platos y pasé la aspiradora.
Marián:	¿De verdad? Qué bueno eres. ¿Viste *Gran Hermano* por la tarde?
Alberto:	No, no vi la tele. Vi una película en el portátil y luego saqué al perro a pasear.

2

Fermín:	Oye, Carla, ¿viste el partido entre el Real Madrid y el Barcelona en la tele anoche?
Carla:	Sí, fue un partido fenomenal, ¿verdad?
Fermín:	¡Y tanto! ¿Jugaste aquel videojuego que compraste la semana pasada?
Carla:	Sí, sí, jugué con mi padre.
Fermín:	¿Quién ganó?
Carla:	Yo, claro, es que mi padre juega fatal.

3

Eva:	Hola, José Luis. ¿Recibiste mi mensaje ayer? ¿Por qué no me llamaste?
José Luis:	Pues llegaron David y Martí a mi casa a mediodía y empezamos a escuchar música y a tocar la guitarra. Pasamos toda la tarde así. Luego jugamos al fútbol en el jardín hasta las siete, por ahí, y después comimos una pizza.

3 🎧 Copy the table, then listen to the conversations and tick the boxes to show what each person did at the weekend.

Three short conversations between friends about what they did last weekend / yesterday, etc. The recording could be paused after each section to allow students to note down the information about that person before they move on to the next section. To consolidate students' recognition of the preterite forms, ask them to highlight these on a printout of the transcript, and to write the infinitive of each verb.

Once they have completed the activity, abler students could be asked to re-present the information in the completed table, as third person sentences. For example, *Alberto ayudó en casa*.

You could also follow up with some questions in English for the whole class, for example:

1 Why do you think Alberto's friend is a little surprised about his account of what he did on Saturday morning?
2 What did Alberto do after lunch? Did he watch Big Brother?
3 What do you know about Carla from the conversation? (there are three things they could mention)
4 What do you think is the relationship between José Luis and the girl who phones him?
5 Why didn't José Luis return the girl's call?

Answers:

Alberto: helped at home, took the dog for a walk.
Carla: played a video game, watched TV.
José Luis: listened to music, played a sport, played a musical instrument.

Answers to follow-up questions:

1 Because he was so good! He did the washing up and hoovering.
2 He didn't watch Big Brother. He watched a film on his laptop.
3 She likes football. She bought a new video game recently. She's quite competitive and she's better than her dad at playing videogames.
4 Girlfriend and boyfriend.
5 He didn't return her call because two of his mates came round.

> ✏️ Some guidelines on how to improve fluency by learning complete phrases. Some examples are given, but you could ask students to produce a few more examples (for instance, they could practise referring to specific films using *ver*; how many sports / games / musical instruments can they recognise / mention? The strategy should then be applied in writing activity 4. **Estrategia**

> Students are instructed to use time expressions in writing activity 4, and they could add more from this list. **Consejo**

4 ✏️ 🌐 Write a diary or blog entry about a day at home last weekend. Include the following time expressions.

Some time expressions are given in the activity but there are several others in the *Consejo* which students could be encouraged to use. Abler students should also be asked to extend their sentences using linking phrases (as recently studied in 1.7).

Plenary activity

Students work in pairs. Without showing their partner, they write a list of five things that they did at home at the weekend. They then write a list of five things they guess their partner did. The partners then compare lists by asking questions to see if their guesses were correct (e.g. *¿Te despertaste tarde el sábado? ¿Viste una película en la tele?*)

Alternatively, the Speaking worksheet provides a structure for consolidation of leisure vocabulary and support for speaking using the preterite, and could be exploited for a plenary activity.

Pages 60–61

2.2 Fuera de casa

Free-time activities

Subject	Discussing free-time activities outside the home
G 1	Using irregular preterites: *ir*, *ser*
G 2	Learning some time and place expressions
	Using time expressions to recognise whether a statement is in the past tense or the present

kerboodle!
- Audo file for core reading text
- Audio file and transcript for listening activity 4
- Listening activity and transcript: *¿Qué tal tu fin de semana?*
- Grammar activity: Using regular preterites *ir*, *ser*
- Writing worksheet
- Extension listening worksheet
- Audio file and transcript for extension listening activity

1 **V** Look at the photos and answer the question: *¿Qué es para ti un fin de semana genial?*

This can be used as a starter activity to elicit from students, for example: *Para mí un fin de semana genial es ir a un partido de fútbol / salir con los amigos*, etc. Elicit further ideas using photos as stimulus – e.g. *jugar al tenis / al rugby / al voleibol, ir a la playa / a la piscina*, etc.

Core reading text

The text, *Un fin de semana genial*, consists of two descriptions by young people (Guillermo and Montse) of their (different) weekends: where they went and with whom, and what they did. They also mention what they usually do at the weekend, so this provides examples of the use of the present tense contrasted with the preterite used to recount past events. There are a good number of examples of *ir / ser* in the preterite. Display the text and use (or ask students to use) one colour for *ser* and one colour for *ir* to highlight the two verbs and demonstrate how, with the preterite of these two verbs, the context tells you which verb is being used.

The reading text is also available online as an audio file.

> 📖 Explain why the recognition of time expressions gives a clue as to the tense, but remind students also that the verb form is usually the main clue. They should look for time expressions in the reading text and tell you 'past' or 'present' for each one – then look at the verb to see if it is the tense they expect.
>
> *Estrategia*

> The paradigm of the shared preterite forms for *ser* / *ir*, which students need to understand for activities 2a and 2b, and to apply in activity 3.
> The secondary grammar point refers to learning some time and place expressions. Remind students of the expressions supplied for activity 4 in 2.1, for example. They could usefully list the time expressions they can think of under 'past', 'present' and 'future'.
>
> *Gramática*

2a 📖 🎧 🌐 Who usually does these activities, Guillermo, Gerardo and / or Montse?

Before they begin, ask students whether the answers to the questions are likely to be in the present tense or the preterite tense (answer: present tense). You could also ask them to give you a couple of time expressions they will be looking for to locate the answers.

Answers:

1 Guillermo
2 Guillermo, Gerardo and Montse
3 Guillermo
4 Gerardo
5 Montse

2b 📖 🎧 🌐 Who did these activities last weekend, Guillermo, Gerardo or Montse?

As with activity 2a, ask students whether the answers to the questions are likely to be in the present tense or the preterite tense (answer: preterite tense). You could also ask them to give you a couple of time expressions they will be looking for to locate the answers.

Answers:

1 Guillermo and Gerardo
2 Guillermo watched, Gerardo took part
3 Guillermo and Gerardo
4 Montse
5 Montse

3 **G** Copy and complete the dialogue using the correct parts of *ser* / *ir* in the preterite.

As well as supplying the missing forms, students could be asked to write the infinitive of the verb in brackets after each one to show that they know which verb they are using even though the forms are the same.

Answers: fuiste (ir), fui (ir), fuisteis (ir), fuimos (ir), fue (ser), fueron (ir)

4 🎧 *Transcript:*

A

DJ: Hola y buenos días. Espero que hayáis pasado todos un fin de semana estupendo. Hola, Laura, ¿qué tal tu fin de semana?
Laura: Hola, pues muy bien. El sábado fui a Valencia con unos amigos.
DJ: A Valencia, fenomenal.
Laura: Y además fuimos a un concierto de Maná en el estadio.
DJ: Un concierto de Maná, un grupo de rock genial.
Laura: Sí, sí, son fantásticos en directo – fue un espectáculo impresionante.
DJ: Me alegro, Laura. Gracias por llamarnos. Hasta luego.

B

DJ:	Hola, Pablo. ¿Cómo estás?
Pablo:	Bien, más o menos.
DJ:	¿Más o menos? Hmm. Me parece que quizás no te salió bien el fin de semana.
Pablo:	Bueno, es que fui con mi club de ciclismo, a un campeonato. En la primera carrera me caí y tuve que ir al hospital.
DJ:	¿Al hospital? Mala suerte.
Pablo:	Y no puedo volver a montar hasta dentro de tres meses.
DJ:	Bueno, Pablo. Tenemos que animarte un poco. Chicas, a ver si llamáis a Pablo. Y vamos a mandarte un CD, ¿vale?
Pablo:	Vale, gracias.

C

DJ:	Hola, Noelia. ¿Cómo estás?
Noelia:	Hola. Bueno hoy estoy muy cansada.
DJ:	¿Por qué? ¿Trabajaste mucho este fin de semana?
Noelia:	No, ¡qué va! El sábado fue mi cumpleaños y para celebrarlo, salí con mis amigos a bailar.
DJ:	Estupendo. ¿Y a qué hora llegaste a casa?
Noelia:	A las tres.
DJ:	Fenomenal. Bueno, hoy tienes que echarte una buena siesta.
Noelia:	Eso es.

D

DJ:	Hola, Raúl. ¿Qué tal tu fin de semana?
Raúl:	Genial. Fui a Londres.
DJ:	¿A Londres? ¿Durante el fin de semana?
Raúl:	Sí.
DJ:	¿Con quién fuiste?
Raúl:	Fui con mis padres y mis hermanos. Fuimos de compras a unos grandes almacenes, a Harrods y a Oxford Street.
DJ:	Fenomenal. Oye, Raúl, de compras el fin de semana a Londres, ¿es que te tocó la lotería?
Raúl:	No, ¡qué va! Fue una oferta especial – vuelo y hotel todo incluido.
DJ:	¡Fantástico! Bueno, la próxima vez que vayas, me avisas y te acompaño. ¿vale?
Raúl:	Vale.

4a 🎧 Listen to the conversations. Did each of these people have a good weekend or not?

Four people call a radio phone-in programme and tell the DJ about their weekend. Students should make two lists: the person / people who had a good weekend, and the person / people who didn't.

Answers:
Had a good weekend: **A** Laura, **C** Noelia, **D** Raúl.
Didn't have a good weekend: **B** Pablo.

4b 🎧 Listen again and answer the questions in English.

Remind students to refer to the *Estrategia* and think about how time expressions and verb forms reveal which statements refer to the past and which ones to the present or usual routine events.

Answers:

1 Laura went to a rock concert in Valencia.
2 Pablo took part in a cycle race but he fell off his bike and had to go to hospital.
3 Pablo's fed up because he can't cycle for three months.
4 It was a special weekend for Noelia because it was her birthday.
5 She's tired but happy.
6 Raúl went to London for the weekend with his family.
7 Because he went to London just for the weekend and went shopping in Harrods.
8 He hadn't won the lottery. They had got a special offer package which included the flight and the hotel.

> A reminder that verb form patterns have to be learned. Students should follow the advice to learn by heart the preterite-tense forms of *ser / ir* before they attempt activity 5.
>
> *Consejo*

5 💬 Work in pairs. Take turns to be Marián and José Luis. Adapt the dialogue by changing the underlined words. Refer to the online worksheet for a language structure box to help you.

Students should use the language structure box and the *Vocabulario* on page 72 for help. Higher-ability students could, after completing the activity as instructed, then adapt it in written form in the plural (Marián talks to José Luis and his brother Miguel), thus practising plural first and second person forms. And / Or students could write up a couple of sentences describing José Luis's weekend, thus practising third person (singular) forms.

Plenary activity

Play a cumulative game (along the lines of the 'I went out to dinner …' game): One student starts off a sequence by saying '*El fin de semana pasado, fui a ….*' The next student repeats this but adds another destination, and so on until someone gets stuck, at which point you can start again. This can be done in teams with the other team being given a chance to continue if a member of one team gets stuck. If you feel it would also be a worthwhile way to practise present-tense forms, elicit a contrasting series prompted by '*Normalmente, los sábados, me despierto tarde …*', etc.

Pages 62–63

2.3 ¿En qué gastas tu dinero?

Shopping, money, fashion and trends

Subject	Talking about money and shopping
G 1	Using direct object pronouns
G 2	Learning about gerunds
🔧	Learning colloquial language

kerboodle!
- Audio file for core reading text
- Audio file and transcript for listening activity 2
- Listening activity and transcript: *El dinero y tú*
- Grammar activity: Using direct object pronouns
- Speaking worksheet
- Extension reading worksheet
- Audio role play activity

Starter activity

Ask students to skim read the text and find the phrases for:

(they) spend half
(they) are more influenced by
leisure is what is important
they enjoy the free time more
(they) save more

Answers:

gastan la mitad
se dejan influir más
el ocio es lo que importa
disfrutan más del tiempo libre
ahorran más

Core reading text

The core text, *El consumismo y los jóvenes*, compares the spending habits and priorities of girls and boys in Spain. The language used provides expressions of agreement / disagreement which should be noted and reused by students, as recommended in the *Estrategia*. (The *Gramática* point, Using direct object pronouns, is exemplified in the listening content.)

The reading text is also available online as an audio file.

1a 📖 🎧 Read the article and match up these Spanish expressions taken from it with their English equivalents.

You could follow up the activity by asking students to find in the text the Spanish for 'they're always having to go and ask for more "dosh"' and see if they can tell you what is a bit 'different' about the word *pasta*. Draw their attention to the *Consejo* about using colloquial expressions.

Answers:

el consumismo – consumerism
la moda y las marcas – fashion and designer labels
la paga (semanal media) – (average weekly) pocket money
mejorar su autoestima – to improve their self-esteem

1b 📖 🎧 Read the article again and answer the following questions in English.

Students now read the text in full to extract the details required for this activity. If you think your students would benefit from the help, do the first two questions as a whole-class exercise, then point out that for the rest of the activity there is one question for each bullet point in the text.

Answers:

1 Boys spend more.
2 Girls spend half their money on clothes.
3 Boys are more influenced by fashion, designer labels and advertising than girls.
4 Young Spaniards spend around 30 euros a week.
5 Enjoying their free time is more important to young people.
6 Young people who work have a better sense of the value of money.
7 The average weekly allowance for 16–17-year-olds is about 11.50 euros.
8 People become addicted to shopping to improve their self-esteem and to be admired.

2 🎧 *Transcript:*

Entrevistador:	Buenos días. ¿Podría hacerte algunas preguntas? Es para una encuesta sobre los jóvenes y las compras.
Joven:	Bueno, sí.
Entrevistador:	La primera pregunta, sección A: ¿En qué gastas tu dinero? Es decir, ¿lo gastas en salir con los amigos? ¿En ropa? ¿En CDs?
Joven:	A ver, pues lo gasto en salir por ahí, con mis amigos, en el bus o el metro para ir al insti y en ir al polideportivo …
Entrevistador:	Vale.
Entrevistador:	Pregunta B: ¿De dónde recibes tu dinero? ¿Te lo dan tus padres? ¿Lo ganas trabajando? ¿Lo recibes de regalo?
Joven:	Mis padres me dan la paga y trabajo los fines de semana así que gano un poco.
Entrevistador:	Muy bien. Tus padres te dan dinero y lo ganas.
Entrevistador:	Pregunta C: ¿Ahorras dinero regularmente?
Joven:	Sí, intento poner veinte euros al mes en mi cuenta del banco.
Entrevistador:	Ahorras siempre que puedes.
Entrevistador:	Pregunta D: ¿Crees que el dinero que tienes es suficiente?
Joven:	Normalmente sí basta, pero si lo gasto todo, mis padres me dan un poco más.
Entrevistador:	Muy bien. Eso es todo. Gracias.
Joven:	De nada. Adiós.
Entrevistador:	Adiós.

Context 2 Leisure 47

2 🎧 Listen to a Spanish teenager being interviewed for a market research survey. Note his responses to the survey by answering these questions.

The boy answers four survey questions about his spending habits. The transcript includes a number of object pronouns (see notes on the *Gramática*, below).

For speaking practice students could act out the survey using a transcript; if you highlighted replaceable phrases such as *salir por ahí, al polideportivo, veinte euros al mes*, students could adapt the dialogue with personal or invented information.

With higher-ability students you could follow up by asking if they think this boy is a typical representative of spending habits as described in the reading text and if so / if not, then what is different about him.

Answers:
1 He spends money on
  – going out with friends
  – transport (getting to school)
  – sports (going to the sports centre).
2 His parents give him pocket money; he works at the weekend.
3 He tries to save regularly; he puts 20 euros a month into his savings account.
4 a (understanding / generous)

> **Gramática**
> The listening transcript contains numerous examples of the direct object pronouns that are the focus of the *Gramática*, so if you want to draw these out, you could supply a transcript and ask students to identify them. They will need to understand that they should identify only direct object pronouns (e.g. in the phrase *te lo dan* … only *lo* should be highlighted).
> The secondary grammar point – learning about gerunds – points out to students that where English uses a gerund, Spanish often uses an infinitive. There are examples in the reading text: *gastan el dinero en salir … y en comer*. Students could also be shown the use of the gerund in expressions such as *los que siguen recibiendo la paga*, and *hay que ir pidiendo más pasta*.

3 Ⓖ Match up each question with the correct answer.

Direct object pronouns are a difficult point to learn and this activity tests them only receptively. Abler students could be asked to produce one or more extra question / answer pairs, in which the answer must contain an object pronoun – they could do this working in pairs.

Answers: 1 c, 2 d, 3 a, 4 b

> **Estrategia**
> ✏️ This strategy, encouraging students to learn and use 'real' or colloquial language, is directed at writing activity 4 but applies just as importantly to speaking tasks. The first two activities on the Writing worksheet provide structure / support for a speaking activity which gives good opportunities for this, and would complement students' work on activity 4.

4 ✏️ 🌐 Create your own financial profile using expressions from the language structure box.

As well as the expressions in the language structure box, students could be given a few more time expressions to practise in the context of this writing task (e.g. *siempre, a veces, de vez en cuando, los fines de semana*). They can use the *Vocabulario* on pages 72–73 for support.

> **Consejo**
> A note on how and when to use (or not use) colloquial expressions.

Plenary activity

Learning colloquial expressions is fun so you may want to come up with a few more items for which students could guess the meaning if you present them in a short contextual sentence.

For a more grammar-based round-up activity you could display two prompt questions: *¿En qué gastas tu paga?* and *¿En qué gastas tu dinero?* and ask students to come up and write invented answers in the appropriate column; they must begin their answer with *lo* (for *dinero*) or *la* (for *paga*).

Pages 64–65

2.4 ¿Te gusta estar de moda?

Shopping, money, fashion and trends

Subject	Discussing your views on fashion and trends
Ⓖ 1	Using demonstrative pronouns (*éste, ése, aquél*)
Ⓖ 2	Learning some indefinite adjectives
🌐	Using a variety of words and phrases to express preferences

kerboodle!
- Audio file for core reading text
- Video and transcript for activity 2
- Activity to accompany video
- Grammar activity: Using demonstrative pronouns
- Speaking worksheet
- Extension listening worksheet
- Audio file and transcript for extension listening activity

Starter activity

Ask the class to come up with as much Spanish vocabulary as they can for clothes, accessories, colours, styles (*manga corta / larga, ajustado, ancho, tacón alto, sudadera con capucha*), etc. You could cut out photos of two different teenagers from a magazine, stick them on the board and ask students to describe what they are wearing.

una blusa	un cinturón	unos pantalones
unas botas	un collar	unos pendientes
una bufanda	una corbata	unas sandalias
unos calcetines	unas gafas de sol	un sombrero

una camisa	una gorra	unos vaqueros
una camiseta	unos guantes	un vestido
un chandal	unas medias	unas zapatillas de deporte
una chaqueta	un pañuelo	unos zapatos

Core reading text

Four young people give their views on the importance of clothes, fashion and personal style.

The reading text is also available online as an audio file.

1 📖 🎧 Read the accounts of personal style and fashion preference. Match up each person with one of the following descriptions, giving reasons for your choices.

This is a gist reading activity, where the students' task is to identify each speaker's overall attitude to fashion.

For closer follow-up work on this text you could ask students to rewrite the opinion which most reflects their own attitude to fashion (their answer to question 5 in this activity), in the third person. They may need reminding about the correct use of personal pronouns (e.g. *a mí* becomes *a él / a ella*).

Answers:

1 Nicolá   2 Alba   3 Mateo
4 Juan   5 (student's own choice)

2 🎥 *Transcript:* _____

Asistenta:	Hola.
Chica:	Hola. Quisiera probar aquel vestido que está en el escaparate.
Asistenta:	¿Aquél? ¿O éste?
Chica:	Ése.
Asistenta:	Vale. ¿Qué talla lleva usted?
Chica:	Treinta y ocho.
Asistenta:	Aquí lo tiene.
Chica:	Gracias.
Asistenta:	Éste, en azul, también es muy bonito. Y éstos van muy bien con los vestidos. ¿Quiere probárselos?
Chica:	Sí, me los pruebo todos.
Asistenta:	Estupendo. Los probadores están allá, al fondo.
Asistenta:	¿Cómo le van? ¿Quiere probárselos en otros colores o en otra talla?
Chica:	No, éstos me van bien. Pero no me decido. Los dos me gustan.
Asistenta:	¿Qué tal le van?
Chica:	Ése, no. Y ése tampoco. Éste y éste, me los llevo.
Asistenta:	Muy bien.
Asistenta:	Son setenta y cinco euros en total. ¿Cómo quiere pagar, con cheque, en efectivo, o con tarjeta de crédito?
Chica:	En efectivo. Aquí tiene.
Asistenta:	Vale. Cien euros … son veinticinco euros de cambio.
Chica:	Gracias.
Asistenta:	A usted.
Chica:	Hola. ¿Compraste algo?
Chico:	Sí, compré una camiseta y algunos calcetines.

2a 🎥 Watch the video clip and choose the correct option to complete each of the following sentences.

The video shows a girl trying on and choosing clothes in a shop. It is full of examples of demonstrative pronouns which you can use to illustrate the *Gramática*. Students should watch once before attempting the activity and then again if they need to while they answer the questions.

Answers: 1 b,   2 c,   3 b,   4 c

2b 🎥 Watch again and answer the following questions in English.

The questions in this activity require closer attention to detail so you may need to pause the video at the appropriate points while students jot down their answers before moving on to the next question.

To make use of the range of demonstrative pronouns in the text, you could provide students with a transcript and each student is told to highlight one particular kind of pronoun, for this / these or for that / those. They should also indicate the gender of the pronouns they find.

Answers:

1 She asks to try on the dress in the window.
2 The changing rooms are at the back of the shop.
3 The girl pays with cash.
4 She gets 25 euros change.

> **Gramática**
> The video includes numerous examples of the demonstrative pronouns that are the main grammar point here. So after looking at the grammar box with the class, you could play the video again, pausing it after each sentence containing the demonstrative pronouns, and ask the class what each one refers to. Students should then be able to tackle activity 3. The secondary grammar point refers to indefinite adjectives – the most useful ones at this point are *alguno, cada, mismo, otro* and *todo*.

3 Ⓖ Copy the sentences and fill in the gaps with the correct demonstrative pronoun.

Instruct students to ask themselves three questions each time:

- Where is the thing that the pronoun refers to (here, there, over there?)
- Is it feminine or masculine?
- Is it singular or plural?

These questions could be displayed as a reminder while students are working on the activity.

Answers: 1 ésta   2 ésos   3 éste   4 aquéllos

> **Estrategia**
> ✏️ Some important expressions for giving personal likes / dislikes / opinions as students will need to do in writing activity 4.

Context 2 Leisure 49

> **Consejo**
> A reminder that the position of adjectives in Spanish sentences differs from English, which may be useful to students in preparing their personal style statement (writing activity 4).

4 Write your own personal style statement. Use some of the ideas and expressions from the four texts on page 64.

Students are given a series of prompt points which they should include in their personal style statement. Remind them that they can model their statement on any of the core reading text pieces, but that they must make it personal and change as many of the details as they can, also adding some of their own. Draw their attention to the *Consejo* which reminds them about the position of adjectives in Spanish.

Students could use the Speaking worksheet at this point either as preparatory to the writing activity or to follow it up with complementary speaking practice.

Plenary activity

Find a few images from a magazine of different outfits and practise expressions of like / dislike and demonstrative pronouns by eliciting comments and criticisms from the students about the outfits shown in the photos. If some of the photos can be of unconventional or high fashion outfits that will enliven the discussion!

Pages 66–67

2.5 Los jóvenes y la tecnología

Advantages and disadvantages of new technology

Subject	Talking about the advantages and disadvantages of new technology
G 1	Using indirect object pronouns
G 2	Learning about comparative and superlative adverbs
	Justifying your opinions and adding extra information

kerboodle!
- Audio file for core reading text
- Audio file and transcript for listening activity 2
- Reading activity: *Las ventajas y desventajas de la nueva tecnología*
- Grammar activity: Using indirect object pronouns
- Writing worksheet
- Extension reading worksheet
- Foundation reading worksheet
- Foundation listening worksheet
- Audio file and transcript for foundation listening activity

Starter activity

Use the first of the series of questions that appears in the reading text as an opener: *¿Cuáles de los siguientes aparatos son más importantes para ti?*

Then as an introduction to the reading matter, ask students to find the Spanish words in the article which match the following English expressions.

advantage	(phone) call
disadvantage	instant messenger
mobile phone	to surf the internet
laptop	to download
message	junk mail, spam
email	broadband

Answers:

- advantage – *la ventaja*
- disadvantage – *la desventaja*
- mobile phone – *el móvil*
- laptop – *el portátil*
- message – *el mensaje*
- email – *el correo electrónico*
- call (phone call) – *la llamada*
- instant messenger – *el mensajero instantáneo*
- to surf the internet – *navegar en la red*
- to download (e.g. music from the internet) – *descargar*
- junk mail – *el correo basura*
- broadband – *banda ancha*

Core reading text

This magazine article, *Encuesta: la tecnología y tú*, is in three sections as three young people explain what use they make of new technology. All three are addressing the prompt questions shown in the middle of the text. Ask students to give you one suggestion for each of the last two central questions, i.e. to mention (in Spanish) one advantage and one disadvantage of new technology.

To further familiarise students with the vocabulary (building on the starter activity), divide the class into two teams: the teams take turns to find (in the text) and tell you a Spanish word related to new technology.

There are plenty of examples in the text to back up your teaching of the main *Gramática* point, using indirect object pronouns. The secondary grammar point, comparative and superlative adverbs, can be practised in the context of this spread if you wish, by using comparative and superlative forms of the familiar adverbs *frecuentemente, rápidamente / rápido, fácilmente*.

Although the *Estrategia* is aimed at the writing task, it can be related directly to several examples in the text showing students ways to justify their opinions and add extra information.

The reading text is also available online as an audio file.

1 Read the article and for each person write down:

If you feel that students will find the length of the text daunting, allocate one of the three sections of the text to one-third of the class, etc., ideally by going round the class members pointing at each student in turn and saying the name of one of the three young people, Sara,

Jorge or Isabel. Then each student must find the answers to the questions for their particular person. You could run through a few students' answers orally afterwards so that the whole class finds out the answers for the whole text.

Answers:

	Sara	Jorge	Isabel
1 most important item	mobile phone	games console	laptop
2 how acquired	Her parents gave it to her for her birthday.	He bought it with the money he earned from his weekend job.	It was passed down to her by her brother when he got a new one.
3 advantages	It's good for keeping in touch with friends. Her parents feel happier knowing they can keep in touch with her when she's out.	It's fun and he never gets bored. He's heard that playing videogames can improve concentration, coordination and reactions.	She can connect to the internet easily. Surfing the net is entertaining and educational. She doesn't have to go to the library or bookshop to look up information. She can download music which works out cheaper than buying CDs. She can keep in touch with friends by email or Instant Messenger. It's good for doing homework.
4 disadvantages	They're quite expensive and are easy to steal.	His parents complain that he spends too much time playing videogames.	Junk mail.

2 🎧 Transcript:

Entrevistadora: Hola, ¿te puedo hacer algunas preguntas sobre la tecnología?
Chica 1: Bueno, sí.
Entrevistadora: ¿Cuáles de los siguientes aparatos son más importantes para ti? ¿El teléfono móvil, el ordenador portátil, el MP3, la cámara digital o la videoconsola?
Chica 1: El móvil, más que nada el móvil.
Entrevistadora: ¿Por qué te es imprescindible el móvil?
Chica 1: Porque me permite estar en contacto con mis amigos.
Entrevistadora: Estar en contacto con los amigos, vale.
Entrevistadora: ¿Y, cómo lo utilizas? ¿Haces llamadas con el móvil o envías mensajes?
Chica 1: Sobre todo mando mensajes. Es muy fácil y sale más barato.

Entrevistadora: Hola, ¿me contestarías algunas preguntas sobre la tecnología y la comunicación?
Chico: Sí, sin ningún inconveniente.
Entrevistadora: De los siguientes aparatos, ¿cuáles son más importantes para ti? ¿El teléfono móvil, el ordenador portátil, el MP3, la cámara digital o la videoconsola?
Chico: Pues … para mí es más importante el portátil.
Entrevistadora: ¿Por qué es tan importante el portátil?
Chico: Bueno, me es imprescindible porque lo utilizo mucho.
Entrevistadora: ¿Para qué lo utilizas?
Chico: Para conectarme a Internet, para descargar música, para enviar y recibir correo electrónico.
Chica 2: Para mí es más importante el MP3.
Entrevistadora: ¿El MP3? ¿Por qué?
Chica 2: Porque me encanta la música y con un MP3 puedes escuchar música en cualquier lugar.
Entrevistadora: ¿Cómo usas el MP3?
Chica 2: Bueno, pues, elijo la música que me gusta. La bajo de Internet y la escucho en el MP3. Sale mucho más barato que comprar discos compactos.

2a 🎧 Listen to three people being interviewed about communication technology. Write down which of the following items each interviewee mentions.

The three interviewees are all stating which technology they use most. The questions and replies provide some clear models for question forming and sentence forming within this topic, including some key adverbial phrases as well as useful models of the position and form of indirect object pronouns, the main grammar point on the spread (see *Gramática*). You could refer to the *Estrategia* and encourage students to make their own lists of key phrases from the transcript and from the texts which they think they are likely to want to use when speaking or writing about communication technologies.

Answers: 1 D: mobile 2 E: laptop 3 B: MP3

2b 🎧 Listen again. Make a list of the uses mentioned for each item, e.g. keeping in touch with friends, for security reasons, etc.

Students should be able to do some predicting before they listen again – they may remember some information from the first time they listened, and they should be able to guess what the speakers are likely to say, so they could note down key Spanish words to listen out for.

Answers:

1 Mobile – good for keeping in touch with friends and for sending texts.
2 Laptop – good for connecting to the internet, downloading music and for email.
3 MP3 – good for listening to the music you like wherever you are.

Following on from the work on direct object pronouns in 2.3, the main point here is now indirect object pronouns. Make sure students are clear on the vital difference between direct and indirect object pronouns. Revisit direct object pronouns by asking them to highlight in a given colour all the direct object pronouns in the text (and / or in a copy of the listening transcript). Then they should use a different colour to highlight the indirect object pronouns. This is quite tricky and will require some class discussion: it could be done as a whole-class exercise, with the text displayed and students telling you which is the next word to highlight and in which colour.
As preparation for grammar activity 3, ask students to translate and then adapt a couple of key short extracts from the transcript, such as:
*¿Por qué **te** es imprescindible el móvil?*
*Porque **me** permite estar en contacto con mis amigos.*
which clearly show the role and form of indirect object pronouns.

3 Copy the sentences and fill in the gaps with the appropriate indirect object pronoun.

Students will need to spend some time on the *Gramática* as suggested above before they attempt the gap-fill exercise. You will also need to remind them that in Spanish, object pronouns can be tacked onto infinitives (as is the case in questions 2 and 4). This was covered for direct object pronouns in the 2.3 *Gramática* but you should point out that it applies equally to indirect object pronouns. There is one example of this construction in the reading text (i.e. *puedo llamarles* in Sara's text).
Answers: **1** me, **2** le, **3** te, **4** les

Students are required to use these skills – 'justify their opinions and add extra information' – in activity 4, but they should study this strategy guideline and note down some model phrases from the reading text before they try the activity.

4 Write notes to answer the questions included in the magazine article on page 66. Then work in pairs. Use your notes as prompts for talking to your partner for one minute about the advantages and disadvantages of new technology.

This task combines writing and speaking skills, and can be supported via the Writing worksheet as well as the language structure box.

This advice helps students to build more varied verbs into their work for writing and speaking tasks such as activity 4.

Plenary activity

The Writing worksheet can be used as a final consolidation task. Alternatively, hold a show-of-hands class survey to find out:
- the technology they use most frequently and why it is important to them (*me ayuda a hacer mis deberes*)
- the technology that is most important at home and why it is important to different members of the family (*le permite hacer el trabajo … me ayuda a …*)
- what item of communication technology they would like to buy if they had £100 to spend … (practising *me gustaría*).

Pages 68–69

Reading and listening

Free time and the media

- Audio files for core reading texts

Core reading text

The reading text is a Leo Verdura cartoon in which he (unsuccessfully, naturally) tries his hand at windsurfing. Students may be pleasantly surprised to find that although there is unfamiliar language, they can understand and deduce enough to answer some questions. You may want to test students' reading skills of deduction and word family recognition by finding out whether they can work out the meaning of *Cruz Roja* and *arrecifes*. (See also activity 1b.)

The reading text is also available online as an audio file.

1a Read the cartoon and answer the following questions in English.

Emphasise that students can find out as much from the pictures as the text – they should use visual clues and not worry too much about understanding every single word.
Answers:
1. a Dad: Leo Verdura
   b Mum: Katya
   c Two sons: Stanley and Livingstone
2. Yes, because Katya refers to the last time he tried it (when he ended up needing first aid).
3. Be careful! or Watch out!
4. Leo's watersports adventure / his windsurfing attempt (or equivalent answer)
5. He can see the tentacle of a giant octopus reaching out towards his dad who is stranded on the rock.

1b 📖 🎧 Read the cartoon again. Match up each Spanish expression with its English equivalent.

This activity tests some useful time phrases as well as new vocabulary items which students should be able to work out from the context and their similarity to familiar words.

Answers:

un rato – a little while
la última vez – the last time
acabamos en – we ended up in
la Cruz Roja – the Red Cross
fue bonito mientras duró – it was good while it lasted

1c 📖 🎧 Choose the sentences which correctly describe the characters in the cartoon. Then choose a sentence from the cartoon to support each of your choices.

Students could also refer to what they see in the pictures, not just the sentences, to back up their interpretation of the characters.

Answers:

1 b: 'La última vez …' etc. (Katya shows no signs of alarm, just keeps on sunbathing)
2 a: 'Voy a divertirme un rato …' etc. (He looks pleased to be going off to have some fun and doesn't look where he's going)
3 b: 'Fue bonito mientras duró …' (He is grinning about it)

> The box provides a reminder of the preterite tense, with examples that relate back to the content of the cartoon. It also points out the use of the indirect object pronoun *le* in *La última vez que le oí decir eso*.
>
> **Gramática**

2 🎧 *Transcript:*

1 Creo que pasar todo el día en el Internet o jugando videojuegos puede llevar a problemas de salud, como, por ejemplo, dolores de cabeza y problemas con la espalda.
2 Con un portátil y un móvil, todo se hace más fácil. Son muy prácticos.
3 El móvil es imprescindible ahora tanto para comunicarse con los amigos, como para el trabajo. Nunca salgo sin él.
4 Puedes hacer casi todo ahora por Internet, es decir, buscar información, comprar y vender cualquier cosa, descargar música, todo. Lo encuentro muy útil.
5 Nunca puedes desconectarte. La gente espera que contestes a los mensajes y a los correos electrónicos enseguida. Esto es muy pesado y conduce al estrés.

2 🎧 Listen to the five people talking about communication technology. What is the attitude of each person? Choose the correct letter.

Ask students to write down the numbers 1–5 in a list before they hear the five speakers, so that they can then just add the letters as they listen.

Answers: **1** C, **2** B, **3** A, **4** B, **5** C

3 🎧 *Transcript:*

– Tiene un mensaje nuevo. Para escucharlo, pulse 1.
– Hola, Eva. Soy Carlos. Oye, compré dos entradas para el concierto el viernes. ¿Quieres venir?
– Empieza a las diez y media, en el estadio. José y Alba fueron ayer y dijeron que fue fantástico.
– Podemos tomar unas tapas primero. Puedo pasar por tu casa a eso de las ocho y media. Llámame o mándame un mensaje. Hasta luego.

3 🎧 Listen to the recorded message and answer the following questions.

Students will almost certainly need to listen more than once to pick up all the details.

Answers:

1 a   2 b   3 b   4 c
5 b   6 b   7 c

Pages 70–71

Grammar practice

G Free time and the media

> **Regular verbs with spelling changes in the preterite**
>
> A reminder of the sound consistency reason for spelling changes, and the typical patterns, to support activities 1a and 1b.
>
> **Gramática**

1a 📖 Choose a sentence (1–4 from Activity 1b below) to match each picture.

Answers: **1** B, **2** C, **3** A, **4** D

1b ✏️ Copy and complete the sentences with the correct preterite form of the verb *jugar*, *llegar*, *sacar* or *tocar*.

Answers:

1 tocaron   2 llegué
3 saqué   4 jugaron

Context 2 Leisure 53

Time and place expressions
Advice about the use of *aquí*, *ahí*, *allí* and *allá* and time expressions which can be used to add detail in writing and speaking tasks. These are practised in activity 2.

2 Complete the letter with the following words.
Answers:
- a aquí
- b allí
- c allá
- d ahora
- e ahí

Present participles, the gerund and infinitives
An explanation of the differences in usage where English uses a gerund and Spanish uses an infinitive; the point is then practised in activity 3.

3 Copy and complete the Spanish with the words below. Then translate the sentences into English.
Answers:
1. *hacer*: Doing sport is a good way to keep fit.
2. *tocar*: Playing the guitar is my favourite pastime.
3. *ir*: Going to the cinema is quite expensive.
4. *disfrutar*: Enjoying your free time is important for a healthy life.

Indefinite adjectives
A reminder of the form, agreement and position of indefinite adjectives *alguno/a*, *cada*, *mismo/a*, *otro/a*, *todo/a* to support activities 4a and 4b.

4a Work with a partner. Read the dialogue aloud, completing it with the correct forms of the indefinite adjectives.
Answers:
- a algunas
- b Todas
- c mismo
- d todas
- e otro

4b Work in pairs. Adapt the dialogue in activity 4a to ask for a different item.
Answers:
  Students' own answers

Comparative and superlative adverbs
The information here is a reminder of the formation of regular adverbs and their comparative / superlative forms; you may wish to remind students also of the irregular comparatives of *bien*, *mal*, *mucho* and *poco*. Regulars and irregulars are practised in activities 5a and 5b.

5a Identify the comparative or superlative adverb in each of the following sentences.
Answers:
1. mejor
2. más
3. más responsablemente
4. más rápidamente

5b Copy the sentences and fill in the missing words to complete the English translations of the sentences from activity 5a.
Answers:
1. better
2. more
3. responsibly
4. faster

Pages 72–73

Vocabulary

V Free time and the media

kerboodle! • MP3 files for each vocabulary list

The essential vocabulary used within Topic 1, Context 2 is presented on this vocabulary spread.

Here students can learn the key words for the topic area *Free time and the media*. You may also want to direct students to the online audio files of these vocabulary lists, so they can hear how the words are pronounced by a native speaker.

Some words are in light grey on the vocabulary spreads in the Student Book. This indicates items that are not included in the GCSE specification vocabulary list, so students do not need to learn these items for Listening and Reading assessment. However, you may wish students to use them in Speaking and Writing Controlled Assessments.

Pages 74–75

2.6 Las vacaciones

Plans, preferences, experiences

Subject	Talking about holiday preferences and experiences
G 1	Using irregular preterite verbs
G 2	Learning how to avoid the passive
🔧	Showing off the language you know

kerboodle!
- Audio file for core reading text
- Audio file and transcript for activity 2
- Reading activity: *Las vacaciones de Lucía, Cristóbal y Eduardo*
- Grammar activity: Using irregular preterite verbs
- Writing worksheet
- Extension listening worksheet
- Audio file and transcript for extension listening activity

Starter activity

As a gentle introduction to holiday vocabulary, make the link from the first topic of this Context by asking students what leisure activities they like to do when they are on holiday. Follow up with questions about what they did on a recent holiday, to elicit some preterite forms (including *ser / ir* as learned in 2.2).

You could also do some work with the photos (as good preparation for activity 1a), simply asking students to call out the correct photo number in response to phrases you say, e.g. *es una ciudad grande, fueron unas vacaciones románticas, llevan mochilas*, etc.

Core reading text

Three young people describe where they were and what they did on their holiday. The texts combine key language for talking about holiday activities and experience, with plenty of examples of irregular preterite verbs which will be the main grammar focus of the spread.

The reading text is also available online as an audio file.

1a 📖 🎧 Match up each speech bubble with the correct photo. (There is one extra photo.)

The starter work should have prepared students for this matching activity, but students will need to read the texts carefully to make sure they identify the correct activities and places. They should write the three names and add a photo letter to each one.

Answers: Lucía **A**, Cristobal **C**, Eduardo **B**

1b 📖 🎧 Write the name of the person who …

Students read the texts again looking for the specific detail requested. They could use the *Vocabulario* on page 86 to help identify the key nouns and verbs they need to find.

Answers: **1** Cristobal   **2** Lucía   **3** Cristobal
              4 Cristobal   **5** Lucía   **6** Eduardo

2 🎧 *Transcript:*

Mujer:	¿Qué tal el viaje a Irlanda, Gema?
Gema:	Fíjate, el avión estaba averiado y cancelaron el vuelo. Pusieron otro avión y llegamos a Dublín con tres horas de retraso. Pero no llegó mi equipaje. Sin la ropa lo pasé mal. Tuve que comprar zapatos, chaqueta, pantalones … Me salió cara la cosa.
Mujer:	Antonio, ¿cómo pasaste tus vacaciones en Tarifa?
Antonio:	Pues, es un lugar de veraneo muy bonito pero lo pasé mal.
Mujer:	¿Por qué?
Antonio:	Hizo mucho sol y cuando estuve en la playa, cogí una insolación. Tuve fiebre, vómitos, dolor de cabeza … Fui al médico y me recomendó guardar cama. Así que pasé las vacaciones en la cama.
Mujer:	¿Y tú, Paloma, fuiste al extranjero?
Paloma:	Sí, fui a los Estados Unidos y lo pasé estupendamente. Es un país magnífico. Visité museos y monumentos. Fui de compras. Fui a hamburgueserías y heladerías.
Mujer:	¿Y qué tiempo hizo?
Paloma:	No hizo buen tiempo. Hizo frío y llovió pero no me afectó.
Mujer:	¿Qué tal tus vacaciones, Joaquín?
Joaquín:	Fui a Alemania, a Berlín. Lo pasé bastante bien. Hay mucho que ver.
Mujer:	¿Qué tal el hotel?
Joaquín:	Ni bueno ni malo, regular. Lo malo fue que me robaron el pasaporte.
Mujer:	¿Qué hiciste?
Joaquín:	Informé a la policía, rellené una ficha y me dieron un documento. No hubo problema.

2a 🎧 Listen to Gema, Antonio, Paloma and Joaquín talking about their holiday experiences. Are their comments positive (P), negative (N) or both (P + N)?

On the first time of listening students are only required to identify the speakers' attitudes, so they should listen for tone of voice but also for specific positive and negative adjectives / adverbs / expressions. Ask students to predict some of these (e.g. *lo pasé mal / bien*, etc.).

Answers: Gema N, Antonio N, Paloma P, Joaquín P + N

2b 🎧 Listen again and write the name of the person who …

On the second hearing students have to pick up very specific information. You could pause the audio after each interview to give students time to consider whether that person is the one who suffered from any of the problems listed.

Answers:

1 Antonio got sunstroke.
2 Gema lost her luggage.
3 Gema had her flight cancelled.
4 Joaquín had his passport stolen.

Context 2 Leisure

> **Gramática**
>
> The irregular preterite forms of the four very common verbs *estar*, *hacer*, *tener* and *dar*, plus a note about radical changing *-ir* preterites. Having presented the paradigms and rehearsed them with students, ask the class to translate into English the following four phrases in the reading text that contain preterite forms of the verbs listed here:
>
> *Cuando estuve allí …*
> *Estuve de vacaciones en los Picos de Europa*
> *Hicimos barbacoas*
> *Tuvimos mala suerte*

3 **G** Copy the sentences and fill in the gaps with the correct form of the verb in the preterite tense, using the words below.

All the forms that students need to fill the gaps are provided but they will need to take care to choose the correct verb. You may need to remind them that the verb used in Spanish may not be a literal translation of the English one (e.g. question 3 – which verb do they need for weather phrases like this one?).

Abler students could be asked to make up another couple of sentences using forms chosen from the *Gramática* lists.

Answers: **1** Estuve, **2** dio, **3** hizo, **4** tuvo

> **Estrategia**
>
> Particularly important for speaking tasks such as activity 4, this advice reminds students that when prompted to speak on a topic they need to make the most of any phrases they know, rather than worry about whether they have the vocabulary to give a literally truthful answer. Practise this with them by firing quick questions about what they did on holiday – they have to answer as quickly as they can, using any leisure activity verb.

4 Do a class survey. Find out what sort of holidays your classmates like. Add reasons to your own answer. If you can, give an example of a recent holiday.

Prepare for the survey itself by having students work for five minutes on pairwork speaking tasks like the model exchange shown in the activity. The survey could be done in groups and then the results pooled, so long as a list of holiday types is agreed in a whole-class forum at the start. Each group appoints a spokesperson / note taker who notes down (or ticks boxes for) the preferences of all the group members including him / herself. Students should use the language structure box for help.

Reassure students that even in this context it is more important to use and practise key language from the topic than to worry about whether you know the exact vocabulary for the activity or place you want to mention. (Refer them to the *Estrategia*.) However, there is no reason why this task could not also be used as a vocabulary extension exercise if some students want to talk about knitting or bobsleighing.

As a written follow-up the results of the survey should be drawn up as a graph, which students could then describe in a paragraph of written text.

> **Consejo**
>
> There is just one example of a passive form (*La Cueva de Nerja fui descubierta en 1959*) in the text; if drawing students' attention to this it should be made clear that this form is not one they should try to use – on the contrary, day-to-day Spanish avoids it (as referred to in the secondary *Gramática* point).

Plenary activity

The survey could be followed up with more work on the preterite: make guesses as to where students went / what they did on a recent holiday, or use a few photos of very contrasting people (sporty girl, grumpy old man) and ask students to invent a few sentences about that person's last holiday. They could use the language structure box for help.

Pages 76–77

2.7 ¿Adónde vas?

Plans, preferences, experiences

Subject	Talking about holiday plans
G 1	Using the immediate future
G 2	Learn about disjunctive pronouns
	Noting prefixes that are the same in Spanish and English
kerboodle!	• Audio file for core reading text • Audio file and transcript for activity 3 • Listening activity and transcript: *Una visita de intercambio* • Grammar activity: Using the immediate future • Speaking worksheet • Extension reading worksheet • Audio role play activity

Starter activity

Before students look at the text, you could start with some map work if you have access to a world map: can students find Cuba? And on a map of Spain, can they find the Sierra Nevada and Costa del Sol? Find out if they know anything about either place, and ask them to mention some things (in Spanish) that they think they are going to do if they go on holiday to these places.

Core reading text

Two people describe their contrasting holiday plans (skiing in the Sierra Nevada and a holiday in Cuba). (Students may be surprised to read about a skiing holiday so close to the Costa del Sol.) Both use the immediate future to talk about their plans and the texts provide a good range of holiday activity language, some familiar and some new, for students to assimilate.

The reading text is also available online as an audio file.

1a 📖 🎧 Who is going to do what on holiday this year? Write S (Sergio) or M (Marisa).

A skim-reading task, which students can mainly guess once they know which type of holiday the two speakers are describing, but they should check their expectations against the text.

Answers: **1** M, **2** S, **3** M, **4** M, **5** S, **6** S

1b 📖 🎧 Using the immediate future, write two more things that Sergio and Marisa are each going to do.

Students can take the information directly from the text but need to refer to the *Gramática* for the third person form they need for their answers. Less able students may need the support of sentence starters *Sergio va a … Marisa va a …*.

> **Gramática**
>
> This is not the students' first encounter with the immediate future tense so they should be able to find the examples in the text relatively easily, but tell them to be careful to distinguish between *ir a* with a noun (destination) and *ir a* with an infinitive (future tense verb), pointing out that the difference is just the same as in English.
>
> Consolidate the verb forms with a question-and-answer session linking destinations to activities. For example, *El sábado, voy a ir al cine. A vuestro ver, ¿qué voy a hacer? Este verano, mis amigos y yo vamos a ir a Tenerife. ¿Qué vamos a hacer?*
>
> (To a student – this would be good preparation for activity 4) *¡Enhorabuena, has ganado un premio en la Lotería! ¿Qué vas a hacer?*
>
> The secondary grammar point refers to disjunctive pronouns i.e. pronouns after a preposition, as in *conmigo* (seen in the reading text) and *para mí* (found in the listening); see also the *Consejo*.

2a Ⓖ Copy the sentences and fill in the gaps with the correct form of the verb *ir* and the correct infinitive.

The gap-fill words are used once each to complete the sentences. Students may need help with *coger*, although they can work it out by process of elimination.

Answers:

1 va, jugar   2 vamos, ir   3 vais, pasar
4 van, coger   5 vas, hacer   6 voy, alojarme

2b Ⓖ Translate the sentences in Activity 2a into English.

A check that students fully understand the meaning of the immediate future construction.

Answers:

1 Consuelo is going to play tennis.
2 This Easter week Emilio and I are going to go to Seville.
3 Where are you going to spend your holidays?
4 Lorenzo and Luisa are going to catch the 6 o'clock train.
5 What about you? What are you going to do in the evenings?
6 I'm going to stay in a two-star guesthouse.

3 🎧 🌐 Transcript: _____

1
Chica: ¿Qué vas a hacer estas vacaciones, Benjamín?
Benjamín: Generalmente voy a la costa con mi familia pero este verano voy a ir al extranjero, a Irlanda. Voy a hacer un intercambio.

2
Chica: ¿Vas a hablar en inglés todo el tiempo?
Benjamín: Espero que sí. Para mí va a ser difícil. Pero Patrick está estudiando el español en el colegio. Sus padres, sin embargo, no hablan nada de español.

3
Chica: ¿Cómo vas a ir?
Benjamín: Preferiría ir en el ferry porque no me gusta volar, pero volar es la manera más barata de viajar. Así que voy a ir en avión a Dublín. Sus padres van a recogerme al aeropuerto.

4
Chica: ¿Cuánto tiempo vas a pasar allí?
Benjamín: Voy a pasar quince días en Irlanda. Pero Patrick sólo va a quedarse diez días conmigo.

5
Chica: ¿Y qué vas hacer allí?
Benjamín: Pues un fin de semana voy a ir al campo con ellos, a la granja de sus abuelos. Para mí, va a ser genial porque me encanta estar al aire libre. Vamos a practicar senderismo, montar a caballo y visitar a los tíos de Patrick.

6
Chica: ¿Qué tiempo va a hacer?
Benjamín: Pues es Irlanda. No va a hacer buen tiempo como hace en Málaga en verano, tampoco va a hacer mucho calor. Pienso que va a llover así que voy a llevar un paraguas en mi equipaje.

> 🎧 **Estrategia**
> The example given uses the verb *reconocer* but you could ask students to work out how this strategy applies to *descansar* at the end of Marisa's part of the reading text (can they link it to *cansado*?).

3 🎧 🌐 Listen to Benjamín talking about his holiday plans. Decide whether the following statements are true (T) or false (F). Correct the false statements.

Benjamín describes his planned holiday at his Irish friend's home. Almost all his statements are in the immediate future, as are the questions in the activity. Once students have completed the activity, you could ask them to identify their evidence for all the 'true' statements, i.e. to tell you what he said, if they can, or to highlight and number the relevant text in the transcript.

Answers:

1 F: He is going to Ireland.
2 T
3 F: He is going to fly.
4 F: Patrick is going to stay for 10 days.
5 T
6 F: He thinks it will rain.

4 Work in pairs. Imagine you have won the lottery. Take turns asking and answering about where you are going to go on holiday and what you are going to do.

Students may have already touched on this (see *Gramática*) but they now follow the model given and invent their own dialogues. Emphasise that all the questions and answers must contain an example of the immediate future tense. They should refer to the language structure box and the *Vocabulario* on pages 86–87 for help.

> **Consejo**
> An explanation of how to use pronouns after *para* and *con*, which students should apply to writing task 5.

5 Prepare an itinerary for an ideal five-day holiday for you or your classmates.

Students could be asked to explain their choices using language they have recently worked on in 2.5 to say what is (most) important to them, e.g.

para mí es imprescindible, para nosotros lo más importante es poder …

This is supported by the *Consejo* and provides practice of the secondary grammar point, disjunctive pronouns. They can also refer to the language structure box and the *Vocabulario* on pages 86–87 for help.

Plenary activity

Students swap itineraries and you could ask questions to find out what seems to be the most important element of a holiday for everyone. Imagine that the class have been given a budget to go on a group holiday and try to agree a list of where they will go and what they will do.

Pages 78–79

2.8 He ido a la fiesta

What to see and getting around

Subject	Talking about what to see and do on holiday
G 1	Using the perfect tense to talk about what you have done recently
G 2	Learning about interrogative pronouns
	Using time phrases in your written work

kerboodle!
- Audio file for core reading text
- Audio file and transcript for listening activity 2
- Reading activity: *Las Fallas de Valencia*
- Grammar activity: Using the perfect tense
- Speaking worksheet
- Extension listening worksheet
- Audio file and transcript for extension listening activity

Starter activity

Write the following words on the board and ask students to explain them to you, in English, based on what they can find in the text.

| las Fallas | castillas de fuegos artificiales |
| ninots | Falleros y Falleras |

Core reading text

Marcos's account is a description of the *Fiesta de las Fallas* in Valencia. Although the text contains a good amount of new vocabulary, much of it is cognates or is fairly easy to work out from the context, so students should be able to find their way through it. You could display it on the screen or board and, following on from the Starter suggested above, help students to pick apart some of the harder items in the text e.g. *queman todos los ninots de la ciudad al mismo tiempo*. You may wish to focus specifically on phrases that use time expressions (as explained in the *Estrategia*).

The reading text is also available online as an audio file.

1a Read Marcos's account of his visit to the Fallas festival. Find the Spanish for these words and phrases in the text.

If you have used the suggestions under Starter and / or Core reading text, above, students should be well prepared to do this activity independently.

Answers:

1 El ambiente is muy festivo.
2 A partir de la una de la madrugada.
3 Queman todos los ninots.
4 Llevan trajes típicos.
5 He ido a las corridas de toros.
6 He visto los desfiles.
7 La especialidad de la región
8 ¡No te la pierdas!

1b 📖 🎧 Answer the following questions in Spanish.

Point out that students need to use exactly the same perfect-tense verb forms in their answers as are found in the questions – it would be worth modelling question 1 as an example.

Answers:

1 Ha ido a Valencia.
2 Ha durado casi veinte días.
3 Ha visto concursos de grupos pirotécnicos / 'castillos de fuegos artificiales'.
4 Han quemado (todos) los ninots.
5 Ha comido (muchos platos de) paella.

2 🎧 *Transcript:*

1
Marcos: Hola Sara, ¿qué tal?
Sara: Hola, Marcos. No te he visto en mucho tiempo.
Marcos: He estado de vacaciones en Valencia.
Sara: ¡Qué maravilla!

2
Sara: ¿Lo has pasado bien?
Marcos: Sí, estupendamente. He visitado la Ciudad de las Artes y las Ciencias. He ido tres días seguidos. Hay mucho que ver. La arquitectura es impresionante con jardines muy bonitos.

3
Sara: ¿Hay museos en la Ciudad?
Marcos: Sí, he ido al Museo de las Ciencias. ¡El museo tiene forma de dinosaurio! Es interactivo y muy interesante. También hay un museo de arte pero no he ido allí.

4
Sara: ¿Has visitado el acuario?
Marcos: Sí, me ha impresionado mucho porque es el acuario más grande de Europa. Tiene peces de todo el mundo.

5
Sara: Ponen conciertos en la Cuidad de las Artes y Ciencias, ¿no?
Marcos: Sí, he ido a un concierto de música clásica y un espectáculo de flamenco que me impresionó por la técnica de los bailarines y sus bonitos trajes.

6
Sara: ¿Qué te ha gustado más?
Marcos: Ay, creo que para mí ha sido el planetario porque he aprendido mucho sobre el espacio y la astronomía. Pero me ha gustado todo lo que he visto.

2 🎧 Listen to the conversation and answer the following questions in English.

Marcos meets his friend Sara after his holiday and she asks him all about it. Plenty of examples of the perfect tense can be used here to present the *Gramática*, but first these English comprehension questions ensure that students are grasping the content of the text. They should listen once to the whole conversation – tell them that it is the same Marcos talking about the same holiday as in the reading text – before attempting the questions. They then read the questions, and listen again, section by section if necessary, to find the answers. Each numbered section of the transcript provides the answer to one question.

Answers:

1 He's been away on holiday.
2 three
3 the *Museo de las Ciencias* – Science Museum
4 It's the biggest one in Europe.
5 The dancers' technique and their beautiful costumes.
6 He learned a lot about space and astronomy.

> **Gramática**
> A summary of how the perfect tense is formed (students can see the paradigm of *haber* on page 182.) Use a copy of the listening transcript to present a series of examples. You may wish to use this process to build up the paradigm of *haber* on the board or screen, so that students can easily refer to it while doing activity 3. The secondary grammar point, interrogative pronouns, is also well supported by Sara's questions in the listening text. If you want to do so draw it out, but it would be best to do this in preparation for speaking task 4, once students have completed grammar activity 3.

3 **G** Copy the sentences and fill in the gaps with the correct form of the verb *haber* and the correct past participle.

Practice of perfect-tense forms – probably best done with the paradigm of *haber* displayed on the screen or board (see *Gramática*). Mention that there may be more than one acceptable choice of past participle.

Answers:

1 han comido   2 habéis visto
3 he visitado / visto   4 has estado
5 ha gustado   6 hemos estado / ido

> **Consejo**
> A reminder about interrogative pronouns which students will need for speaking activity 4.

4 💬 Work in pairs. Look at the pictures and ask each other about recent holidays to the places in the pictures.

Three prompt questions are supplied for this activity, but students could also work on a transcript of Marcos and Sara's conversation first, to build up a bank of question and answer phrases that they will use (see also the *Consejo* which reminds them about the use of interrogative pronouns). Emphasise that each question and answer should contain one example of the perfect tense.

> **Estrategia**
> ✏️ Various time phrases can be picked out in the reading and listening texts to illustrate this *Estrategia* so that students can see how to apply it in writing activity 5.

5 ✏️ Write a postcard about a recent holiday.

Students have the language structure box for support, but you may also wish to display a list of prompts to make sure students make full use of the language learned on this spread. For example:
- Where have you been?
- When did you go?
- What you saw
- What you liked and why

Plenary activity

Combine practice of the perfect tense with revision of how to form negatives, by imagining a really boring summer holiday where someone just stayed at home, didn't do anything, didn't see anyone, etc.

Pages 80–81

2.9 ¡Vamos de viaje!

What to see and getting around

Subject	Talking about getting around on holiday
G 1	Using imperative verb forms
G 2	Learning how to say 'Let's …'
🔊	Using high numbers and 24-hour time

kerboodle!
- Audio file for core reading text
- Audio file and transcript for activity 2
- Listening activity and transcript: *De viaje*
- Grammar activity: Using imperative verb forms
- Speaking worksheet
- Extension reading worksheet
- Foundation reading worksheet
- Foundation listening worksheet
- Audio file and transcript for foundation listening activity

Starter activity

Before students start looking at the spread, tell them they are going to be working on two dialogues, one in a car rental office, one in a train ticket booking office. Display two headings: *En la oficina de alquiler de coches* and *En la taquilla de RENFE*

and ask students to sort the following words / phrases under the two headings:

taquilla, autopista, tren, conducir, billete, ¿A qué hora sale …?, alquiler, la llegada, 75 euros por día, máquina de auto-check-in … add more from the dialogues as you wish.

Core reading text

Two dialogues: in *En la oficina de alquiler de coches* a customer arranges the hire of a Seat Ibiza; in *En la taquilla de RENFE*, a young client books a return journey to Barcelona. The dialogues are of course in formal register so students have the chance to see the *usted* form in use, including imperatives (the focus of the *Gramática*).

Times and charges also throw up some 24-hour clock figures and higher numbers (as referred to in the *Estrategia*).

The reading text is also available online as an audio file.

> 📖 **Estrategia** A reference to the importance of practising high numbers and the 24-hour clock. To do this with the reading text, which includes several examples, you could make use of the audio recording of the text. Once students have done the initial activity 1, you could play the audio of the file and pause the recording just before each numbered item – students have to say aloud the number / time that is about to come up, before you restart the audio so they can hear whether they were correct.

1 📖 🎧 🌐 Read the dialogues and find the correct word for each gap from the lists below. Then listen and check.

The gapped words include some of those suggested for use in the pre-reading starter activity.

You may want to extend this by blanking out other words when you display the text. Alternatively, to support comprehension, do an additional 'find the Spanish' whole-class task to pin down the meaning of key language for this topic. Students could be given a copy of the dialogues with interchangeable items underlined (make of car, train departure time, etc.) and they adapt it with their own information for a pairwork roleplay.

Answers:

En la oficina de alquiler de coches:
1 acondicionado   2 ficha   3 conducir
4 documento   5 autopista

En la taquilla de RENFE:
6 viaje   7 directo   8 descuento
9 billete   10 tren

2 🎧 *Transcript:*

1
Viajero 1: ¿De qué andén sale el tren a Málaga?
Taquillero: Sale del andén número nueve.
Viajero 1: ¿Y el tren a Badajoz?
Taquillero: Sale de la vía dos.

2
Viajero 1: ¿Es ésta la carretera a Santander?
Taquillero: Sí, pero en el cruce, gira a la izquierda.

3
Viajero 1: Vamos a coger un autobús.
Viajera 2: Vale, es más barato que conducir.
Viajero 1: Pues, vamos a la estación de autobuses.

4
Viajera 1: Necesitamos gasolina.
Viajera 2: Hay una gasolinera después del semáforo.

5
Viajero 1: Tenemos que esperar mucho tiempo por el autocar.
Viajera 2: ¿Dónde está la sala de espera?
Viajero 1: Baja por el paso subterráneo. Está frente a la salida.

Context 2 Leisure **59**

6
Viajera 1: Vamos a viajar en el AVE en primera clase.
Viajero 2: ¿Por qué?
Viajera 1: Porque te ofrecen una bebida de bienvenida y te sirven desayuno.
Viajero 2: Pero hay que pagar un suplemento.

2 🎧 Listen to the conversations and answer the questions in English.

Students listen to a series of short conversations about different journeys or travel-related matters and answer a question on each one.

Answers:

1 platform 9
2 turn left
3 the bus
4 a petrol station
5 the waiting room
6 by high-speed train, first class

> **Gramática**
> Imperative forms, familiar singular and plural. A difficult grammar point and you may want to concentrate on familiar forms first, before working on the formal ones with the support of the reading dialogues which contain numerous examples.
> To consolidate the formal / familiar differences, you could write a series of contrasting instructions, and ask e.g. is this Wallace talking to Gromit, or is it a travel guide talking to her clients? Some possible phrases:
> *Traeme el periódico, por favor.*   *Déme su pasaporte.*
> *¡Siéntate!*   *Siéntense aquí, por favor.*
> *Pon ésto en el coche.*   *Pongan su equipaje en la consigna.*

3 **G** Copy the sentences and fill in the gaps with the correct form of the verb in the imperative.

Students should refer closely to the *Gramática* to work out the answers. Alternatively, work through this activity as a whole-class task.

Answers: **1** trae   **2** tomad   **3** dejad   **4** bajad   **5** mira

> **Consejo**
> The reference to *vamos* complements the *Gramática* on imperatives, and puts this familiar word into its grammatical context.

4 🔄 Work in pairs. Take turns to make up an instruction to go with each picture.

You could prepare students for this task by working from an infinitive prompt. Tell them first of all that all the instructions are to be in the familiar form, and for each picture, set the scene, e.g. *Mirad el primer dibujo … Esteban va de vacaciones. ¿Qué debe hacer Esteban?* (to elicit *debe poner el equipaje en el coche*). *Bueno, ¿qué decimos a Esteban?* (to elicit *¡Pon el equipaje en el coche, Esteban!*) Once students have come up with the answers for the pictures, you could run through a series of simple scenarios along the same lines. One or two could include the use of *vamos* (see the *Consejo*).

5 ✏️ Write an email to a friend giving instructions for a journey to meet you. Tell your friend what to do if you aren't there on time.

Students should use the language structure box to help them with this task. You may also wish to write up a list of infinitives of relevant verbs, with some kind of symbol or special colour to highlight those that are irregular.

You could draft one example of an email with the whole class before they attempt their own; less able students may need to adapt this model. You may wish to suggest the context of a train journey, because then they can use or adapt language from the second reading dialogue, and in addition it will produce some practice of 24-hour times.

Plenary activity

Download some example journey details from the RENFE website and display these on the whiteboard or hand out copies. Ask questions about departure times, changes, etc.

Ask students to match Spanish to English for a series of bossy tour guide instructions in formal imperative form: Follow me! Show me your tickets! Take a photo! Choose a postcard!

Pages 82–83

Reading and listening

Holidays

kerboodle! • Audio files for core reading texts

Core reading text

The reading text is quite a long letter from Guadalupe, who is on holiday with her parents in Cancún, Mexico, to her cousins. You could start to access the text by use of the photos – can students find in the text any information about what is shown in the pictures?

The reading text is also available online as an audio file.

1a 📖 🎧 Read Guadalupe's letter about her holiday in Cancún. What opinion does she have about the following aspects of her trip? Write P (positive), N (negative) or P + N (positive and negative).

If students need some help because of the length of the text, point out in which paragraph they will find the answer to each question (1 – paragraph a; 2 – paragraph c; 3 – paragraph e; 4 – paragraph f).

Answers: **1** P,   **2** N,   **3** P + N,   **4** P

> **Gramática**
> A brief reminder of perfect tense and immediate future tense forms, with reference to examples in the reading text.

Context 2 Leisure 61

1b 📖 🎧 Answer the following questions in English.

Students reread the text for the details required.

Answers:

1 It's her first trip abroad; she's always wanted to visit a Latin American (South American) country.
2 b
3 a
4 Lots of discos and clubs are open all night.
5 b
6 Knowledge about the culture and customs of the Mayans.

2 🎧 *Transcript:*

1 Restaurante Ándale, dígame.
   Quisiera reservar una mesa para esta noche.
   ¿A qué hora?
   A las nueve.
   ¿Para cuantas personas?
   Para cuatro. ¿Hay mesas libres en la terraza?
   Lo siento, no hay.
   Pues, cerca de la ventana entonces.
   Muy bien.

2 ¡Camarera! Me trae la carta?
   Tomen ustedes.
   ¿Hay un menú del día?
   Sí, y hay también un menú turístico.
   ¿Cuál recomienda?
   Pues el menú turístico es más económico pero el menú del día tiene más variedad.

3 ¿Qué es un plato combinado?
   Es un plato con mucha cosas.
   O sea, en vez de sólo carne tienes también un taco, guacamole, arroz …
   Eso es, ponen un poco de todo en el mismo plato.
   Es una buena idea. Así puedes probar varias cosas.

4 ¡Camarera! Tengo una queja.
   ¿Qué pasa?
   Falta un tenedor. Y el cuchillo está sucio.
   Lo siento. Traigo otros ahora mismo.

5 ¿Van a querer postre?
   Qué hay de postre?
   Hay helado, ensalada de fruta fresca o flan.
   Pues, un helado de vainilla. Tráiganos dos cucharas.
   ¿Van a compartir?
   Exactamente.

6 ¡La cuenta, por favor!
   Tengan ustedes.
   ¿Está incluido el servicio?
   Sí, está incluido el servicio y el IVA.
   Vamos a dejar una propina.
   Vale, el servicio ha sido excelente.

2a 🎧 Listen to the conversations in a Mexican restaurant. Match up each conversation with the correct picture.

Answers: **1** E, **2** B, **3** F, **4** C, **5** D, **6** A

2b 🎧 Listen to the conversations again and answer the following questions in English.

Answers:

1 c
2 a
3 You can try different dishes.
4 No: there is a fork missing and the knife is dirty.
5 In order to share the dessert.
6 Yes: they leave a tip and say the service was excellent.

Pages 84–85

Grammar practice

G Holidays

Recognising the passive voice

A reminder of what the passive voice looks like and means, and how it is formed, to support activity 1.

1 📖 Identify which of the following sentences are in the passive voice. Translate the sentences into English.

Answers:

1 The cathedral is admired all over the world.
2 The traveller's cheques were changed at the bank.
4 The museum was closed for two months.

How to say 'for me' / How to say 'with me'

A note on prepositional pronouns and how to use them, to support activity 2.

2 ✏️ Copy the sentences and fill in the gaps with the correct prepositional pronoun.

Answers:

1 La paella es **para nosotros**.
2 Esta postal es **para ti**.
3 ¿Las limonadas son **para vosotros**?
4 Va ir a la montaña **con ellos**.
5 ¿Quieres venir **conmigo**?
6 Yo hablé **con él**.

Interrogatives

A reminder of the main interrogative pronouns, to support activity 3.

3 📖 💭 Choose the correct interrogative pronoun to complete these questions. Then work in pairs and make up more questions.

Answers:

1 Cuál   2 Quién   3 De dónde   4 Por qué
5 Cómo   6 Cuándo   7 Para qué   8 Qué

The perfect tense

A reminder of the formation and use of the perfect tense, to support activity 4.

4 ✏️ Copy the sentences and fill in the gaps with the past participles of the verbs in brackets. Then translate the sentences into English.

Answers:

1 *invitado*: My friend has invited me to spend a week in Bilbao.
2 *visto*: Julia, have you seen Penélope Cruz's new film?
3 *comido*: They haven't had the roast lamb in that restaurant.
4 *hecho*: Have you been on a trip to the Costa Azul?
5 *ido*: I haven't been on holiday this year.
6 *quedado*: We have stayed at home.

Imperatives

A table of regular positive imperative forms (familiar and formal), to support activity 5a.

5a 📖 Choose the appropriate form of the imperative by deciding whether the requests are formal or familiar.

Answers:

1 bebas   2 Vaya   3 Cruza
4 Rellene   5 visiten   6 pon

How to say 'let's'

A reminder of how to use *vamos* to say 'let's', to support activity 5b.

5b ✏️ Look at the pictures and write a caption for each one using *vamos a* ... Then write five more sentences using *vamos (a)* ...

Answers:

A Vamos a esquiar (vamos a la montaña).
B Vamos de compras.
C Vamos al parque temático.

Pages 86–87

Vocabulary
V Holidays

- MP3 files for each vocabulary list

The essential vocabulary used within Topic 2, Context 2 is presented on this vocabulary spread.

Here students can learn the key words for the topic area *Holidays*. You may also want to direct students to the online audio files of these vocabulary lists, so they can hear how the words are pronounced by a native speaker.

Some words are in light grey on the vocabulary spreads in the Student Book. This indicates items that are not included in the GCSE specification vocabulary list, so students do not need to learn these items for Listening and Reading assessment. However, you may wish students to use them in Speaking and Writing Controlled Assessments.

Pages 88–91

Controlled Assessment

Refer to the section on Controlled Assessment, pages 107–112 in this Teacher's Book.

Page 92

2 Context summary

- Interactive multiple-choice quiz

The closing page for Context 2, Leisure, provides a multiple-choice quiz which tests the key language learnt in this Context.

A longer version of this quiz is also available online as an interactive, self-marking multiple-choice test.

Answers:

1 toco, escucho, juego, veo
2 mal / fatal
3 jugaron, ganaron
4 On Saturday I went to a concert with Nieves. Our friend Juan went too.
5 éstas / aquéllas
6 El dinero que te dan tus padres cada semana.
7 Student's own choice, e.g. Una desventaja es que nunca puedes desconectarte.
8 tuve, hice
9 Student's own choice, e.g. Voy a visitar a mis primos. / Voy a estudiar para mis exámenes.
10 Have you ever been to Seville (Sevilla)?

3 Home and environment

Home and local area
Special occasions celebrated in the home

KS3 Revision: Rooms in the house, things in the house; House types and locations; Normal routine; Helping at home	*Online materials* • Audio files for core reading texts	
3.1 De fiesta ■ Using the imperfect tense ■ Making use of social and cultural contexts	• Audio file for core reading text • Audio file and transcript for listening activity 3 • Listening activity and transcript: *Una fiesta quinceañera* • Grammar activity: Using the imperfect tense • Extension reading worksheet • Writing worksheet	
3.2 ¿Cómo es tu casa? ■ Using possessive pronouns ■ Remembering to use quantifiers and intensifiers	• Audio file for core reading text • Audio file and transcript for listening activity 3 • Reading activity: *El blog de Trini* • Grammar activity: Using possessive pronouns • Writing worksheet • Extension listening worksheet • Audio file and transcript for extension listening activity	

Home, town, neighbourhood and region, where it is and what it is like

3.3 ¿Cómo es tu barrio? ■ Using relative pronouns ■ Using common patterns within Spanish	• Audio file for core reading text • Audio file and transcript for listening activity 3 • Listening activity and transcript: *Los barrios de Cristina e Isidro* • Grammar activity: Using relative pronouns • Speaking worksheet • Extension reading worksheet • Audio role play activity	
3.4 Mi región ■ Describing past weather conditions ■ Recognising percentages, common fractions and temperatures	• Audio file for core reading text • Audio file and transcript for listening activity 2 • Reading activity: *Mi región* • Grammar activity: Describing past weather conditions • Speaking worksheet • Extension listening worksheet • Audio file and transcript for extension listening activity • Foundation reading worksheet • Foundation listening worksheet • Audio file and transcript for foundation listening worksheet	

Reading and listening

Home and local area	• Audio file for core reading text • Audio file and transcript for listening activity 3 • Audio file and transcript for listening activity 4

Grammar

Home and local area ■ *ser* and *estar* ■ When to use the imperfect and preterite tenses	■ *hay* and *había* ■ Using possessive pronouns ■ *cuánto, cuánta, cuántos, cuántas* ■ Relative pronouns

Vocabulary

Home and local area	• MP3 files for each vocabulary list

Environment

Current problems facing the planet

3.5 La contaminación
(Includes video)
- Using *por* and *para*
- Learning complete phrases to promote fluency

- Audio file for core reading text
- Video and transcript for activity 3
- Activity to accompany video
- Grammar activity: Using *por* and *para*
- Writing worksheet
- Extension listening worksheet
- Audio file and transcript for extension listening activity

3.6 El futuro del planeta
- Using the future tense
- Expressing ideas: use phrases you know

- Audio file for core reading text
- Audio file and transcript for listening activity 2
- Reading activity: *El planeta*
- Grammar activity: Using the future tense
- Speaking worksheet
- Extension Reading worksheet

Being environmentally friendly within the home and local area

3.7 Cómo cuidar el medio ambiente
- Using verbs of obligation: *deber, haber de, hay que, tener que*
- Introducing variety to make your Spanish more interesting

- Audio file for core reading text
- Audio file and transcript for listening activity 3
- Listening activity and transcript: *¿Qué haces para proteger el medio ambiente?*
- Grammar activity: Using verbs of obligation: *deber, haber de, hay que, tener que*
- Speaking worksheet
- Extension reading worksheet
- Foundation reading worksheet
- Foundation listening worksheet
- Audio file and transcript for foundation listening worksheet
- Audio role play activity

Reading and listening

Environment

- Audio file for core reading text
- Audio file and transcript for listening activity 3
- Audio file and transcript for listening activity 4

Grammar

Environment
- The perfect tense
- The present continuous tense
- Avoiding the passive by using the reflexive pronoun *se*
- Indefinite pronouns: *algo, alguien*
- Avoiding imperatives

Vocabulary

Environment
- MP3 files for each vocabulary list

Summative assessment

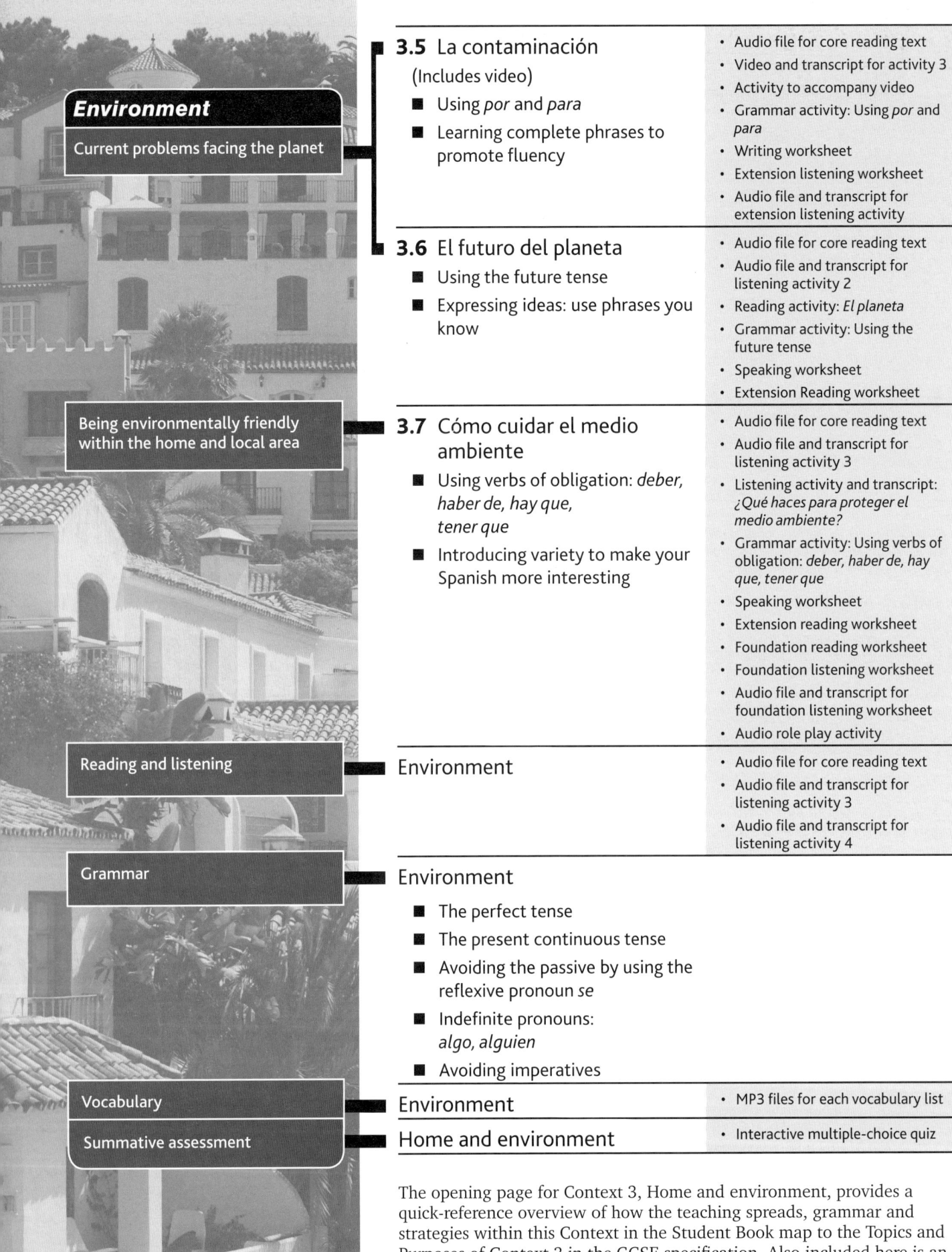

Home and environment
- Interactive multiple-choice quiz

The opening page for Context 3, Home and environment, provides a quick-reference overview of how the teaching spreads, grammar and strategies within this Context in the Student Book map to the Topics and Purposes of Context 3 in the GCSE specification. Also included here is an overview of the online resources available for each of these spreads in the Student Book.

Context 3 Home and environment 65

Page 94

Revision

Rooms in the house, things in the house

kerboodle! • Audio files for core reading texts

> A reminder of the most common prepositions for use with *estar*. Students will need to refer to this reminder to help them with activity 1.
>
> **Gramática**

1a 📖 🎧 Read the following descriptions of houses and match up each one with the correct plan.

The quickest students may answer the question from the first sentence, so to ensure that they read the texts thoroughly, follow up with a test of the prepositions in the *Gramática* by displaying the text with the prepositions blanked out for students to supply.

Answers: **1** B, **2** A

1b ✏️ Look at the picture of the room and say if the following sentences are true or false.

You could extend this activity by adding more sentences for students to identify as true or false. Correct the sentences that are false.

Answers: **1** T, **2** T, **3** T, **4** F (las cortinas son azules)

1c 💬 Work in pairs. Partner A asks questions about the room and Partner B answers. Then swap roles.

You could extend this activity by applying the same idea to the plans in activity 1.

2 ✏️ Write a description of your own house in Spanish.

Prompt students to include some or all of the following information:

- what the house is like: how many floors, what rooms
- where the rooms are in relation to each other
- some detail about one particular room, what is where.

Page 95

Revision

House types and locations

kerboodle! • Audio files for core reading texts

1 📖 🎧 Read the descriptions and name the person who says each of the sentences below.

Answers:
| 1 Ignacio | 2 Elvira | 3 Ignacio | 4 Matilde |
| 5 Elvira | 6 Ignacio | 7 Elvira | 8 Matilde |

> A reminder of when to use *ser* and when to use *estar*, which students can see in place in the reading texts and which they will need to put into practice in activity 2.
>
> **Gramática**

2 ✏️ 💬 Write some questions in Spanish to ask other students about their houses.

Prompt students to write questions that will find out from their classmate(s):

- how long they have lived in their house (provide models with *desde* and *desde hace*)
- what type of house it is
- the location
- whether they like their house, giving a reason
- where they would like to live (provide a model with *me gustaría*)

Then students should work in pairs to interview each other.

Page 96

Revision

Normal routine

kerboodle! • Audio files for core reading texts

> A reminder of the *u > ue* and *e > ie* patterns of common radical-changing verbs. There are six such verbs in the reading text; how quickly can students find them all?
>
> **Gramática**

1a 📖 🎧 Read Miguel's account of his daily routine. Match up the two halves of the sentences below.

You could prepare for this task and revise how to ask and answer questions about the time by asking questions such as *¿A qué hora se despierta Miguel?* etc. This would also be relevant as preparation for activity 1b, and would ensure that all the singular parts of the radical-changing verbs are rehearsed.

Answers: **1** g, **2** b, **3** e, **4** c, **5** h, **6** f, **7** a, **8** d

1b ✏️ 💬 Make up an interview with Miguel about his daily routine. Work in pairs. Partner A plays the part of the interviewer and Partner B plays the part of Miguel. Then swap roles.

The *Vocabulario* on the page gives good support for this task. You could challenge students to prepare and enact an interview that is long enough to include all these verbs. It may be worth running through the pairs of 2nd person questions / 1st person answers for a few verbs, and possibly leaving one or two of these pairs displayed as reminders while students work on the task.

1c ✏️ Write a letter to Miguel telling him about your own routine.

Page 97

Revision

Helping at home

kerboodle! • Audio files for core reading texts

> **Gramática**
> Some support to help students mix their present and past tense references using the present and preterite, and some time expressions which flag up the tenses.

1a 📖 🎧 Read Enrique's account and write the letters of the pictures in the order in which the household tasks are mentioned.

The *Vocabulario* lists all the tasks depicted, so you could prepare for this task by asking students first of all to match the vocabulary listings with the pictures before they read the text. This can be done at a very simple level – students can see the English so it is purely a reminder of which Spanish phrase has which meaning – alternatively mime the actions and ask for the Spanish phrases.

You could warn the students that not all the tasks mentioned in the text are shown in the pictures (missing from the pictures are *quitar la mesa* and *cambiar las sábanas*).

Answers: G, C, D, A, H, F, E, B, I

1b 📖 🎧 Read Enrique's account again and indicate who does each of the household tasks in the pictures: Enrique (E), father (F), mother (M), older sister (OS), younger brother (YB), other brothers (OB).

Check that students know which family member nouns to look out for, to find the people referred to in the instruction.

Answers:

A E	B M	C YB	D OB, YB	E F
F OS	G F, OS	H E	I M	

2 💬 Who does what in your house? Work in pairs. Partner A asks the questions and Partner B answers. Then swap roles.

Instruct students to:

- say what they usually do, and when (practising the present tense and appropriate time expressions from the *Gramática*)
- give examples of what they did to help in the house last week / weekend, using the preterite tense and appropriate time expressions from the *Gramática*.

3 ✏️ Adapt Enrique's description to write, in Spanish, about how you help at home.

Encourage students to say also what other members of the household do or don't do (some may be able to use negatives other than *no*). To prompt inclusion of the preterite tense and past time expressions, ask them to describe who did what in the house last week / last weekend. Remind them that they can invent, and if they would rather talk about an imaginary household instead of their own, they could write about an impossibly virtuous family, *La familia Ángel*, who are obsessive about housework and team work.

Pages 98–99

3.1 De fiesta

Special occasions celebrated in the home

Subject	Talking about special occasions
G 1	Using the imperfect tense
G 2	Learning about when to use the imperfect and preterite tenses
🌐	Making use of social and cultural contexts

kerboodle!
- Audio file for core reading text
- Audio file and transcript for listening activity 3
- Listening activity and transcript: *Una fiesta quinceañera*
- Grammar activity: Using the imperfect tense
- Writing worksheet
- Extension reading worksheet

1a 📖 🎧 Match up each photo with the correct paragraph.

This simple matching exercise can be used as a starter activity before students read the text in more detail for activity 1b.

Answers: **1** C, **2** B, **3** D, **4** A

Core reading text

Four paragraphs about Christmas, couched mainly in the imperfect tense (the main focus of this spread's *Gramática*) as the passage is describing what childhood Christmases used to be like. Some of the less familiar terms in the text can be unpicked using contextual social and cultural knowledge students may have, as explained in the *Estrategia*.

The reading text is also available online as an audio file

Context 3 Home and environment **67**

📖 A tip that social and cultural information you already know can be used as clues to help you work out the meaning of new language.

Estrategia

1b 📖 🎧 🌐 Answer the following questions in English.

Students now read more closely – they should bear in mind the *Estrategia* as well as using the *Vocabulario* on page 110 for help in finding the answers to the comprehension questions.

Answers:

1 in the street
2 in the living room
3 midnight
4 for good luck
5 6 January
6 5 January

To introduce the imperfect tense, draw stick figures of a child and an adult and indicate that they both represent you. Make contrasting statements about what you used to do at Christmas (or any other chosen special occasion), contrasted with now. For example:
Cuando era pequeño/a, me encantaba la fiesta de Navidad. Ahora que soy mayor, sí me gusta pero ....
Cuando era pequeño/a, no podía dormir, porque esperaba a Papá Noel. Ahora, no puedo dormir porque preparo los regalos para los niños.

Gramática

Allocate one paragraph of the reading text to each student (by 'lettering' students A, B, C, D, A, B, C, D, etc. round the class), then ask each student to look in his / her paragraph for examples of the imperfect tense. The reading text also includes some examples of the time expressions mentioned in the *Consejo*. Can students give you an explanation to show they understand why the time expressions here might work well with the imperfect tense? (= because they refer to things that happened repeatedly, frequently or routinely in the past).

2a 🅖 Copy the sentences and fill in the gaps with the correct verb from the list.

This activity helps to familiarise students with the imperfect verb endings.

Answers:

1 comía
2 hacían
3 ibais
4 ponía
5 tomabas
6 esperaban

2b 🅖 Make a list of the verbs in the imperfect tense in Nicolás' memories of Christmas celebrations in Activity 1.

Students may have begun this process by working on one of the paragraphs (see the suggestion in the *Gramática*). They should now work through the whole text, singly or in pairs – unless you prefer to allocate parts of the text to students or groups and then pool their findings.

Answers:

A Cuando **era** pequeño las fiestas de Navidad **eran** las mejores del año. **Era** cuando la familia **se reunía** y mis padres **preparaban** comida especial y **comíamos** dulces como el mazapán y el turrón que contiene almendras y miel. A veces mis primos y yo **íbamos** por la calle cantando villancicos – canciones típicas de Navidad – y la gente nos **daba** algo de dinero. En el salón siempre **poníamos** un belén que es una escena en miniatura del nacimiento del Niño Jesús.

B El 24 de diciembre es la víspera de la Navidad y se celebra la Nochebuena. Todos los años **cenábamos** con los abuelos, los tíos y los primos. El plato principal **solía** ser pescado. Después de la cena **íbamos** a la iglesia a celebrar la Misa de Gallo a medianoche.

C La Nochevieja se celebra el 31 de diciembre. A las 12 de la noche, **tomábamos** 12 uvas para tener suerte los próximos 12 meses. Después, los adultos **brindaban** con cava, sidra o champán. Muchas veces **poníamos** música y **bailábamos** toda la noche. Lo **pasábamos** muy bien.

D Los Reyes Magos es el 6 de enero. Es un día mágico para los niños, pues los tres Reyes nos traen los juguetes que han pedido en una carta. Cada año en nuestra ciudad el 5 de enero, víspera de Reyes, a las seis de la tarde, los Reyes **se paseaban** por las calles a caballo o en camello, cargados de paquetes de juguetes. **Repartían** caramelos entre la gente, que los **esperaban** por las calles para verlos pasar. Luego, de madrugada, cuando **estábamos** en la cama, **pasaban** casa por casa repartiendo regalos. **Ponían** los regalos en los zapatos que **se dejaban** en el balcón.

3 🎧 *Transcript:* _____

1 Me llamo Guadalupe y soy mexicana. Para las jóvenes mexicanas la celebración de los quince años es un evento muy importante. Cumplí 15 años en junio. Mis padres me hicieron una fiesta quinceañera fabulosa.
2 En México es costumbre despertar a la quinceañera por la mañana con una canción. Un grupo de mariachis, músicos tradicionales, me cantaron una canción de cumpleaños.
3 Luego fuimos a la iglesia para empezar la celebración con una misa. La iglesia estaba decorada con flores. Después de la misa un fotógrafo me sacó fotos y mis amigas me dieron regalos.
4 Fuimos al salón de fiestas en coche, una limusina enorme que alquiló mi tío. Yo llevaba un vestido de marca color rosa (que es mi color preferido), era largo y muy bonito.
5 En el salón de fiestas había varias mesas para el banquete. Yo me senté con mis padres y mis tíos en la mesa de honor y el resto de los invitados se sentaron en las otras mesas.
6 Después de la cena hubo un baile. Para mí, era lo mejor de la fiesta. Primero bailé con mi padre. Y después mis amigos y yo bailamos toda la noche. Bailamos salsa, cumbia, merengue, pop, reggae, de todo. La fiesta acabó a las tres de la madrugada. Lo pasé muy bien.

3a 🎧 Listen to Guadalupe's account of her 15th birthday celebrations. Which of the following does she mention?

This activity can be done on a first listen, especially if you ask students to give you one key word for each picture before they listen out for those key words in the audio.

Answers: B, D, E

3b 🎧 Decide whether the following statements are true (T), false (F), or not mentioned (?). Correct the ones that are false.

Students need to listen more closely this time as they have to pick out differences of detail. There is one question for each of the six sections of the account so you could pause the audio after each section.

Answers:

1 F: the party was in June, not July
2 T
3 ? A photographer took some pictures but she doesn't say what kind of presents she received.
4 T
5 F: she sat at the top table with her family, not with her friends
6 F: it finished at 3 in the morning.

4 Work in pairs. Take turns to ask and answer questions about how you celebrate a special occasion now, and how you used to when you were younger. Then write about the occasion you chose to talk about. Refer to the online worksheet for a language structure box to help you.

Students should use the vocabulary on page 110 for help, and could note down phrases from the reading passages that they can use / adapt for their own description. They should also try to use some of the time expressions in the *Consejo* along with their imperfect tenses for the part of their text referring to the past. They could plan their task by drawing two spider diagrams, one with the centre heading *cuando era pequeño/a* and the other one headed *ahora*.

> **Consejo**
> A note about time expressions, in particular ones that are suitable for use with the imperfect tense to talk about how frequently / when you used to do certain things.

Plenary activity

Students could be asked to invent questions (using the imperfect tense) for an interview with an older person about how they used to celebrate their birthday when they were younger. Higher-ability students could extend this to contrasting present-tense questions about what is different now.

Pages 100–101

3.2 ¿Cómo es tu casa?

Home, town, neighbourhood and region, where it is and what it is like

Subject	Describing what your home is like
G 1	Using possessive pronouns
G 2	Learning about interrogative adjectives
🧠	Remembering to use quantifiers and intensifiers

kerboodle!
- Audio file for core reading text
- Audio file and transcript for listening activity 3
- Reading activity: *El blog de Trini*
- Grammar activity: Using possessive pronouns
- Writing worksheet
- Extension listening worksheet
- Audio file and transcript for extension listening activity

Starter activity

As a whole-class vocabulary gathering exercise, ask students to give you as many words as they can to do with describing a home, inside and out. To make it more competitive, divide the class into four teams and ask each team in turn.

Core reading text

In *El blog de Trini*, Trini describes in some detail the fabulous home of her favourite singer, Julia Pérez, and contrasts it with her own (the contrast throws up a good number of possessive pronouns, as referenced in the *Gramática*), though she is not unhappy with her own home and concludes that she would not want to swap. Quantifiers and intensifiers (see *Estrategia*) are also used by Trini to convey the extremes she is contrasting. Students will of course also need to recognise the comparative constructions with *más* and *menos*, as the *Consejo* reminds them.

The reading text is also available online as an audio file.

1 📖 V Read the following blog and find the Spanish words in each paragraph which match the English expressions. Work in pairs: test each other on these words and phrases from the text.

You could extend this exercise by choosing more phrases in the text that use possessive pronouns, and giving English prompts and asking students to find the phrases.

Answers:

1 Es igual que un palacio.
2 Hay muchas escaleras que subir.
3 La nuestra es alquilada.
4 Sólo hay una ducha.
5 Es muy acogedora.

Context 3 Home and environment 69

2 📖 🎧 Read the sentences and identify which home, if any, is being referred to in each case. Write J for Julia's house, T for Trini's flat or N for neither of them.

This activity tests comprehension of the detail of the text but also serves to refamiliarise students with comparative language (as mentioned in the *Consejo*).

Answers: **1** J, **2** N, **3** T, **4** T, **5** N, **6** J, **7** T, **8** J

> **Estrategia**
> 🎧 Both the reading text and the listening text include several examples of quantifiers and intensifiers such as the common ones noted here. Students could be asked to identify and translate phrases using these quantifiers and intensifiers from a copy of the transcript, to increase their awareness of the usefulness of these words which they should try to use in their own speaking and writing, as in Activity 5 on this spread.

3 🎧 🌐 *Transcript:* _____

a
Entrevistador:	¿Dónde vives, María Ángeles?
María Ángeles:	Vivo en un pueblo que se llama San Miguel.
Entrevistador:	¿Es grande el pueblo? ¿Cuántos habitantes tiene?
María Ángeles:	Uf, no, no es grande. Es pequeño, sólo tiene unos doscientos habitantes. Hay granjas y casas viejas pero no hay mucha gente.

b
Entrevistador:	¿Y cómo es tu casa?
María Ángeles:	La nuestra es bastante antigua. Tiene trescientos años.
Entrevistador:	¿Y es grande o pequeña?
María Ángeles:	Es bastante grande. Es de tres plantas.
Entrevistador:	¿Cuántos dormitorios hay?
María Ángeles:	Hay cinco dormitorios. El mío está en el ático. Es muy cómodo. Tiene vistas muy bonitas de los campos y el bosque.

c
Entrevistador:	¿Cuántas plantas hay?
María Angelés:	Es de tres plantas. Antes era una granja. Los animales vivían en la planta baja y la familia vivía arriba.
Entrevistador:	¿Tenía luz eléctrica?
María Angelés:	No tenía ni luz ni calefacción.
Entrevistador:	¿Y ahora tenéis calefacción?
María Ángeles:	Sí, sí tenemos calefacción y dos chimeneas.

d
Entrevistador:	¿Y cómo es ahora?
María Ángeles:	Ahora la casa está totalmente reformada y ahora tenemos una cocina muy grande con cocina de gas, lavaplatos, microondas y todo. También hay un salón, un comedor y un despacho.
Entrevistador:	¿Y no había cuartos de baño antes, verdad?
María Ángeles:	No, pero ahora hay cuatro cuartos de baño arriba y un aseo abajo.

e
Entrevistador:	¿Qué te gusta más de tu casa?
María Ángeles:	Que en invierno es caliente y acogedora. Y en verano es muy fresca por dentro porque las paredes son muy gruesas.
Entrevistador:	¿Qué no te gusta de vivir allí?
María Ángeles:	Que a veces es demasiado tranquilo.

3 🎧 🌐 Listen to the interview with María Ángeles about her house. In which section of the interview (a–e) are the following mentioned?

The interview is in five sections, a–e: the questions each relate to one section. Pause the audio after each section to give students time to identify which is the relevant question and write down the letter of the section next to the question number.

You could consolidate imperfect tense work from the previous spread by asking students to describe what the house is like now and what it used to be like. (It was a farm, the animals used to live on the ground floor and the family upstairs, it didn't have electric light, heating or bathrooms. Now it has been modernised, it has light and heating, it has lots of mod cons, four bathrooms upstairs and a toilet downstairs.)

The listening also provides a good opportunity for some number practice. Ask students what the following figures refer to (answers given in brackets):
200 (= number of inhabitants), 300 (= age of house in years), 3 (= number of floors), 5 (= number of bedrooms), 4 (= number of bathrooms).

Answers: **1** e, **2** c, **3** a, **4** d, **5** b

> **Gramática**
> Refer students also to the full table of possessive pronouns on page 179.
> You could underline how these pronouns work by demonstrating a few examples with classroom objects in students' possession (or yours), contrasting for example: *mi mochila es muy vieja – ¿y la tuya? ¿es más nueva?* (pointing to someone else's) *me parece que la suya es más vieja* … etc.
> The secondary grammar point is interrogative adjectives. You could remind students that *¿Cuánto/a(s) …?* must agree with its noun (as exemplified in the listening text); students can later make use of this point in speaking activity 5.

4 **G** Choose the appropriate possessive pronoun and copy out the sentences correctly.

Students can, in theory, choose the correct pronoun purely on the basis of recognising the gender and number agreement with the noun, so you may wish to follow up by asking them to translate the completed sentences into English to prove their understanding.

Answers:

| 1 la vuestra | 2 el suyo | 3 la tuya |
| 4 el nuestro | 5 el mío | |

5 🗨 Work in pairs. Look at the pictures and each choose a house. Partner A asks Partner B questions to work out which is their chosen house. Also ask which your partner prefers and why. Then swap roles.

You may want to encourage each student to think of the house they choose as their own house, as this will mean that they can explain why *la mía* is better than their partner's, how it contrasts with his or hers (i.e. using constructions as in the *Consejo*). Demonstrate a dialogue with a student as your Partner B.

To make sure the dialogues are varied and that students 'own' contrasting houses, you could tell each student which photo is theirs.

Students can use the language structure box and the *Vocabulario* on pages 110–111 for support.

> **Consejo**
> A reminder of how possessive pronouns are useful for making comparisons between 'mine' and someone else's.

Plenary activity

Follow up on speaking activity 5 with a similar activity: distribute photos of different homes, e.g. from a magazine, to students and ask two of them to come out to the front. They compare 'their' two homes. Alternatively, label the photos as e.g. *la casa del Señor Ibañez*, and the student's task is to write e.g. three sentences comparing their own house with the one in the photo, using *la mía, la suya*, etc.

Pages 102–103

3.3 ¿Cómo es tu barrio?

Home, town, neighbourhood and region, where it is and what it is like

Subject	Talking about your neighbourhood
G 1	Using relative pronouns
G 2	Learn to use *hay* and *había*
🌐	Using common patterns within Spanish

kerboodle!
- Audio file for core reading text
- Audio file and transcript for listening activity 3
- Listening activity and transcript: *Los barrios de Cristina e Isidro*
- Grammar activity: Using relative pronouns
- Speaking worksheet
- Extension reading worksheet
- Audio role play activity

Starter activity

Ask students to skim through the texts and note down any vocabulary that could be useful for describing their own neighbourhood. Then ask them to come up with short sentences using the following openers:

- *Mi barrio es …*
- *Mi barrio tiene …*
- *Para los jóvenes hay …*
- *Mi barrio necesita …*

Core reading text

The *Mi barrio* text is in two parts: text A describes an urban home area while text B describes a small coastal village.

The main grammar point of this spread, relative pronouns, is seen in phrases such as *no hay mucho que hacer*. The text also has plenty of instances of the construction *lo* + adjective, not new to students but referred to in the reminder *Consejo*. Likewise there are some useful examples of *hay* and *había* in context (see secondary grammar point).

The *Estrategia* gives some indicators about word families which can be drawn out using some of the lexical content of the text (see notes in *Estrategia* below).

The reading text is also available online as an audio file.

> 📖 **Estrategia**
> The advice here about recognising and using patterns in Spanish refers to word families and common endings typical of nouns and adjectives. To add to these examples, see if students can remember or guess at other words related to the following ones from the reading text, e.g.:
> *contaminación* – what's the related verb?
> *seguridad* – what's the adjective?
> *diversión* – what's the verb?
> *construir* – what's the noun?
> etc.

Context 3 Home and environment

1 Make notes for each local area described in the texts: location, what it is like, what it has, what there is for young people and what it needs.

Students could prepare a table for their findings and work in pairs, each working on one of the texts, then each checks the other's list to make sure they have not missed anything. Test their lists by asking random questions in Spanish such as ¿Qué hay para los jóvenes en el barrio B? (See also speaking activity 2.)

Answers:

	barrio A	barrio B
Location	outskirts of city	coast
What it is like	Residential, ugly, dirty, noisy, polluted, rather dangerous	Pretty, touristy, historic, boring in winter
What it has	Unemployment, traffic, a motorway, CCTV cameras, shopping centre with multiplex cinema	Beaches near by, fishing port, fun fair, narrow streets, tourist shops, town square, craft market, bars and restaurants
What there is for young people	shopping centre with multiplex cinema	In summer: beaches, fun fair, bars
What it needs	Pedestrianised streets, green spaces, sports centre	Disco, amenities for young people, youth club, swimming pool, efficient transport system

2 Work in pairs. Each choose one of the texts and take turns to ask each other the following questions about the neighbourhoods being described.

This provides spoken follow-up to activity 1. It could be extended to include consolidation of the previous spread's grammar work on possessive pronouns e.g. ask students to invent comparative statements such as *Tu barrio es menos sucio que el mío. Sí, pero ¡el tuyo es más aburrido!*

3 Transcript:

Isidro

Entrevistador: Hola Isidro. ¿Dónde vives?
Isidro: Vivo en una chabola, un barrio pobre de Lima, la capital del Perú. El barrio está en las afueras de la ciudad.
Entrevistador: ¿Cómo es tu barrio?
Isidro: Hay mucho paro. No hay mucha infraestructura. Lo peor es que no hay hospital, ni biblioteca, ni supermercado, ni nada. Además, está lleno de basura y es muy sucio.
Entrevistador: ¿Qué hay que hacer para los jóvenes?
Isidro: No hay nada que hacer para los jóvenes. Antes había un club de jóvenes pero ahora está cerrado. Hay mucho crimen y mucha droga. La zona es peligrosa. Ni viene la policía aquí.
Entrevistador: ¿Qué necesita tu barrio para mejorarlo?
Isidro: Lo que necesitamos es dinero para construir casas, para establecer tiendas y pequeños negocios y para dar algo que hacer a la gente.

Cristina

Entrevistador: Cristina, ¿dónde está tu barrio?
Cristina: Está cerca de Madrid. Hay un bosque cerca donde vamos a hacer footing, montar a caballo y merendar al aire libre.
Entrevistador: ¿Cómo es la zona?
Cristina: Es moderna, las casas son adosadas o chalets. Fue construido hace diez años así que todo está nuevo y muy limpio. Lo bueno es que es muy seguro, hay cámaras de seguridad en las esquinas. No hay crimen, no hay pintadas. Es un lugar ideal para las familias.
Entrevistador: ¿Qué hay que hacer para los jóvenes?
Cristina: Pues hay una piscina, canchas de tenis, un campo de fútbol. Pero si quieres animación tienes que cruzar el río e ir al centro. Lo malo es que no hay una buena red de transportes y tienes que llevar el coche.
Entrevistador: ¿Te gusta tu barrio?
Cristina: Pues no mucho. Preferiría vivir en el centro donde hay más animación y hay más movida. Aquí no hay clubes ni discotecas, no hay tiendas buenas ni galerías de arte. Para mí vivir aquí es bastante aburrido.

3a Listen to Isidro and Cristina talking about their neighbourhoods and answer the questions.

You could link this into the *Gramática* by supplying students with a transcript and asking them to find examples of constructions using *lo que* and note these down with their English meanings.

Answers:

1 Isidro lives in Lima, Peru / in the suburbs
2 Cristina lives near Madrid

3b Listen again and put the information each speaker gives into the order in which you hear it.

Answers:

Isidro: **c, a, b**   Cristina: **b, c, a**

Gramática

You could present the grammar by starting with the *Consejo* which reminds students of the previously-learned *lo* + adjective construction. This will then lead naturally into seeing how to use *lo que* with a verb to refer to an idea, if you ask them to find in text A the Spanish for:

- the good thing is …
- what I like (about my neighbourhood) is …
- what we need (as well) is …
- the most important thing

Ask them to find and translate into English, similar constructions in text B.

For the usage of the relative pronoun *que*, you can again point out examples in the text, asking students to translate phrases in context and showing them that *que* is needed in Spanish in these constructions when 'what' is not always used in English.

no hay nada que hacer   there's nothing to do

4 (G) Translate the following sentences into English.

This translation process underlines the important point that although the relative pronoun always has to be present in Spanish, it is often omitted / taken as read in English.

Answers:

1. The pool (that) they are going to build is an Olympic one.
2. What we need are tennis courts.
3. The policeman I was talking with (= the policeman with whom I was talking), gave me directions.
4. The sight (that) I like best is the castle.
5. The rubbish in the streets is what I don't like.
6. The girl (whom) I invited is Argentinian.

> **Consejo**
> This tip complements the *Gramática* to help students understand and use relative pronouns, which they need for activities 4 and 5.

5 ✎ Write a report about your neighbourhood.

Students are prompted to include information about their neighbourhood under the following points:

- where it is
- what it's like
- what facilities it has for young people
- what it used to be like (for practice of the imperfect tense)
- what it needs to improve it.

They should refer carefully to the *Gramática* and the *Consejo* and try to use these relative constructions in their answer. They can use the reading text and transcript for ideas, and the language structure box for support.

Plenary activity

If you can download relatively simple information about a tourist destination in Spain, you could display this and ask students questions based on and developed from the questions they have been using on the spread.

Alternatively, take the school / college as your *barrio* and discuss on a whole-class basis what is good and bad about the place and its facilities.

Pages 104–105

3.4 Mi región

Home, town, neighbourhood and region, where it is and what it is like

Subject	Talking about your region
(G) 1	Describing past weather conditions
(G) 2	Learning more about the imperfect tense
🌐	Recognising percentages, common fractions and temperatures

kerboodle!
- Audio file for core reading text
- Audio file and transcript for listening activity 2
- Reading activity: *Mi región*
- Grammar activity: Describing past weather conditions
- Speaking worksheet
- Extension listening worksheet
- Audio file and transcript for extension listening activity
- Foundation reading worksheet
- Foundation listening worksheet
- Audio file and transcript for foundation listening activity

Starter activity

Brainstorm vocabulary for describing where your own region is and its geographical features: *el norte / este / sur / oeste / centro; la costa / el pueblo / la ciudad / el barrio / las afueras; la zona industrial / las carreteras / las autopistas / las fábricas; las montañas / los bosques / el campo / el río / el lago*, etc. This discussion could also revise weather vocabulary.

Core reading text

Two texts *En el norte* and *En el sur* contrast the climate and landscape of northern Spain (the Pyrenees) and southern Spain (Andalusia). The texts should be read in conjunction with studying the *Estrategia*.

You may be able to download from tourism sites, or find in magazines, further images of areas of Spain which you could discuss with students, e.g. whether they think the picture is likely to be in the south or north, what the climate is like there. This may also be a good opportunity to do some map work to familiarise students with the main regions of Spain, perhaps also using a weather forecast map.

The reading text is also available online as an audio file.

> **Estrategia**
> 📖 Some hints on recognising percentages, common fractions and temperatures, using context and similarity to English to help with meaning.

1a 📖 🎧 Match up each caption a–f with one of the two parts of the article.

For the matching activity, ask students to copy out the two text headings *En el norte* and *En el sur* and then to write the letters of the appropriate captions under the headings.

Answers: En el norte: a, e, f   En el sur: b, c, d

1b 📖 🎧 Answer the following questions in English.

For this activity students will need to understand the figures in the text and they should refer to the *Estrategia*.

Answers:

En el norte
1 The valley is 500 metres above sea level.
2 It is 30 °C or above in summer.
3 It can be as low as 15 ° below zero in winter.

En el sur
1 Yes, it's sunny most of the year in Seville. It says that more than 90% of the days in a year are sunny.
2 It's sometimes over 40 °C in summer.
3 The winters are usually mild and the temperature rarely drops below zero.

2 🎧 Transcript:

1
Natalia: Hola, Carlos, ¿Qué tal tus vacaciones?
Carlos: Pues, muy bien.
Natalia: ¿Adónde fuiste?
Carlos: Fui a Galicia.
Natalia: ¿A Galicia? Estupendo. ¿Y qué hiciste?
Carlos: Fui a la playa.
Natalia: ¿Son buenas las playas?
Carlos: Sí, sí, hay playas preciosas, muy tranquilas, con muy poca gente.
Natalia: ¿Y qué tal el tiempo?
Carlos: Bueno, en realidad no hacía buen tiempo: llovía bastante.
Natalia: Claro, en Galicia llueve mucho.
Carlos: Pero no hacía frío.
Natalia: Menos mal.

2
Gustavo: Hola, Sandra. ¿Qué tal tu fin de semana en los Pirineos?
Sandra: ¡Genial! Me encanta ir a las montañas y como están tan cerca los Pirineos, pues hay que ir.
Gustavo: ¿Fuiste a esquiar?
Sandra: Claro, en invierno, si hay nieve, hay que esquiar. Pero también me gusta ir en verano a pasear.
Gustavo: ¿Cómo es para esquiar?
Sandra: Bastante bien pero lo que me gusta más de los Pirineos, para esquiar o para pasear, son las vistas y el paisaje.
Gustavo: Tienes razón, las vistas y el paisaje son impresionantes allá en las montañas. ¿Hacía mucho frío?
Sandra: Sí, la estación de esquí está a dos mil metros sobre el nivel del mar, hacía mucho frío por la noche – hasta 20 grados bajo cero.
Gustavo: ¡Uf! ¡Qué frío! ¿Y nevaba?
Sandra: Sí, sí, nevaba pero durante el día hacía sol y el cielo estaba despejado.

3
Teresa: Hola, José María. Te veo muy moreno pero estamos en pleno invierno. ¿Cómo puede ser?
José María: Pues acabo de pasar unas vacaciones estupendas en las Islas Canarias.
Teresa: ¡Qué suerte! ¿A qué isla fuiste? ¿A Tenerife? ¿A Gran Canaria?
José María: Fui a Lanzarote.
Teresa: ¿A Lanzarote? ¿Qué se puede hacer allí?
José María: Se pueden practicar muchos deportes como el surfing y el windsurf.
Teresa: No sabía que te gustaran estos deportes.
José María: Sí, sí, lo mejor de Lanzarote es que puedes practicar el surfing y el windsurf allí todo el año.
Teresa: Ah, sí, en las Islas Canarias hace buen tiempo todo el año.
José María: Eso es. No hace frío en invierno y como es una isla, también hace viento.

4
Marco: Hola, Noemí. Hace mucho que no te veo.
Noemí: Estuve unas semanas en Barcelona.
Marco: ¿En Barcelona? Pues, muy bien. Es una ciudad muy interesante, ¿verdad?
Noemí: Sí, hay mucho que hacer en la ciudad – hay museos, galerías de arte, conciertos, teatro.
Marco: ¿Qué te gusta más? ¿Te gusta todo eso – museos, galerías de arte?
Noemí: Pues, sí me gusta pero lo que más me gusta de Barcelona son las tiendas.
Marco: ¿Por qué?
Noemí: Porque me encanta ir de compras. Las tiendas en Barcelona son fantásticas.
Marco: ¿Hacía buen tiempo?
Noemí: Bueno el clima es un poco variable. Algunos días hacía buen tiempo – hacía sol pero a veces estaba nublado y no hacía calor.

2 🎧 Listen to four people (Carlos, Sandra, José María and Noemí) talking about places they have visited. For each person, note down in English the place visited, activities they could do, some positive aspects and what the weather was like.

Before students listen, pick out vocabulary from the transcript. Write it on the board and elicit meanings from students. For example: *precioso, tranquilo, poca gente, los Pirineos, las vistas, el paisaje, museos, galerías de arte, conciertos, teatros, tiendas*.

Point out the *Consejo*, which is relevant to the several examples of *hacía* in the text which gives plenty of practice in recognising weather phrases in the past (see also *Gramática*).

Students could prepare a table for their answers using the speakers' names and the prompts in the instructions as headings, i.e.:

	place visited	activities	positive aspects	what weather was like
Carlos				
etc.				

Apart from noting what the weather was like (tying in with the *Gramática*), students could also be asked to identify what the speakers say about the climate of the regions.

Answers:

	place visited	activities	positive aspects	what weather was like
Carlos	Galicia	went to the beach	beaches were beautiful and very quiet	It rained a lot but it wasn't cold
Sandra	Pyrenees	went skiing but also likes to go walking there in summer	views and scenery	It was cold when she went, about –20 °C at night, and it snowed but it was bright and sunny during the day
José María	Lanzarote in the Canary Islands	surfing and windsurfing	You can do these sports all year round because the weather is always good	Good weather
Noemí	Barcelona	lots of interesting places to visit, cultural activities such as museums, art galleries, concerts and theatre	great shops	It was sometimes cloudy and it wasn't hot

Gramática

Guidance on the constructions needed for describing past weather conditions: the past form *hacía* and the imperfect forms of other weather verb forms and usage. Use the transcript of the listening text to work on recognising / predicting these forms.
The secondary grammar point links this information to more general learning of imperfect tense.

3 **G** Copy and complete the sentences using the appropriate verbs in the past: *hacía* (use three times), *estaba* (use once), *nevaba* (use once).

All the words students need for this gap-filler are in the *Gramática* box. Point out also the *Consejo* to remind them that it is always the third person singular that is used.

Answers:

1 hacía
2 nevaba
3 hacía
4 hacía
5 hacía
6 estaba

4 Decide whether these descriptions are true or false for where you live.

Students could work in pairs to work out the meaning of each statement and discuss their answers. You could follow up by seeing whether the class are generally in agreement about points that refer broadly to the region.

Answers: Students' own answers.

5 Write a description of your region for a Spanish-speaking visitor. Use the following questions as a guide.

For this activity students will need mainly present tenses, so practise in a whole-class discussion some present-tense weather statements for describing climate. Encourage them to add intensifiers or quantifiers such as *bastante, mucho, poco*. More able students may be able to add some time expressions such as *frecuentemente, raramente* or *siempre*, or even to make use of *soler*.

Students should concentrate first of all on their own region, then as a second part of the activity, they should use *Me gustaría vivir en …* giving reasons which can relate to weather but also to activities that can be done in that area.

The transcript could be used as a source of useful phrases for both stages of the activity, but provide students with the prompts:

¿Dónde te gustaría vivir?

Me gustaría vivir en … .

The Speaking worksheet will also help students with this activity, as will the *Vocabulario* on page 111.

Students could write up their statements afterwards.

Consejo

A note about the use of third person singular forms for weather expressions, which should be used in conjunction with the *Gramática* and as a useful reminder for activities 3 and 5.

Plenary activity

Students could use the Speaking worksheet as a round-up of the work on this spread. You could also download or copy information from a guide to a region of Spain, or a Latin-American country for students to read the section on climate. This would be particularly useful if it includes guidance on what the weather is like at particular times of year, especially if the region or country has a variable climate (e.g. Galicia, Chile).

Pages 106–107

Reading and listening

Home and local area

• Audio files for core reading texts

Core reading text

The text is an advert for a seaside holiday apartment. The reading text is also available online as an audio file.

Context 3 Home and environment 75

1 📖 🎧 Read the advert for the holiday apartment and choose the correct pictures to answer the following questions.

A skim-reading task requiring only the recognition of vocabulary (if students need to remind themselves, they can refer to the *Vocabulario* on page 107 and on pages 110–111).

Answers:

1 a, b, d   2 a, b, c

2 📖 🎧 Read the advert again and decide which of the following statements are true.

Students now need to read more closely for factual details about the apartment. You could ask them to correct the false statements.

Answers:

2, 4, 5 and 6 are true.
(Corrections of false statements if done:
1 There is a view of **the sea**.
3 There are bars and restaurants **close by**.
7 It costs **513€** for a month in the low season. *or*
It costs 431€ for a **week** in the **mid / standard** season.
8 It costs **531€** for a week in the high season. *or*
It costs 513€ for a **month** in the **low** season.)

3 🎧 *Transcript:* _____

1
Entrevistador: ¿Dónde vives, Miguel Ángel?
Miguel: Vivo en un pueblo en La Sierra Nevada. Es muy bonito. En invierno hay mucha nieve y es muy popular con los turistas que vienen a practicar el esquí.

2
Entrevistador: ¿Qué tiempo hace en verano?
Miguel: Pues en el verano normalmente hace mucho calor con temperaturas de unos 30 grados. Pero el verano pasado hacía mal tiempo casi todos los días, había tormentas y mucho viento.

3
Entrevistador: ¿Cómo es la red de transporte?
Miguel: Pues hay una estación de ferrocarril con dos trenes al día a la capital. También hay un servicio de autobuses muy barato y eficiente. La autopista está cerca pero en invierno a veces está cerrada por la nieve.

4
Entrevistador: ¿Qué te gusta de tu pueblo?
Miguel: Lo bueno es que hay mucho que hacer para los jóvenes. Hay discotecas e instalaciones deportivas y tenemos una bolera. El año que viene van a construir un cine.

3 🎧 Listen to the interview with Miguel and answer the following questions.

There is one numbered section of the interview for each question, so the audio can easily be paused as required.

Answers: 1 a 2 b 3 b 4 c

4 🎧 *Transcript:* _____

1
Entrevistador: ¿Hay fiestas en tu pueblo?
Penélope: En mi pueblo hay muchas fiestas. Hay las Cruces de Mayo y las fiestas patronales el 15 septiembre. Las más divertidas para mí son las fiestas de mi barrio el primero de agosto. Las puedo disfrutar sin ir muy lejos.

2
Entrevistador: ¿Por qué son tan divertidas?
Penélope: Ponen actividades para todo el mundo. Me gusta cantar y este año voy a presentarme en el concurso de talento en la categoría de cantante.

Entrevistador: ¿Hay cambios este año?
Penélope: Siempre había un mercado de artesanía que tiene lugar en la plaza. Pero este año van a poner el mercado a las afueras del pueblo. Lo malo es que está lejos. Si quieres comprar muchas cosas tienes que llevar el coche.

3
Entrevistador: ¿Qué haces en las noches de fiesta?
Penélope: Todas las noches hay baile en la plaza, hay un grupo de música diferente todas las noches y un DJ toca música de diferentes estilos. Es muy divertido y lo paso muy bien bailando. No acaba hasta las tres o las cuatro de la madrugada. No me voy a casa hasta que termine la música.

4
Entrevistador: ¿A qué hora vuelves a casa?
Penélope: Vuelvo a casa muy tarde pero mis padres son guay y no se preocupan porque ellos también lo pasan bien bailando en la plaza.

5
Entrevistador: ¿Qué beneficios trae la fiesta a la comunidad?
Penélope: Lo bueno es que muchos turistas vienen al barrio y también que mucha gente gasta dinero en las tiendas y en los bares.

4 🎧 Listen to the interview with Penélope about a festival in her neighbourhood and answer the following questions.

There is one numbered section of the interview for each question, so the audio can easily be paused as required.

Answers:

1 a
2 b
3 c
4 a
5 Tourists come to the neighbourhood. They spend money in the shops and bars.

Pages 108–109

Grammar practice

G Home and local area

> **Ser and estar**
> A reminder of the usage of *ser* and *estar*, to support activities 1a and 1b.

1a Copy and complete the following sentences with the appropriate form of *ser* or *estar*.

Answers:

1 es
2 está
3 están
4 soy
5 son
6 estamos

1b Work in pairs. Use *ser* and *estar* to make up a conversation about your home and local area. Take turns to ask and answer the questions.

Students are given a few prompts to start them off but should be encouraged to produce additional questions and answers.

> **When to use the imperfect and preterite tenses**
> A reminder of useful time expressions which are best used with either the imperfect tense or the preterite tense. These guidelines should be used for help with activities 2a and 2b.

2a Choose the correct verb forms to complete the following text.

Answers:

1 comíamos
2 fuimos
3 probamos
4 gastaban
5 regalaron
6 salíamos
7 celebrábamos
8 viajamos
9 pasamos

2b Write three sentences in the imperfect tense and three in the preterite tense, using the time expressions in the grammar box.

Answers:

Students' own answers, but they should include all the time expressions in the *Gramática* box with correctly chosen tenses.

> **Hay and había**
> A reminder of the present and imperfect forms of *haber* (there is / are and there was / were) to support activity 3.

3 Translate the following sentences into English.

Answers:

1 In winter there is a lot of snow.
2 There was always a lot of noise in the street.
3 Now there is a pedestrianised area in the centre.
4 Ten years ago there was a bowling alley in my town.
5 This summer there were storms.

> **Using possessive pronouns**
> A reminder of the form and agreement of possessive pronouns, to support activities 4a and 4b.

4a Copy and complete the following sentences with the correct form of the possessive pronoun.

Answers:

1 mío
2 suyos
3 nuestro
4 suyas
5 tuyo
6 vuestra

4b Make up some sentences of your own using possessive pronouns, writing the Spanish and the English. Work in pairs. Partner A gives Partner B the English version to translate into Spanish, then checks with their own Spanish translation. Then swap roles.

You could model this with a student taking the role of Partner A, to demonstrate how it works.

> **Cuánto, cuánta, cuántos, cuántas**
> Students should read this reminder before doing activities 5a and 5b.

5a Copy the sentences and fill in the gaps with *cuánto, cuánta, cuántos* or *cuántas*.

Answers:

1 Cuántos
2 Cuántos
3 Cuántas
4 Cuántos
5 Cuánto

Context 3 Home and environment 77

5b Using *cuánto, cuánta* or *cuántos, cuántas* write a question for each of the following answers.

Answers:

Variations are acceptable provided that the agreement of *cuánto* is correct.
1 ¿Cuántos jardines tiene la casa?
2 ¿Cuántas plantas tiene la casa?
3 ¿Cuántos cuartos de baño hay?
4 ¿Cuántos años tiene tu madre?
5 ¿Cuántos hermanos tienes?

> **Relative pronouns** *Gramática*
>
> Students should study this information before doing activity 6.

6 Translate the following sentences into English.

This activity emphasises the fact that English often omits the relative pronoun but Spanish always includes it.

Answers:
1 The house on the left is pretty.
2 The dress (that) Marina bought is cheap.
3 The girl Marcos is talking to / with is French.
4 The person (that) I'm buying the present for is my grandmother.
5 The friends (that) I'm calling live in another part of town / neighbourhood.
6 The information (that) I need is in my diary.

Pages 110–111

Vocabulary

V Home and local area

kerboodle!
- MP3 files for each vocabulary list

The essential vocabulary used within Topic 1, Context 3 is presented on this vocabulary spread.

Here students can learn the key words for the topic area *Home and local area*. You may also want to direct students to the online audio files of these vocabulary lists, so they can hear how the words are pronounced by a native speaker.

Some words are in light grey on the vocabulary spreads in the Student Book. This indicates items that are not included in the GCSE specification vocabulary list, so students do not need to learn these items for Listening and Reading assessment. However, you may wish students to use them in Speaking and Writing Controlled Assessments.

Pages 112–113

3.5 La contaminación

Current problems facing the planet

Subject		Understanding and giving opinions about pollution
G	1	Using *por* and *para*
G	2	Learning about the perfect tense
🔧		Learning complete phrases to promote fluency

kerboodle!
- Audio file for core reading text
- Video and transcript for activity 3
- Activity to accompany video
- Grammar activity: Using *por* and *para*
- Writing worksheet
- Extension listening worksheet
- Audio file and transcript for extension listening activity

1 Work in pairs. Read the opinions on the banners and put them in order of priority according to your own views. Compare your ideas with your partner.

This activity can be used as a starter before students begin to tackle the main reading text.

Core reading text

The texts are taken from newspaper reports and present current pollution issues in Spain. There are examples to illustrate the grammar point, using *por* and *para*, as well as vocabulary and expressions for giving opinions about the issues.

The reading text is also available online as an audio file.

2 Read the newspaper cuttings and answer the following questions in English.

You could lead into this activity by making one short statement about each text (not in the order in which the texts appear) and asking students to say which text you are talking about. Say the statements quite slowly, and repeat them if necessary. For example:

(text 3): *Ese texto dice que tenemos que reducir las emisiones contaminantes.*

(text 1): *Esa persona no está contenta porque en las calles de su barrio hay papeles y basura por todas partes.*

(text 2): *Ese texto dice que el ruido daña al medio ambiente.*

(text 4): *En ese texto se habla de las industrias que emplean sustancias tóxicas.*

The comprehension questions focus in part on the statistics in the articles.

Answers:
1 20.9% of people surveyed complained about rubbish (e.g.: paper, bags and plastic containers) in the streets.
2 Light pollution which disrupts sleep and visual pollution such as badly-designed buildings and excessive advertising.
3 Noise pollution from aircraft flying low over their houses.
4 Air pollution.
5 Mercury leaked from a factory into the river.

3 🎥 *Transcript:*

Presentadora:	¿Qué aspectos de la contaminación y el medio ambiente te afectan más a ti?
Jaime:	El tráfico. El ruido a todas horas del día molesta mucho. Te pone de los nervios.
Esther:	Además hay mucha contaminación del aire. Si vas a pie o en bici te sientes mal respirando aire contaminado. Te pican los ojos, la nariz y la garganta.
Presentadora:	Aparte del ruido y la contaminación del aire, ¿qué más os preocupa?
Esther:	La suciedad en las calles. Mira. Hay sitios donde se puede tirar, por ejemplo, botellas y envases de plástico o de cartón, para el reciclaje. Pero la gente sigue tirando la basura donde les da la gana.
Esther:	Aquí estamos en el barrio antiguo, que es muy bonito, con todo muy bien conservado pero mira, allá hay anuncios y pintadas que son muy feos.
Presentadora:	¿Qué hay que hacer para solucionar estos problemas?
Jaime:	Hay que reducir el tráfico en el centro de la ciudad para disminuir el ruido y la contaminación.
Esther:	Hay que crear más zonas para peatones, donde no hay coches.
Esther:	Hacen falta más caminos para bicicletas.
Esther:	Hay que realizar más campañas para animar a la gente a reciclar basura.
Esther:	Tenemos que conservar la belleza de nuestro medio ambiente.

3 🎥 Watch the video clip, then answer the following questions.

Play the whole video once, and then again while students attempt the activity. If they need more time to work out their answers, you could pause the video as follows:

Pause after the first scene (after *Te pican los ojos, la nariz y la garganta*) for students to answer question 1.

Pause after the second scene (after *donde les da la gana*) for students to answer question 2.

Pause after the third scene (after *carteles que son muy feos*) for students to answer question 3.

Students should then read question 4 carefully before you play the rest of the clip which contains the information they need to answer this question.

Answers:

1. Noise; air pollution from traffic.
2. b
3. b
4. a and b

Gramática

To present the grammar point (using *por* and *para*), take examples from the text and video. Work with students on finding and explaining the uses of *por* in reading texts 2, 3 and 4. Can they match them to any of the usages explained in the *Consejo*? The transcript of the video clip can then be used to do similar work on the uses of *para*. You could also draw attention to the *Estrategia* and apply it to learning off by heart some of these *por* and *para* expressions. Students should then be well prepared to attempt grammar activity 4.

4 **G** Copy and complete the sentences with *por* or *para*.
Students should refer to the *Gramática* guidelines for support for this activity.

Answers: **1** por, **2** por, **3** para, **4** por, **5** para

Estrategia

💬 This advice about learning set phrases should be taken in the context of memorising uses of *por* and *para* (see also the *Gramática* and *Consejo*). It can also be applied to the useful expressions of obligation in the video transcript: *hay que, tenemos que, hace(n) falta* … which are worked on in more detail in 3.7.
Display a copy of the video transcript to show these in context. There are a few useful idiomatic phrases in the transcript – can students find these? For example:

te pone de los nervios

la gente sigue (tirando basura)

¿Qué hay que hacer?

The phrases learned can then be used in speaking activity 5.

Consejo

This builds on the *Gramática* by listing a few standard uses of *por*. As advised in the *Estrategia*, students should learn these by heart and try to use some of them in speaking activity 5.

5 💬 🌐 Prepare a presentation to answer the following questions. Refer to the online worksheet for a language structure box to help you.

Students have to cover the questions:

- ¿Qué aspectos de la contaminación y del medio ambiente te afectan más?
- ¿Qué hay que hacer para solucionar estos problemas?

They should do some work memorising key phrases (as advised in the *Estrategia*) using *por* and *para*, and could also memorise some of the expressions of obligation such as *hay que, tenemos que*, etc. and other idiomatic expressions which are to be found in the video clip (see also 3.7 for more work on this point). The online worksheet also provides language to support this activity, and students can refer to the *Vocabulario* on page 122.

Plenary activity

Ask students to suggest short statements about any pollution or environmental issues in their area, with corresponding suggestions about what needs to be done. Write these up on the board as though for a poster or leaflet.

Pages 114–115

3.6 El futuro del planeta

Current problems facing the planet

Subject	Understanding the main threats to the environment
G 1	Using the future tense
G 2	Learning how to avoid using the passive
🗣	Expressing ideas: use phrases you know

kerboodle!
- Audio file for core reading text
- Audio file and transcript for listening activity 2
- Reading activity: *El planeta*
- Grammar activity: Using the future tense
- Speaking worksheet
- Extension reading worksheet

Starter activity

Ask students to find in the texts the Spanish equivalent of the following phrases, some of which will familiarise them with simple future verb forms:

In Natalia's letter: the greenhouse effect (*el efecto invernadero*); sea levels will rise (*subirá el nivel del mar*); there will be floods (*habrá inundaciones*).

In Jorge's letter: the balance of the ecosystem (*el equilibrio de nuestros ecosistemas*); endangered species (*las especies en peligro de extinción*).

In Alex's letter: there will be more storms (*habrá más tormentas*); it will be hotter in future (*hará más calor en el futuro*).

In Cecilia's letter: the population of the world keeps on growing (*la población mundial sigue creciendo*); renewable energy (*energías renovables*).

Core reading text

Four people express their concerns about threats to the environment. Several use simple future expressions (see the *Gramática*) to predict problems. Use the Starter activity to access the text before students attempt activities 1a and 1b.

The reading text is also available online as an audio file.

> **Consejo**
> Reassurance that although this topic may seem dauntingly full of new language, the meaning of many of the terms can be deduced from similarities to English.

1a 📖 🎧 Read the letter extracts and say which of the following environmental problems each person addresses. There may be more than one answer for some speakers.

This does not require close reading but does involve the skill of skim reading and looking out for key words, and students need to be aware that some speakers mention more than one problem.

Answers:

Natalia: 1 (*las catástrofes naturales*) and 2 (*el calentamiento global y el cambio climático*)
Jorge – 3 (*la deforestación*)
Alex – 1 (*las catástrofes naturales*)
Cecilia – 4 (*la escasez de recursos y la sobrepoblación*)

1b 📖 🎧 Identify the person who expresses each of the following opinions.

This follows on from the skim reading in activity 1a but now requires students to identify more detail and to understand statements in the simple future tense.

Answers:

1 Jorge 2 Natalia 3 Cecilia 4 Natalia
5 Natalia 6 Cecilia 7 Jorge

2 🎧 *Transcript:*

1
Entrevistador:	Hola, ¿Nos puedes decir tu nombre y de dónde eres?
Ignacio:	Hola, Me llamo Ignacio y soy de Huelva en el sur de España.
Entrevistador:	Bienvenido Ignacio. Estamos preparando un programa sobre el cambio climático. ¿Nos contestarías a algunas preguntas?
Ignacio:	Sí, sí.

2
Entrevistador:	¿Crees que está cambiando el clima? ¿Qué efectos has notado en tu región?
Ignacio:	Bueno, últimamente los veranos han sido más calurosos.
Entrevistador:	Entonces crees que el cambio climático ya existe.
Ignacio:	Sí, definitivamente.

3
Gloria:	Hola, yo me llamo Gloria y también soy de Huelva.
Entrevistador:	Bueno, Gloria, dinos: ¿crees que ya existe el cambio climático?
Gloria:	Es que últimamente el tiempo ha sido muy variable. Había inundaciones en el sur el año pasado y en otras partes de España.
Entrevistador:	Inundaciones, sí, tienes razón.

4
Gloria:	Pero no creo que ya exista el cambio climático. Creo que el tiempo y el clima pueden variar.
Entrevistador:	Bueno, Gloria e Ignacio, dos puntos de vista muy diferentes. ¿Qué pensáis vosotros, los oyentes de este programa? Esperamos recibir vuestros mensajes y vuestros emails.

2 🎧 Listen to the interviews and choose the correct option.

Play the entire recording once, then play it again, pausing if necessary after each exchange while students make their choices.

You could follow up by playing the interview again and asking 'How would you summarise Ignacio's and Gloria's views?' (Students answer in English).

Answers: **1** c, **2** a, **3** b, **4** b

> *Gramática*
>
> Introduce the grammar point (the simple future tense) using activity 3a. Consolidate this after students have done both grammar activities by showing a gapped version of the texts: ask students to predict the missing verbs and to tell you the meaning of the phrase in which they fall.
> The secondary grammar point, avoiding the passive, could be practised by giving students jumbled versions of the following three extracts from Jorge's and Alex's texts (most of which also give further practice of the simple future forms): students reconstruct the sentences in the correct word order.
> *se destruirá el hábitat de muchos animales*
> *lo único que se puede hacer es estar alerta*
> *se cree que habrá más tormentas*

3a **G** Find 10 verbs in the future tense in the letters on page 114.

This activity serves as an introduction to the grammar point which is then practised more actively in activity 3b.

Answers: será, serán, desaparecerá, subirá, habrá, faltará, se destruirá, desaparecerán, hará, faltarán

3b **G** Copy the sentences, putting the verb in brackets into the future tense.

Students should refer to the *Gramática* for help with this activity.

Answers:

1 Si reducimos el tráfico en las ciudades, el aire **estará** menos contaminado.
2 Si se organizan campañas para erradicar las bolsas de plástico, **habrá** menos basura en las calles.
3 El calentamiento global y el cambio climático **serán** irreversibles si no se reducen las emisiones de CO_2.
4 La deforestación **matará** a muchos animales.
5 Dicen que **hará** más calor en verano y menos frío en invierno.
6 **Faltarán** alimentos, agua y combustibles si la población mundial sigue aumentando.

> *Estrategia*
>
> ✏️ Some guidance to remind students to make the most of the language they know; they should try to apply this as they work on writing activity 4.

4 ✏️ 🌐 Summarise the main environmental threats to the planet.

Students should take the advice in the *Estrategia*, and refer also to the language structure box and the *Vocabulario* on pages 122–123 for help with this activity.

Plenary activity

The support Writing worksheet could be used as a round-up activity.

Alternatively, developing the advice given in the *Consejo*, you could ask students to find examples in the reading texts and / or in the audio transcript of terms related to the topic whose meaning can be worked out by thinking about similarities with English words.

Pages 116–117

3.7 Cómo cuidar el medio ambiente

Being environmentally friendly within the home and local area

Subject	Giving suggestions for being environmentally friendly
G 1	Using verbs of obligation: *deber, haber de, hay que, tener que*
G 2	Learning about indefinite pronouns
🌐	Using variety to make your Spanish more interesting

kerboodle!
- Audio file for core reading text
- Audio file and transcript for listening activity 3
- Listening activity and transcript: *¿Qué haces para proteger el medio ambiente?*
- Grammar activity: Using verbs of obligation: *deber, haber de, hay que, tener que*
- Speaking worksheet
- Extension reading worksheet
- Foundation reading worksheet
- Foundation listening worksheet
- Audio file and transcript for foundation listening activity
- Audio role play activity

Starter activity

Before students start to work on the reading text, write the names of the rooms (*En el salón*, etc. as used for headings in the text) and then read aloud a few sentences from the text. For each sentence, students have to tell you which room it applies to. For example:

- *No tires todo a la basura. Reutiliza y recicla los residuos.*
- *No pongas alimentos calientes en la nevera.*
- *No dejes los grifos abiertos cuando te lavas los dientes.*
- *Usa un buen edredón nórdico en invierno.*

Core reading text

The advice in the leaflet text provides language and ideas to enable students to give opinions on and suggest solutions for protecting the environment at home and in their local area. It includes several examples of the grammar point (verbs of obligation).

The reading text is also available online as an audio file.

1 📖 🎧 Read the leaflet and match up each section with the appropriate English sentences (1–10).

Suggest that students think about which room is most likely, before they start searching for the answer.

Answers:

En el salón: sentences 3, 6, 9
En la cocina: sentences 2, 4, 8
En el dormitorio: sentences 1 and 10
En el baño: sentence 7
En el garaje: sentence 5

2 💬 📖 Work in pairs. Partner A reads out one of the statements below and Partner B decides whether the speaker is eco-friendly or not. Then swap roles.

Higher-ability students should be asked to invent a couple of additional speech bubbles. To practise the grammar point, students could also be asked to suggest – in response to the non-eco-friendly statements – more eco-friendly ways for people to behave.

3 🎧 *Transcript:* ─────────────

1

Entrevistadora:	Hola y bienvenidos a nuestra serie sobre el medio ambiente. Hoy hablamos con dos jóvenes estudiantes de secundaria, Daniel y Nati. Hola, Daniel. ¿Qué haces tú para cuidar el medio ambiente?
Daniel:	Hola. Bueno, yo lo que intento hacer es conservar energía, es decir, apagar las luces al salir, apagar la tele y el ordenador también. Cosas así.
Entrevistadora:	Es decir, que ahorras energía. Muy bien, Daniel.
Entrevistadora:	¿Y tú, Nati? ¿Qué sueles hacer para cuidar el planeta?
Nati:	Tiro lo menos posible a la basura. Reciclo envases de vidrio y de plástico, también las latas, el cartón y el papel. En casa tenemos varios contenedores de reciclaje y separamos todo. Así se tira muy poco.
Entrevistadora:	Reciclas todo. ¡Estupendo!

2

Entrevistadora:	¿Conoces a alguien que sea un buen protector del medio ambiente? ¿Cómo es? ¿Qué hace?
Daniel:	¡Sí, tengo un amigo super ecológico! Siempre va a todos lados en bici. Le interesa todo lo relacionado con el medio ambiente. Si vamos de excursión no nos deja tirar nada, ni la piel de un plátano.
Entrevistadora:	¡Ja,ja,ja! Un amigo super ecológico.
Nati:	Mi padre. Sólo pone la calefacción cuando hace mucho frío.
Entrevistadora:	Así son los padres.

3

Entrevistadora:	¿Qué medidas o instalaciones hay en tu instituto para cuidar el medio ambiente?
Nati:	Hay placas solares para calentar el agua.
Entrevistadora:	¿Placas solares? Pues, muy bien.
Daniel:	Hay persianas en las ventanas.
Entrevistadora:	Persianas – para mantener frescas las aulas en verano.
Daniel:	Sí, eso es.

4

Entrevistadora:	¿Qué crees que se debe hacer para reducir emisiones en tu ciudad o región?
Daniel:	Bueno, se deben crear más carriles para bicicletas. Es que con todo el tráfico es muy peligroso ir en bicicleta en nuestro barrio.
Nati:	Hay que reducir el tráfico. Se podría prohibir el tráfico en el centro de la ciudad, por ejemplo.

3 🎧 Listen to Daniel and Nati. What are their answers to the following questions? Select the correct option for each person.

The questions are reproduced from the audio text so this should help students to pinpoint the answers. However, you may need to pause the recording to allow them time to make their choices, as they have to go through two processes to identify which answers are correct, and who said which one. For slower students it may be necessary to ask them to concentrate on one speaker only on each time of listening.

Answers:

1 a D, c N   **2** b D, c N   **3** b N, c D   **4** a D, c N

> **Gramática**
>
> Students may have done some work on expressions of obligation in 3.5, but this *Gramática* now focuses on key verbs of obligation *haber de*, *tener que* and *deber*. The use of different (or no) prepositions make these difficult, so it would be worth making good use of the examples in the reading text. For instance, first display the text and work through it highlighting the three verbs in three different colours (prompted by students). Then show a copy of the text with the verbs in place but with the prepositions *de* and *que* after *haber* and *tener* blanked out. Can students remember – and if not, can they work out, with reference to the *Gramática* – which preposition is missing?

4 Ⓖ Copy the sentences and fill in the gaps with the correct verb from the list.

The preparatory work on the reading text described in the *Gramática* notes should support students in this task, but in any case they need to refer closely to the *Gramática* as they work though the activity.

Answers:

1 Mis padres me dicen: 'No **debes** llevar ropa ligera en invierno. Ponte un jersey.'
2 El último alumno que salga del salón **debe** apagar las luces.
3 Siempre **hemos** de apagar el televisor y el ordenador cuando no estamos usándolos.
4 En verano en el instituto **tenemos** que cerrar las persianas si queremos mantener fresca el aula.

Estrategia

In the reading text there is one example of this strategy (using questions to vary the way you introduce an idea). Students may be able to think of questions that could have been used to introduce some other paragraphs in the text. They then apply the strategy in writing activity 5.

5 Write a leaflet giving 10 tips on ways to reduce CO_2 emissions and save energy at home and at school. Refer to the online worksheet for a language structure box to help you.

Students should use the core text as a model to adapt, and refer to the language structure box on the online worksheet for support. Give students examples of how to use the verbs of obligation with the suggestions in the core text. For instance:

Para ahorrar energía y para reducir emisiones de CO_2:
- *Debes apagar las luces al salir del salón.*
- *Tienes que llevar manga larga en invierno y ropa ligera en verano.*
- *Sólo hemos de poner el lavaplatos cuando esté lleno.*
- *Hay que usar un buen edredón nórdico en invierno.*

Plenary activity

Practise the verbs of obligation along with imperatives: you say an imperative e.g. *¡Apaga las luces!*, and students have to come up with an alternative, more polite way of saying what must be done, using *tener que*, *haber de* (including *hay que*) or *deber*. You could make the cultural point that although in English we try to avoid using imperatives (orders) because it is considered impolite, this is not the case in Spanish, where simple imperatives are not considered too indirect or rude.

Pages 118–119

Reading and listening

Environment

kerboodle! • Audio files for core reading texts

Core reading text

The reading text comprises three positive news stories on environmental issues: the first describes the cancellation of a $25 million debt owed to the US by Peru, in exchange for the conservation of 54 million hectares of Amazonian forest; the second describes the decision of a small village in Andalusia to install solar panels on its public buildings; the third reports a finding that solar energy could contribute to supplying the energy needs of two-thirds of the world's population. The references to recent events provide examples of the perfect tense which is the focus of the *Gramática*.

The reading text is also available online as an audio file.

1 Read the news stories and match up each one with the most appropriate title below.

Students need to read the headlines carefully to look out for all the key terms (e.g. in title **a**, not just *solar* but also *mundo*). You could also ask which news story each of the two photos illustrates.

Answers: **1** b, **2** c, **3** a

Gramática

A brief reminder of how to use the perfect tense for reporting recent events.

2 Read the news stories again and answer the questions.

Students reread the text for the details required.

Answers:
1 b
2 a
3 solar energy
4 the town hall, the sports centre and the theatre
5 Each child is going to plant a tree.
6 b

3 *Transcript:*

Entrevistadora: Pensamos reducir el tráfico en el centro y se planea hacer un carril para bicicletas. ¿Qué le parece?
Joven: Mala idea. Si va más gente en bicicleta por aquí habrá más accidentes, seguro.
Entrevistadora: El ayuntamiento está considerando un plan para hacer carriles sólo para bicicletas. Es para reducir tráfico y reducir emisiones. ¿Qué le parece esta idea?
Chica: Bueno, yo, por ejemplo, no voy en bici porque hay mucho tráfico y es peligroso pero con un carril sólo para bicicletas, sí, sí, a lo mejor me apunto a pedalear.
Mujer: ¿Un carril para bicicletas, aquí en el centro? Pues, no sé. A mí me da igual porque yo, de todas maneras, siempre voy o en autobús o a pie.

3a Listen to the interviews. What are they about?

Students listen for the general theme of the interviews and choose one of three options.

Answer: b (more people cycling)

3b Listen again and note each person's point of view. Write F (for), A (against) or N (neither for nor against) for each interviewee: the young man, the girl and the older woman.

Students listen again to identify attitudes.

Context 3 Home and environment 83

Answers:
Young man: A
Girl: F
Older woman: N

4 Transcript:

Entrevistadora: Hola, buenos días. ¿A usted le interesa el medio ambiente?
Hombre joven: Bueno, sí. ¿Pero en qué aspecto?
Entrevistadora: ¿Cree usted que se debe reducir la cantidad de bolsas de plástico que se usan, en los supermercados, por ejemplo?
Hombre joven: Francamente, esto no me parece muy importante.
Entrevistadora: ¿Qué aspectos medio ambientales le parecen más importantes?
Hombre joven: El calentamiento global y el cambio climático son los dos problemas que tenemos que enfrentar porque si no los controlamos ahora, pronto serán irreversibles.
Entrevistadora: ¿Y qué cree usted que podemos hacer para frenar el calentamiento global?
Hombre joven: Tenemos que reducir las emisiones de CO_2 y tenemos que proteger los bosques y las selvas.

4a Listen to the market research interview and choose the correct letters of the issues mentioned.
Answers: A, C, D, F, G

4b Listen again and choose the correct letters of the opinions expressed by the interviewee.
Answers: B, C, E

Pages 120–121

Grammar practice

G Environment

1a Choose the correct verb form to complete each sentence.
Answers:
1 ha introducido
2 han reducido
3 he intentado
4 Has notado
5 hemos notado

The perfect tense
A reminder list of irregular past participles, some of which students will need for activity 1b.

1b Use the perfect tense and the prompts below to write six sentences about how you have helped to protect the environment in the last week.
Answers:
A He apagado las luces y he cerrado la puerta y las ventanas al salir del aula.
B He puesto un jersey o una sudadera cuando hacía frío.
C No he tirado todo a la basura.
D He reutilizado / reciclado los residuos.
E He reciclado los envases de vidrio, de plástico y los metálicos.
F No he puesto alimentos calientes en la nevera.

The present continuous tense
A brief reminder of present participle endings for the present continuous tense. Although the example shows the point, you may want to stress that *estar* (not *ser*) is used to form the tense.

2a Write the present participles for the following verbs.
Answers:
1 cambiando
2 creando
3 desapareciendo
4 reduciendo
5 vendiendo

2b Copy the sentences and fill in the gaps with the present continuous of the verb in brackets.
Answers:
1 está creando
2 están reduciendo
3 están desapareciendo
4 están vendiendo

Avoiding the passive by using the reflexive pronoun *se*
A reminder of how the impersonal reflexive construction with *se* is commonly used in Spanish instead of the passive. Students should read this reminder before they do activity 3.

3 Choose the correct English translation for each of the following signs.
Answers:
Se alquilan pisos: Apartments to let
Se vende: For sale
No se admiten menores de 18 años: No entry to under-18s
Se aceptan tarjetas de crédito: Credit cards are accepted
Se habla español: Spanish spoken
El desayuno se sirve a partir de las 7.30: Breakfast is served from seven thirty

> **Indefinite pronouns: *algo, alguien***
>
> A reminder that indefinite pronouns *algo* and *alguien* do not change their form, to support activity 4.

4 ✏️ Copy the sentences and fill in the gaps with *algo* or *alguien*.

All students need to decide is whether it is 'someone' or 'something' that is being referred to.

Answers:

1. algo
2. alguien
3. algo
4. algo
5. alguien

> **Avoiding imperatives**
>
> A reminder of how verbs of obligation can be used instead of imperatives to tell someone they must do something. Students should refer to this for support as they do activity 5.

5 ✏️ Replace the imperatives in the following instructions with a verb of obligation plus an infinitive.

Answers:

Students' choice of verb but the forms must be as listed in the activity instruction, and used with the correct infinitives as follows:

1. regar
2. adaptar
3. apagar
4. dejar
5. reparar
6. cerrar

Pages 122–123

Vocabulary

V Environment

- MP3 files for each vocabulary list

The essential vocabulary used within Topic 2, Context 3 is presented on this vocabulary spread.

Here students can learn the key words for the topic area *Environment*. You may also want to direct students to the online audio files of these vocabulary lists, so they can hear how the words are pronounced by a native speaker.

Some words are in light grey on the vocabulary spreads in the Student Book. This indicates items that are not included in the GCSE specification vocabulary list, so students do not need to learn these items for Listening and Reading assessment. However, you may wish students to use them in Speaking and Writing Controlled Assessments.

Pages 124–127

Controlled Assessment

Refer to the section on Controlled Assessment, pages 107–112 in this Teacher's Book.

Page 128

3 Context summary

- Interactive multiple-choice quiz

The closing page for Context 3, Home and environment, provides a multiple-choice quiz which tests the key language learnt in this Context.

A longer version of this quiz is also available online as an interactive, self-marking multiple-choice test.

Answers:

1. nuestra, suyo
2. Student's own answer
3. From time to time / Occasionally / Sometimes we used to eat fish on Christmas Eve.
4. Student's own answer
5. Student's own answer
6. En invierno hacía frío y nevaba; solía hacer / hacía menos de 0 grados.
7. Tenemos que cambiar el coche **por** la bicicleta **para** reducir el tráfico en las ciudades.
8. El cambio climático
9. En el futuro **subirá** el nivel del mar, no **habrá** agua limpia y el campo se **hará** desierto.
10. Es importante reciclar porque podemos convertir la basura en materiales nuevos.

4 Work and education

School / college and future plans

What school / college is like

	KS3 Revision: School subjects, school buildings; jobs and careers	*Online materials* • Audio files for core reading texts
	4.1 Bienvenidos al colegio ■ Using impersonal verbs ■ Developing answers to questions	• Audio file for core reading text • Audio file and transcript for listening activity 3 • Reading activity: *Mi colegio* • Grammar activity: Using impersonal verbs • Writing worksheet • Extension listening worksheet • Audio file and transcript for extension listening activity • Foundation reading worksheet
	4.2 Colegios británicos y españoles ■ Using different tenses ■ Spotting tense usage	• Audio file for core reading text • Audio file and transcript for listening activity 3 • Listening activity and transcript: *Colegios británicos y españoles* • Grammar activity: Using different tenses • Speaking worksheet • Extension reading worksheet

Pressures and problems

4.3 ¡Cuánto estrés! ■ Using *desde hacía* and the imperfect tense ■ Making sure you give all the information that you are asked to give	• Audio file for core reading text • Audio file and transcript for listening activity 3 • Reading activity: *¡Cuánto estrés!* • Grammar activity: Using *desde hacía* and the imperfect tense • Writing worksheet • Extension listening worksheet • Audio file and transcript for extension listening activity
4.4 ¿Qué piensas de tu colegio? ■ Using the conditional tense ■ Looking for clues to help understanding	• Audio file for core reading text • Audio file and transcript for listening activity 3 • Reading activity: *¿Qué piensas de tu colegio?* • Grammar activity: Using the conditional tense • Speaking worksheet • Extension reading worksheet • Foundation listening worksheet • Audio file and transcript for foundation listening activity • Audio role play activity

Reading and listening

School / college and future plans	• Audio file for core reading text • Audio file and transcript for listening activity 3 • Audio file and transcript for listening activity 4

Grammar

School / college and future plans ■ Demonstrative adjectives ■ The present subjunctive in certain exclamatory phrases	■ Comparative adjectives ■ The personal *a*

Vocabulary

School / college and future plans	• MP3 files for each vocabulary list

Current and future jobs

Looking for and getting a job

4.5 El trabajo a tiempo parcial
- Recognising the pluperfect tense
- Including different tenses in speaking and writing

  - Audio file for core reading text
  - Audio file and transcript for listening activity 2
  - Listening activity and transcript: *El trabajo a tiempo parcial*
  - Grammar activity: Recognising the pluperfect tense
  - Writing worksheet
  - Extension reading worksheet
  - Foundation reading worksheet

4.6 Buscando trabajo
- Asking questions using the preterite tense
- Using context to work out meaning

  - Audio file for core reading text
  - Video and transcript for listening activity 3
  - Activity to accompany video
  - Grammar activity: Asking questions using the preterite tense
  - Writing worksheet
  - Extension reading worksheet

4.7 Poniéndose en contacto
- Using *quisiera*
- Using knowledge of grammatical categories

  - Audio file for core reading text
  - Audio file and transcript for listening activity 4
  - Listening activity and transcript: *Correos electrónicos*
  - Grammar activity: Using *quisiera*
  - Writing worksheet
  - Extension listening worksheet
  - Audio file and transcript for extension listening activity

Advantages and disadvantages of different jobs

4.8 Después de los exámenes
- Using imperatives (commands)
- Finding different ways to say similar things

  - Audio file for core reading text
  - Audio file and transcript for listening activity 3
  - Reading activity: *¿Qué hacer?*
  - Grammar activity: Using imperatives (commands)
  - Speaking worksheet
  - Extension reading worksheet
  - Foundation listening worksheet
  - Audio file and transcript for foundation listening activity

4.9 Comparando empleos diferentes
- Using irregular adverbs
- Checking grammar in written work

  - Audio file for core reading text
  - Audio file and transcript for listening activity 3
  - Listening activity and transcript: *¿Qué trabajo es?*
  - Grammar activity: Using irregular adverbs
  - Speaking worksheet
  - Extension listening worksheet
  - Audio file and transcript for extension listening activity
  - Audio role play activity

Reading and listening

- Audio file for core reading text
- Audio file and transcript for listening activity 3
- Audio file and transcript for listening activity 4

Grammar

Current and future jobs

- Comparative and superlative adverbs
- Possessive adjectives
- Interrogatives with prepositions
- *Usted* and *ustedes*
- The relative adjective *cuyo*

Vocabulary

Current and future jobs
- MP3 files for each vocabulary list

Summative assessment

Work and education
- Interactive multiple-choice quiz

The opening page for Context 4, Work and education, provides a quick-reference overview of how the teaching spreads, grammar and strategies within this Context in the Student Book map to the Topics and Purposes of Context 4 in the GCSE specification. Also included here is an overview of the online resources available for each of these spreads in the Student Book.

Context 4 Work and education 87

Page 130

Revision

School subjects, school buildings

kerboodle! • Audio files for core reading texts

Gramática

A reminder of how to form simple negative statements with *no*, to support comprehension for activity 1 and the question–answer work in writing / speaking activity 2b.

1 📖 🎧 Read Ricardo's text and decide if the following statements are true (T), false (F) or not mentioned (?).

Students have to read quite closely for this activity. You could support their reading by focusing on e.g. adjectives – highlighting them and making sure students can see which noun they qualify and what information the noun + adjective provides. Check that they understand the quantifiers *bastante* and *demasiado*, and ask them to find two phrases that indicate a positive opinion (*me gusta … me encanta …*) and one that indicates a problem (*lo malo es …*). They should then be well equipped to deal with the true / false questions. Ask students to point to the part of the text which justifies their answer; abler ones should, as part of this process, be able to correct the false statements.

Answers: **1** T, **2** F, **3** F, **4** F, **5** F, **6** T, **7** ?

2a 💬 Work in pairs. Partner A starts by naming in Spanish either a school subject or a part of your school. Partner B repeats that word and adds another, then Partner A repeats both words and adds another, and so on. When one of you hesitates or cannot give another word, the other person scores a point. The first to three points is the winner.

Students should close their books once they have read the instruction and attempt the task without the *Vocabulario* being visible. Alternatively, give them two minutes to read / memorise the *Vocabulario*, then they close their books and do the activity.

2b ✏️💬 Write some questions to ask each other about your school. Partner A asks the questions and Partner B answers. Then swap roles.

Encourage students to include opinion questions as well as factual ones, reminding them of the constructions *me gusta / me encanta* and making sure they can use the question forms *¿te gusta / encanta …?* Point out the *Gramática* to remind them how to make negative replies. They could also use the quantifiers *bastante* and *demasiado* from the text (along with *muy, un poco*) and you could provide the question prompt *¿Qué opinas de …?*

Page 131

Revision

Jobs and careers

kerboodle! • Audio files for core reading texts

Gramática

A reminder that most job titles in Spanish have a masculine and a feminine version.

1a 📖 🎧 Match up each job with its correct description. There are two descriptions you don't need. Do you know the Spanish for all these jobs?

This could also be done as a purely listening exercise if you write the English job titles on the board and then read out the descriptions. The two distractor descriptions are E (mechanic / *mecánico*) and F (postman / *cartero*).

Answers: **1** G, **2** H, **3** A, **4** B, **5** D, **6** C

1b ✏️ Make up similar sentences in Spanish for these jobs.

This is quite a challenging task and students may need some support, e.g. gapped sentences to complete. They should keep their sentences for use in speaking activity 1c.

1c 💬 Work in pairs. Partner A reads out a sentence and Partner B says which job it is describing. Then swap roles.

Students should use the sentences from reading activity 1a and the ones they have produced for activity 1b.

4.1 Bienvenidos al colegio

Pages 132–133

What school / college is like

Subject	Describing what school / college is like
G 1	Using impersonal verbs
G 2	Learning more about the words for 'this' and 'that'
	Developing answers to questions

kerboodle
- Audio file for core reading text
- Audio file and transcript for listening activity 3
- Reading activity: *Mi colegio*
- Grammar activity: Using impersonal verbs
- Writing worksheet
- Extension listening worksheet
- Audio file and transcript for extension listening activity
- Foundation reading worksheet

1 **V** In three minutes, see how many of the following words and phrases you can find in Spanish in the text below.

This can be used as a starter activity before students read closely for detail in activity 2.

Answers:

1 alumnos 2 (un) ambiente
3 polideportivo 4 biblioteca
5 tienen lugar 6 clases de apoyo

Core reading text

The text *Bienvenidos al Instituto Cervantes* is the text from a school's home web page, and as such is full of the key nouns for describing school, as well as phrases for mentioning regular school events and routines.

The reading text is also available online as an audio file.

2 📖 🎧 Read the following sentences and decide whether they are true (T), false (F) or not mentioned in the text (?).

This activity focuses on information about what the facilities are like and what happens in the school, so you may wish to do some more preparatory work before students attempt the questions. For example:

- whole-class work on English–Spanish match of nouns for places in the school
- asking students to make a list in English of at least 10 facilities in the school
- giving students a list in English of school facilities, some of which are not mentioned in the text (e.g. shop, music room): students tick off on the list the items that are mentioned.

Answers: **1** T, **2** ?, **3** F, **4** ?, **5** T, **6** T

3 🎧 *Transcript:*

1 En mi colegio los chicos y las chicas llevan su propia ropa. Esto es mejor que tener que llevar uniforme, que es muy caro. La piscina que construyeron el año pasado es fenomenal y el director dice que en el futuro vamos a tener un salón de actos, que actualmente no tenemos.

2 Con el calor que hace, me encantaría tener una piscina al aire libre o incluso una cubierta, pero en mi colegio no hay. Es peor porque nuestro uniforme es muy incómodo, tanto para los chicos como para las chicas, y esta mañana tuvimos que pasar media hora en el salón de actos escuchando a la directora.

3 Me gustaría ir a un colegio mixto, pero mis padres dicen que es mejor estudiar en el mío, que es un colegio masculino con un uniforme muy feo. Sin embargo, tenemos una piscina grande donde hacemos muchos concursos y hay premios que el director presenta en el salón de actos.

4 Cada mañana tengo que decidir lo que voy a llevar para ir al instituto y lo odio. Preferiría tener uniforme porque sería mucho más fácil. Creo que no es tan difícil para los chicos de mi instituto porque generalmente no les preocupa tanto la moda. Me gustaría ir al colegio de mi primo, ya que tiene una piscina y un salón de actos enorme, y el mío no tiene.

3 🎧 Listen to four students speaking about their schools. Copy and complete the table by writing 'yes' or 'no' in each box.

Run through the English headings with students before they listen, to make sure they know which key Spanish word to listen out for, for each heading.

Answers:

	Is it mixed?	Is there a uniform?	Is there a pool?	Is there a hall?
1	Yes	No	Yes	No
2	Yes	Yes	No	Yes
3	No	Yes	Yes	Yes
4	Yes	No	No	No

Gramática

The construction *me gusta* should be familiar from Key Stage 3 and is revised on page 186, but this reminder provides useful support for activity 4 and speaking activity 5. Point out the list of pronouns given as prompts in activity 4, and reinforce students' grasp of this point with some quick-fire translation in both directions, game style: you say e.g. *me gustan*, students respond 'I like them', etc., moving onto harder examples e.g. you say 'we love them', students respond *nos encantan*. Alternatively, write two columns of phrases – Spanish on the left, English translations in jumbled order on the right – and students have to come up and draw lines to pair off the equivalents.

4 **G** Copy the sentences and fill in the gaps with the missing pronoun or verb from the boxes below. Then translate each sentence into English.

Simple practice of the impersonal verb opinion constructions *me gusta / encanta*, etc. Make sure that students understand that they have free choice of pronoun and verb, but the translation must show that they have understood the meaning of the pronoun they have chosen and that they know when to use singular and plural verbs.

Once students have finished the sentences in the book, as extension work they could be asked to make up sentences of their own, including one of the key words. They could then read these to the rest of the class, who could then say what each one meant.

Answers:

1 (any pronoun, so long as the translation is accurate)
2 any plural verb
3 (any pronoun, so long as the translation is accurate)
4 any plural verb
5 (any pronoun, so long as the translation is accurate)
6 any singular verb

> **Estrategia**
> The skill of developing answers to questions can be practised in the context of activity 5. Emphasise that students will greatly increase their score in their spoken work if they can add detail and make their replies more interesting, saying why they like / dislike something or adding some information as well as just the fact(s) asked for.

> **Consejo**
> The reading text can be used to give some examples of how to follow this advice on finding alternative ways of saying things. For example, alternatives to *Hay* …:
>
> *ofrecemos*
> *tenemos*
> *los estudiantes disponen de*
>
> Students should check their draft for their presentation and watch out for repetition, replacing some words with alternatives if they can.

5 Prepare a presentation about your school, to last between one and two minutes. Use the language structure box to help you.

Students should refer to the language structure box for help with this activity. Give them some bullet points to help them structure their presentation, e.g.:

- *Introducción: nombre del colegio, situación,*
- *Gente: mixto / femenino / masculino, cuántos profesores / alumnos*
- *¿Qué hay (edificios, aulas, lugares para el deporte)?*
- *Rutina*
- *Ventajas y desventajas*
- *Conclusión: lo que te gusta / lo que no te gusta en tu colegio*

Before the students prepare the presentation, it is advisable to encourage them to give their own ideas and points of view and to give full descriptions. They should also try to vary the language and verb tenses that they use, according to the ability of the student.

Ask the rest of the class to prepare questions to ask at the end of the presentation. That would probably need previous practice of question forms, as it is something that most students find very difficult.

To complement this activity and to develop the grammar point (impersonal verbs) and the skill referred to in the *Estrategia* (developing answers to questions), students could work on an interview rather than a presentation, in which Partner A plays the role of a new student who wants to know all about the school, and Partner B answers their questions.

Plenary activity

Encourage students to give more than one reason for liking or disliking an aspect of school and to use different adjectives and verbs to enrich their language. You might point out some of the following words and phrases, which show how language can be varied at a fairly simple level:

Positive comments	Negative comments
Es (muy) divertido / interesante / entretenido / fantástico / impresionante / útil.	Es (un poco / bastante) aburrido / fatal / pesado.
Me encanta / me gusta (mucho / muchísimo) / me interesa / me fascina …	Odio / detesto / me fastidia / me molesta / me aburre …

Pages 134–135

4.2 Colegios británicos y españoles

What school / college is like	
Subject	Talking about school routine and comparison with Spanish schools
G 1	Using different tenses
G 2	Revising comparative adjectives
	Spotting tense usage

kerboodle!
- Audio file for core reading text
- Audio file and transcript for listening activity 3
- Listening activity and transcript: *Colegios británicos y españoles*
- Grammar activity: Using different tenses
- Speaking worksheet
- Extension reading worksheet

Starter activity

Before reading the text in the book, you could do an activity to practise adjectives with the class, and to relate those adjectives to school. You call out an adjective and someone has to say an aspect of school life to which it might relate. For example, you say *difícil* and a student may say *la historia es difícil* or you say *fatal* and a student says *la comida es fatal*.

Other possible adjectives could include: *fácil, rico, divertido, emocionante, aburrido, limpio, sucio, largo, entretenido, impresionante, útil, grande, justo, injusto, simpático, antipático, maravilloso*.

Students need to adapt the adjective as necessary to agree with the noun they choose.

The activity can be made more challenging by asking for a justification of the answer given.

1 Work in pairs. Your task is to form a sentence about your school by saying one word each in turn. You must use at least one of the following words in each sentence.

Give students three minutes for this task: their aim is to do three sentences each.

Core reading text

The text is two emails exchanged between an English student and a Spanish one about their schools. Before students read the text, it may be useful to point out the meaning of *privado* and *público* in a school context, because of the possible confusion with 'public school'. Help students to read and understand the text by asking a few questions before they read it. You might ask how to say 'take the register' or 'lunch', for example.

Students should refer to the *Estrategia* before they read, and perhaps do the suggested tense-spotting work on a second read which would also serve to familiarise them with the text as good preparation for reading activity 2. Noticing the tenses is relevant also to the *Gramática* (on using different tenses) which students will be studying later in the spread.

The reading text is also available online as an audio file.

> **Estrategia**
> A reminder that recognising tenses is an important reading skill. Students read though Danny's and Juan's emails noting the tense and person of the verbs they use.

2a Read the emails and decide to which school each of the following statements applies. Write D (for Danny's school), J (for Juan's school) or D + J (for both schools).

As preparation for this task, you could work with the class as a whole, taking them through first one email and then the other to find out what is said about:

- lunchtime
- taking the register
- uniform
- what kind of school (private or state)

Answers: 1 D, 2 J, 3 D + J, 4 J, 5 D

2b Copy the sentences and fill in the gaps with a suitable word from the emails.

To help students to access this task and to develop their reading skills you could ask them what kind of word they are looking for in each case (a noun, a verb, an adjective, etc.)

Answers:

1 voy	2 duro	3 todos
4 vez	5 tuve	6 todavía

3 *Transcript:*
1 Disfruté las clases de español porque los alumnos me hicieron preguntas sobre la vida en España. Por otro lado la mayoría de los profesores eran más estrictos que en mi colegio, lo que me molestó.
2 Incluso los estudiantes que sacan muy malas notas en los exámenes no tienen que repetir curso. ¡Qué suerte! En mi país te suspenden y eso es horrible.
3 La clase que tienen primero cuando pasan lista a mí me parecía inútil. Prefiero el sistema en España, donde pasan lista en cada clase.
4 El uniforme que tienen que llevar es feo e incómodo. No entiendo por qué los estudiantes no pueden ponerse su propia ropa, como en mi colegio.

3 Listen to four Spanish students speaking about the English schools they have visited during an exchange visit. Note whether each person's opinion is positive (P), negative (N) or positive and negative (P + N). Then write a summary in English of what each person says, showing why you have chosen P, N or P + N.

This activity is quite challenging and before students attempt it you may wish to let them listen once to find the Spanish for these phrases:

Speaker 1: I enjoyed the Spanish lessons; on the other hand

Speaker 2: to repeat a year; How lucky!

Speaker 3: when they take the register; I prefer the system in Spain

Speaker 4: it's ugly and uncomfortable; their own clothes

For the activity itself, it is probably most practical for students to concentrate on one speaker at a time, pausing the audio while they do both parts of the task in relation to that person before they move on to the next one.

Answers: 1 P + N,   2 P,   3 N,   4 N

> **Gramática**
> The *Gramática* (using different tenses) complements the *Estrategia*, by focusing on the ability to use verbs in different tenses. Students practise the point in activity 4 and then apply it in writing activity 5.
> The secondary grammar point, comparative adjectives, can be practised if wished by including some comparisons between Spanish and British schools, in activity 5.

Context 4 Work and education 91

4 **G** Choose the correct tense of the verbs.

Remind students to look carefully at the time expressions and words such as *próximas* which tell them which tense is appropriate (they could look back at pages 96–97 for some reminders of present and past time expressions). There is a mix of regular and irregular verbs. When discussing students' answers to the questions, ask how they worked out which tense had to be used, picking out those words that show whether a past tense will be used (*anoche*) or whether it is a current or habitual action requiring the present tense (*actualmente, cuando vuelvo*). Many students prefer to use the immediate future instead of the future tense, and of course there is nothing wrong with that. However, the future tense may still have to be recognised in reading and listening tasks.

Answers:

1 iré   2 comemos   3 hice
4 tuve   5 estudiará   6 leo

> **Consejo**
> A note on the importance of checking verb tense forms when you have drafted a written text. Students should apply this in activity 5.

5 ✎ Write in Spanish what you have found to be some of the differences in Spanish schools compared to your own. Write an imaginative account, focusing on a Spanish student's school day, either in the present tense saying what normally happens or in the past, describing what was done yesterday. Refer to the online worksheet for a language structure box to help you.

This activity will be done better if the teacher has a short oral session prior to students attempting the written work, in which the differences between Spanish schools and the students' own can be drawn out. Students should refer to the *Gramática* before starting the task and to the *Consejo* once they have drafted their text.

Plenary activity

Check students' recognition of different tenses by asking them to produce some short sentences about school life to say e.g. which subjects they studied last year, this year and which ones they will study next year. They can use the language structure box on the online worksheet for support.

Pages 136–137

4.3 ¡Cuánto estrés!

Pressures and problems

Subject	Discussing pressures and problems in school
G 1	Using *desde hacía* and the imperfect tense
G 2	Using the subjunctive in exclamatory phrases
🌐	Making sure that you give all the information that you are asked to give

kerboodle!
- Audio file for core reading text
- Audio file and transcript for listening activity 3
- Reading activity: *¡Cuánto estrés!*
- Grammar activity: Using *desde hacía* and the imperfect tense.
- Writing worksheet
- Extension listening worksheet
- Audio file and transcript for extension listening activity

1 **V** Find the odd word out in the following groups. Then make up one of your own using school vocabulary. Test it out on the rest of the class.

This provides a pre-reading starter; students could work in pairs to compose their own 'odd one out' lists.

Answers:

1 comedor   2 estuche
3 castigar   4 me enfada

Core reading text

The text is a report of survey findings about stress in school, showing what causes most stress. Refer students to the *Consejo* which offers some help on approaching unfamiliar text. The text provides the key language students will need to discuss pressures and problems at school, and an example of how to say how long something has been happening: *Algunos estudiantes sufrían desde hacía muchos años* (as explained in the *Gramática* on using *desde hacía* and the imperfect tense).

The reading text is also available online as an audio file.

> **Consejo**
> Some help on how to tackle longer texts containing unfamiliar language. This is relevant for activities 2a and 2b.

2a 📖 🎧 Find the Spanish equivalent in the text for these words and phrases.

There are other key words and phrases you could ask students to find, for example 'homework' (*deberes*), 'to continue with' (*seguir con*), 'continuous assessment' (*evaluación continua*), 'often' (*a menudo*).

Answers:

1 acoso escolar   2 castigos
3 buenas notas   4 comportamiento
5 presión   6 aunque

2b 📖 🎧 Answer the following questions in English.

Students read the text more closely now to extract the information required. Remind them of the *Consejo*.

Answers:

1. A group of Spanish students aged 14–16.
2. good marks
3. it's less stressful
4. It makes the teacher's work much more difficult; so that those who want to learn can't do so.
5. physical and verbal bullying by other students
6. It can be very expensive buying fashionable clothes.

3 🎧 *Transcript:*

María	¡Hola! Soy María. Generalmente lo paso bien en el colegio, aunque admito que a veces tengo problemas con el acoso escolar. Lo peor son los deberes que son muy difíciles y paso mucho tiempo haciéndolos. Sin embargo, no es culpa de los profesores, que explican bien.
Carlos	Me llamo Carlos. Tengo amigos que sufren acoso escolar pero yo he tenido mucha suerte porque nunca me ha afectado a mí. A decir verdad encuentro que el colegio es un sitio donde siempre me divierto trabajando. Aparte del trabajo estoy en el equipo de baloncesto en el colegio y me encanta.
Lucía	¡Hola! Me llamo Lucía. Lo malo para mí es la presión que siento por parte de mis padres. Ya sé que sólo quieren que saque buenas notas. No obstante, de vez en cuando es demasiado cuando dicen que debería hacer más deberes y salir menos. Por lo menos tengo profesores simpáticos que entienden mi problema.

3 🎧 Listen to the three teenagers. For each person, decide which of the following statements are true.

Each speaker covers two issues, each tested by one question in the activity, so you may want to pause the audio accordingly.

Answers: 1 b, 2 c, 3 a, 4 b, 5 b, 6 a

Guidance on how to use *desde hacía* + imperfect tense if you want to say that something went on for a period of time in the past. Students practise the point in activity 4 and could apply it in speaking activity 5 (though they may be more likely to need the present tense form *desde hace* + present tense, so you could choose to remind them about this form as well).

Gramática

---

4 **G** Change the infinitive of the verb in brackets to the imperfect tense. Translate each sentence into English.

Make sure students are clear about the prompts – they must use the part of the verb indicated by the pronoun given with each infinitive. They should refer to the *Gramática* as they work. Students could be asked to make up their own sentences as an extension activity.

Answers:

1. *estudiaban:* They had been studying at that school / college for four years.
2. *sufríamos:* We'd been suffering from bullying (at school) for a long time.
3. *esperaba:* She had been waiting for her friend in the playground for 15 minutes.
4. *vivía:* He had been living in the house next door to his victim for a month.

💬 Advice on how to tackle speaking or writing tasks that are prompted by bullet points (as in activity 5), to make sure you give all the information you are asked for.

Estrategia

---

5 💬 🔊 With a partner, or in groups of three or four, answer the following questions. You could play the role of someone who is more or less affected by these problems than you are. Refer to the online worksheet for a language structure box to help you.

Students should apply the advice in the *Estrategia* to their work on this speaking task.

You could discuss the first bullet point on a whole-class basis and then divide the class into four groups, each of which has to discuss and agree upon an answer to one of the other four bullet point questions.

Plenary activity

The survey which is the basis of the report in the reading text could be run in the class, with students (anonymously) ticking one of three boxes *no me molesta, me molesta un poco, me molesta mucho* for each of the nine categories of problem. There could be a *Comentarios* box below the questions in which students note down any other source of stress at school.

Depending on the size of your group, you could summarise the results immediately or in the next lesson.

Context 4 Work and education

Pages 138–139

4.4 ¿Qué piensas de tu colegio?

Pressures and problems

Subject	Discussing opinions of school
G 1	Using the conditional tense
G 2	Revising adjectival agreement
🔍	Looking for clues to help understanding

kerboodle!
- Audio file for core reading text
- Audio file and transcript for listening activity 3
- Reading activity: ¿Qué piensas de tu colegio?
- Grammar activity: Using the conditional tense
- Speaking worksheet
- Extension reading worksheet
- Foundation listening worksheet
- Audio file and transcript for foundation listening activity
- Audio role play activity

1 Work in pairs. Partner A gives their opinion, in Spanish, of the following aspects of your school. Then swap roles.

Students could use the language structure box for help: remind them also of the quantifiers / intensifiers *muy, demasiado, bastante* which they may need to express their opinions.

Core reading text

Two manifestos by students standing for the position of chairman of the *Consejo Escolar*. Each puts forward ideas of what they want to change. The *Gramática* explains how the conditional is used and there are a couple of examples in the text which illustrate this *(podríamos comenzar una hora más tarde; sería mucho mejor llevar uniforme)*.

The reading text is also available online as an audio file.

2 Answer the following questions in English.

Before they work in detail on the questions, ask students to skim read the text and tell you briefly, in English, what the main suggestions are from each candidate (three from Natalia, two from Iker). After they have answered the questions, students could work in pairs to come up with one idea they would include in a similar manifesto. They should write a couple of sentences in Spanish:

- one to state the problem, starting *Lo malo es (que)* …
- one to say what has to be done, starting *Podríamos* … or *Deberíamos* …

You could demonstrate this to start them off.

Answers:

1 To find out their ideas.
2 That all students need to be more responsible in keeping them clean.
3 She wants to start school (an hour) later.
4 There is too much junk food / unhealthy food.
5 Because some of them may seem strange.
6 He wore one when he was at the school and there was more respect for teachers and from the public.
7 In favour – because he finds it annoying having to decide what to wear each morning.
8 He wants more severe punishments.

> *Estrategia*
>
> The *Estrategia* gives advice about listening to what surrounds a difficult word in a listening text, and listening out for topic-related words. Students could try it out with the audio for activity 3, listening once for gist and then again to try to pick up detail.

3 *Transcript:*

1 La historia es la asignatura en que tengo que escribir más apuntes. Me gusta mucho pero lo encuentro muy difícil y siempre saco malas notas. Creo que voy a suspender el examen de fin de curso.
2 Mi profesora que tengo de inglés desde hace cuatro años dice que siempre he hablado el idioma con buen acento y que trabajo a un nivel muy alto. Me alegro, ya que es una asignatura obligatoria.
3 Hasta este año nunca había tenido éxito en geografía. Los profesores que tenía me aburrían y tengo que decir que no me comportaba bien en las clases. Sin embargo, este año tenemos un nuevo profesor que es estricto pero apruebo todos los exámenes y todo va bien.
4 Hay un grupo de alumnos desobedientes en mi clase de dibujo y eso hace que sea difícil concentrarse. Es una asignatura optativa y ahora pienso que sería mejor estudiar música. Lo que pasa es que tal vez sea demasiado tarde cambiar.

3 Listen to Manolo talking about school subjects. Match up each subject with the correct comment.

The audio is in four sections, one for each of the four school subjects. Ask students to read the questions carefully before they listen. Pause the audio after each section so that students have time to scan the different comments, because all the comments are paraphrases of what is actually said. You may need to do the first question as a whole-class exercise, explaining that they should not listen out for translations of the English but for something which conveys the same meaning or opinion.

Remind students also that, as in the *Estrategia* advice in 4.2, they need to recognise different tenses in order to know when things happened – for example, Manolo uses the imperfect to talk about his previous geography teachers, and the present to talk about his new one.

As an extension activity, students could be asked to note or say in English any other information given about the four subjects.

Answers: **1** C, **2** F, **3** E, **4** A

Gramática

The conditional tense is introduced here but only in constructions with the infinitive, (as are the examples in the reading and listening texts) to avoid the pitfalls of the subjunctive in *Si* sentences. In activity 4 students simply have to recognise the appropriate person of the verb to complete the sentences.

4 **G** Copy and complete the sentences, choosing the correct part of the conditional tense.

Practice in recognising the forms of the present conditional tense.

Answers:

1 sería
2 gustaría
3 recomendaríamos
4 deberían

Consejo

In activity 5 students are asked to justify the score they allocate, but this tip reminds them that it will help them to achieve a high score in writing or speaking tasks if they can justify their opinion without being asked.

5 You find a 'Rate-a-school' website in Spanish and decide to rate your own school according to the following score ... Justify the score you have given and suggest possible ways of improving each aspect.

Students have the language structure box and the *Vocabulario* on page 145 for support, but it would be a good idea to give students an example of what they might write, for example:

El horario – 3

Creo que el horario está bien porque sólo empezamos a las nueve. Por eso puedo levantarme a las ocho y diez, ya que vivo cerca del instituto. Sin embargo terminar a las cuatro es tarde y quiero tener menos tiempo para la comida, así que podemos terminar media hora antes.

Plenary activity

Elicit, in Spanish, students' ideas to include in a manifesto about things to change or improve in the school. Once 10 ideas have been collected and noted on the board, number them. Ask students to note down the number of their top priority among the ideas. Take a show-of-hands vote for each idea, to find out which are the three most popular.

Pages 140–141

Reading and listening

School / college and future plans

kerboodle! • Audio files for core reading texts

Core reading text

The text is a description by Carmen of her school life, reminiscing about primary school and then describing her current secondary school.

The reading text is also available online as an audio file.

1 Read Carmen's account and complete the following sentences with the correct option.

A task requiring reading for detail only for factual content – no inference is needed. All the answers are to be found in the first half of the text (up to *¡lo odia!*).

Answers: 1 b, 2 c, 3 a, 4 c, 5 c, 6 b, 7 c

2 Answer the following questions in English.

Students now need to read the whole text (except the first paragraph) for broader information about Carmen's experiences and impressions. As an extension, ask students what they can find out about Carmen's teachers' opinions of her ability (= they say she is going to get good results).

Answers:

1 Her older brother was already a student at the school.
2 about 500
3 They are strict but hardworking.
4 chewing gum
5 sports and sciences
6 There's not much space for relaxation at break times, and she'd like it if there were a café where you could buy a sandwich and a drink.
7 an exchange with a school in England
8 whether to do an A-level course in Technology or do a vocational course

3 *Transcript:*

Bueno, Javi, el lunes es tu primer día de instituto. Vamos al pueblo para comprar las cosas que vas a necesitar. Primero, vamos a escogerte una mochila. Tiene que ser cómoda y bastante grande. No habrá que comprar cuadernos ni libros porque el instituto te los dará.

En la papelería, vamos a buscar un estuche, un sacapuntas y una regla. No vas a necesitar un diccionario hasta el tercer curso.

Ya tenemos un montón de bolígrafos y lápices en casa así que no nos hace falta comprar más. Todavía nos queda suficiente dinero para una buena goma y, claro, tienes que tener una calculadora para las clases de matemáticas.

3 Listen to Luis telling his brother what he will need when he starts school. Which six items from below are they going to buy?

Students need to listen closely to the sense of what is said, not only to the items mentioned, in order to distinguish those which the boys are actually going to buy.

Answers: They are going to buy: A (calculator), C (ruler), E (eraser), H (bag), I (pencil sharpener), G (pencil case)

Context 4 Work and education

4 🎧 *Transcript:*

El director: Buenos días, chicos y chicas. Quiero empezar por explicar las cinco reglas principales del instituto.
Uno, todos los alumnos deben comportarse con respeto para sus compañeros y profesores.
Dos, es obligatorio asistir a todas las clases. Si estás enfermo, hay que llevar una carta de los padres.
Tres, está prohibido fumar en todas partes del instituto para los profesores tanto como para los alumnos.
Cuatro, en clase, es importante escuchar y mantener silencio cuando el profesor te está hablando.
Cinco, una cosa fundamental es esto: si ves a otro alumno intimidar o molestar a un compañero, díselo en seguida a uno de los profesores. No vamos a tolerar este tipo de acoso escolar en este instituto.

4 🎧 Listen to the head teacher explaining school rules. Complete the following sentences with the correct option.
Make sure students understand there is one question about each of the five rules.
Answers: **1** b, **2** c, **3** a, **4** a, **5** c

Pages 142–143

Grammar practice

G **School / college and future plans**

Demonstrative adjectives
A reminder of the meaning and form of demonstrative adjectives, to support activities 1a and 1b. *Aquel* forms are not included here.

1a 💬 Work in pairs. Take turns to buy things for school. Follow the examples given.
Students are given prompts to start them off but should be encouraged to produce additional questions and answers. They only require *este / ese* forms, as in the *Gramática* box.

1b ✏️ Translate the following words into Spanish. Use the nouns in the box below and check in a dictionary if you are unsure of the gender.
Answers:

1 este examen
2 esas aulas
3 estas mochilas
4 esa palabra
5 este trimestre
6 esos profesores
7 esa prueba
8 este uniforme
9 estos alumnos
10 ese vocabulario

The present subjunctive in certain exclamatory phrases
A reminder of how subjunctive exclamations are used to convey a hope or wish.

2 📖 Find a suitable expression (1–6) to match each of the following occasions.
Answers: **a** 3, **b** 5, **c** 1, **d** 2

Comparative adjectives
A reminder of how to use *más* and *menos* with adjectives, and of the irregular forms *mejor* and *peor*, to support activities 3a, 3b and 3c.

3a ✏️ Guillermo Sinamigos has to outdo what anyone says. What would he reply to the statements 1–10 below? Follow the example.
Answers:

1 Los alumnos aquí son más inteligentes.
2 El director aquí es mejor.
3 El gimnasio aquí es más grande.
4 Los recreos aquí son más largos.
5 Las aulas aquí son más cómodas.
6 La comida aquí es más deliciosa.
7 Los profesores aquí son más trabajadores.
8 Las actividades aquí son más interesantes.
9 Las notas aquí son mejores.
10 El edificio aquí es más histórico.

3b 💬 Work in pairs. Take turns to compare the following things now with what they were like at primary school.

3c ✏️ Write a paragraph comparing your primary school with the school you are at now. Use *más* and *menos* to compare them. Write about the following things and anything else you would like to mention.

The personal *a*
A note about when the personal *a* needs to be included in front of an object. Students practise the point in activity 4.

4 ✏️ Copy the sentences and fill in the gaps with *a* if you think it is needed.
Answers: Personal *a* should be included in sentences 2 and 5

Pages 144–145

Vocabulary

V School / college and future plans

kerboodle!
- MP3 files for each vocabulary list

The essential vocabulary used within Topic 1, Context 4 is presented on this vocabulary spread.

Here students can learn the key words for the topic area *School / college and future plans*. You may also want to direct students to the online audio files of these vocabulary lists, so they can hear how the words are pronounced by a native speaker.

Some words are in light grey on the vocabulary spreads in the Student Book. This indicates items that are not included in the GCSE specification vocabulary list, so students do not need to learn these items for Listening and Reading assessment. However, you may wish students to use them in Speaking and Writing Controlled Assessments.

Pages 146–147

4.5 El trabajo a tiempo parcial

Looking for and getting a job	
Subject	Talking about part-time jobs and work experience
G 1	Recognising the pluperfect tense
G 2	Learning how to use *cuyo*
🔧	Including different tenses in speaking and writing

kerboodle!
- Audio file for core reading text
- Audio file and transcript for listening activity 2
- Listening activity and transcript: *El trabajo a tiempo parcial*
- Grammar activity: Recognising the pluperfect tense
- Writing worksheet
- Extension reading worksheet
- Foundation reading worksheet

Starter activity

Ask the students what they think the two texts are (= a letter to a problem page and the reply). Ask what work Elena has been doing and where.

You could then ask a few questions about the time frame to see whether students have a basic grasp of the meaning of the tenses and time expressions used in Elena's letter. For example:

Did Elena just recently get the idea of having a job? (= no, she had always thought it was a good idea)

Did Elena have her job two months ago? (= no, she got it a month ago)

Does she work every day? (= no, three nights a week)

When did her mother talk to her about giving up her job? (= yesterday)

Does Elena plan to end the relationship with her boyfriend? (= no, she says it *would* end if they can't go out)

Core reading text

The texts are a letter from Elena to a problem page, and the counsellor's reply. The story in the letter refers to different time frames (see notes on the Starter activity), including use of various tenses: pluperfect (see *Gramática*), imperfect, preterite, perfect, present, and conditional (see *Estrategia* on using different tenses).

If you want to draw out the range of tenses, write these tenses as titles on the board and ask students to find the verbs in the text to write up under each heading. (Concentrate on the letter only rather than the reply, unless you want to explain the subjunctives in the reply!)

The reading text is also available online as an audio file.

1a 📖 🎧 Copy the sentences and fill in the gaps with the correct word from the box.

Students may need telling that they won't need all the words from the box. The questions mostly require facts that can be taken directly from the text without interpretation.

Answers:

| 1 16 | 2 cuatro | 3 sale |
| 4 padre | 5 menos | 6 optimista |

1b 📖 🎧 Answer the following questions in English.

After picking out mainly factual details in activity 1a, students now read again for more subtle points.

Answers:

1 to earn some money while she was studying
2 magazines and make-up
3 She has a boyfriend and they like to go out to cafés and the cinema.
4 because it's affecting her school marks
5 It could mean the end of her relationship with her boyfriend if they can't afford to go out.
6 Lots of people her age are in a similar situation.
7 continue to work, but fewer nights a week and ask her parents for a bit more money
8 to be responsible and not forget the importance of her studies

2 🎧 *Transcript:*

1 Hice mis prácticas en la oficina de un abogado.
 Pasé nueve días allí, porque el lunes de la segunda semana fue día festivo así que no tuve que trabajar. Todos los días trabajaba desde las nueve menos cuarto hasta las cinco y encontré el trabajo difícil.
2 Tuve que ir a mi antigua escuela primaria y me divertí mucho allí.
 Tenía que levantarme a las siete porque el día empezaba a las ocho y media.
 Sin embargo, los diez días que estuve allí pasaron muy rápidamente.
3 Yo trabajé durante tres semanas como mecánico en un taller cerca de mi casa.
 Era aburridísimo porque tenía que hacer lo mismo todos los días.
 Además, no me gustaba nada empezar a las ocho de la mañana.

Context 4 Work and education   97

2 🎧 Listen to three students talking about their work experience. For each one, say:

Run through some of the new vocabulary first in a Spanish–English whole-class matching activity (students should be able to make the matches by using a combination of recognising word similarities with English and by process of elimination):

prácticas – work experience
abogado – lawyer
antiguo – former, old
un taller – a workshop

Students could prepare a table for their answers, as follows, before they listen:

	where	how long	starting time	opinion
1				
2				
3				

Answers:

	where	how long	starting time	opinion
1	solicitor's / lawyer's office	9 days	8.45	difficult
2	primary school	10 days	8.30	good fun
3	garage / mechanic	3 weeks	8.00	very boring

> **Gramática**
> To support the recognition of the pluperfect tense, show students the example of the pluperfect in context, in Elena's letter *(siempre había pensado)*.

3 **G** Copy the sentences, changing the infinitive in brackets into the correct part of the pluperfect tense. Those with a ! have an irregular past participle.

As preparation for the exercise, revise the imperfect tense of *haber* and test students on past participles, including irregular ones, perhaps with a competition: divide the class into groups, write up 20 or so infinitives (including some verbs that have irregular past participles) and ask each group in turn to give you the past participle of any verb.

Answers:
1 había pensado   2 había dejado
3 habían comido   4 habíamos vuelto
5 habías bebido   6 había hecho

> **Estrategia**
> 🖉 See notes on Starter activity – the reading text illustrates the wide range of tenses that you need to express what had happened, did happen, has just happened, and could happen. The transcript of the listening task can also be used to show uses of the preterite and imperfect when talking about an episode in the past. Students should study these alongside this *Estrategia* on including different tenses, before applying the advice as they work on activities 4a and 4b.

4a 🖉 🔊 You want to find out your friends' thoughts about work experience. Plan and write a questionnaire in Spanish which will ask for people's opinions.

Students can use the language structure box for help; you could also give them the transcript of the audio for some ideas.

If students have done work experience already, some of the questions can be about what people did. If they have not yet done it, the questions can ask about:
– what they think of the idea of doing work experience
– what kind of work experience they would like to do.

Students should try to use a range of tenses as explained in the *Estrategia*. Their questionnaire should include space for answers – explain that they are going to use the questionnaire with their classmates.

4b 💬 In groups of three or four ask the questions you have devised in Activity 4a and make notes in Spanish on the answers given. Report your findings to the class in Spanish.

An oral follow-up to activity 4a.

> **Consejo**
> A reminder of the prepositions *a* and *de*.

Plenary activity

As a follow-up activity, students could write a summary of, or discuss as a class, their findings from the survey done in activities 4a and 4b. Give them some questions such as:

Por lo general, ¿estamos a favor de o en contra de hacer prácticas?
¿Qué más nos gustaría hacer como prácticas?
¿Qué es lo malo y qué es lo bueno de hacer prácticas?
etc., depending on the questions students have devised.

Alternatively, go back to the issue raised by the problem letter and group the class in threes – in each group, one person represents Elena's point of view, one represents her mother's, and one represents the counsellor trying to find a compromise. They should prepare what they want to say, and then you choose one group and run a chat show scenario where you are the host and the three people argue out their points of view.

Pages 148–149

4.6 Buscando trabajo

Current and future jobs

Subject	Looking for and applying for jobs
G 1	Asking questions using the preterite tense
G 2	Learning how to use *usted* / *ustedes*
🔧	Using context to work out meaning

kerboodle!
- Audio file for core reading text
- Video and transcript for activity 3
- Activity to accompany video
- Grammar activity: Asking questions using the preterite tense
- Writing worksheet
- Extension reading worksheet

1 🅥 Write down as many Spanish words as you can think of which are associated with the following jobs.

This activity can serve as a starter for the spread. To make the process quicker and more fun, you could allocate the words to different groups in the class, and see which group comes up with the greatest number of words for their job.

Core reading text

A series of short job adverts. Students should skim read once, then read the *Estrategia* on using context to work out meaning before they read again more closely for activity 2.

The reading text is also available online as an audio file.

2 📖 🎧 🔧 These students are looking for work in Spain. Which job would suit each of them? Read the advertisements and write the correct letter for each person.

Ask students to find in each advert the key word that says what the job is, and to tell you it in English. Then ask which jobs ask for some previous experience or knowledge (A, B, E, F) and what that is. Students should then be well prepared to match the people to the jobs, but tell them to read all four personal texts *before* they try to do any matching.

Answers: **1** F, **2** D, **3** E, **4** C

📖 📹 The skill of using context to work out meaning can be equally applied in reading and in listening, so the *Estrategia* can be applied to both here.

Estrategia

3 📹 🔧 Transcript: _____

1
Manolo: Buenos días.
Dueña: Hola.
Manolo: He visto su anuncio en el periódico de ayer. Entiendo que usted busca camareros y cocinero.
Dueña: Sí, es verdad.
Manolo: ¿Puede decirme un poco más del trabajo de camarero?
Dueña: Claro. Buscamos camareros para este restaurante, que es muy popular entre españoles y turistas.
Manolo: Sí, ya veo que es un restaurante impresionante.
Dueña: Abrimos todos los días desde las siete de la mañana hasta la medianoche.
Manolo: Y, ¿tendría que trabajar esas horas?
Dueña: No. Lo que pasa es que está la opción de trabajar por la mañana para servir desayuno y almuerzo, o trabajar por la tarde para terminar de servir el almuerzo y servir la cena. ¿Qué preferirías?
Manolo: Vivo bastante lejos de aquí, así que para mí sería mejor empezar por la tarde.
Dueña: Muy bien. Ya sabes por el anuncio cual es el sueldo. También recibirás todas tus comidas gratis.
Manolo: ¿Qué tendría que llevar puesto?
Dueña: ¿Ves a este camarero de aquí? Todos los camareros tienen que llevar el mismo uniforme.
Manolo: Y, ¿dónde podría comprarlo?
Dueña: No hay que comprarlo. Compramos los uniformes para nuestros camareros.
Manolo: Estupendo.

2
Fátima: Hola, señora.
Dueña: Hola.
Fátima: Mi amiga me ha dicho que usted necesita cocinera.
Dueña: Sí, su amiga tiene razón.
Fátima: ¿En qué consiste el trabajo?
Dueña: Aunque el restaurante ofrece una variedad de platos de todo el mundo, nos especializamos en platos típicos de pescado y marisco, como ve aquí.
Fátima: ¡Qué rica parece la comida!
Dueña: ¿Sabe lo que es este plato?
Fátima: ¡Claro que sí! Es la paella.
Dueña: Y, lo más importante, tendría que saber prepararla.
Fátima: Tengo mucha experiencia.
Dueña: ¿Dónde trabajó usted?
Fátima: Trabajé en la cocina de un restaurante en Málaga. Tengo aquí una carta del jefe de ese restaurante.
Dueña: ¡Qué bien! ¿Podría prepararme una paella?
Fátima: Sí. ¿Cuándo?
Dueña: Ahora mismo.
Fátima: Sí. ¿Dónde están los ingredientes?
Dueña: Aquí a la derecha.
Fátima: Vale. ¡Al trabajo!

3 📹 🔧 Watch the video clip about summer jobs. Answer the questions in English.

The text builds on the six adverts in the reading text, adding more detail about the job requirements.

Answers:

1a 2 (morning or evening)
1b free meals

Context 4 Work and education   99

2a fish and shellfish / seafood
2b She worked in a restaurant in Malaga.

> **Gramática**
> Guidance on how to ask questions using the preterite tense, which students then practise in activity 4 and part of activity 5.

4 🗨 **G** Work in pairs, changing the verbs in the infinitive into the *tú* form of the preterite tense. Answer each question with a sentence that includes a preterite verb in the first person. Take turns to ask and answer the questions.

Once students have done this speaking task, you could make use of it as preparation for activity 5 where students will have to use the *usted* form: ask them to write out the questions using the *usted* form of the given verbs.

Answers:

Questions in *tú* form:
1 ¿Trabajaste el sábado?
2 ¿Ganaste mucho dinero?
3 ¿Por qué decidiste trabajar allí?

Questions in *usted* form:
1 ¿Trabajó usted el sábado?
2 ¿Ganó usted mucho dinero?
3 ¿Por qué decidió usted trabajar allí?

5 🗨 Work in pairs. Your partner is preparing for an interview for one of the jobs advertised on page 148. Ask him / her questions like the ones below: note that these questions use the formal (*usted*) form of the verb in a formal situation. Then swap roles.

You could ask students to discuss which tenses they are going to need in this activity. The questions mainly require the use of the present tense and the immediate future, but the last one will require some preterite, some perfect and some imperfect: you could talk through some examples, and then demonstrate the dialogue with a student playing the part of the interviewer.

Students can use the language structure box on the online worksheet for support.

> **Consejo**
> A general tip about writing down explanations of new grammar points.

Plenary activity

Use the *Consejo*:

Ask students to think of any grammar point that they think they know reasonably well and to write a sentence or two in English to explain it to a new learner.

Then write a couple of recently studied grammar points on the board, and students have to write or say a brief explanation in English.

Pages 150–151

4.7 Poniéndose en contacto

Current and future jobs

Subject	Communicating in the workplace
G 1	Using *quisiera*
G 2	Revising possessive adjectives
🔧	Using knowledge of grammatical categories

kerboodle!
- Audio file for core reading text
- Audio file and transcript for listening activity 4
- Listening activity and transcript: *Correos electrónicos*
- Grammar activity: Using *quisiera*
- Writing worksheet
- Extension listening worksheet
- Audio file and transcript for extension listening activity

1 **V** Write down in Spanish the item of work equipment that your teacher describes.

Read out the following descriptions of work equipment for the students to write down. It would be an ideal opportunity to use 'show me' boards.

1 Es una máquina en que se puede escribir cartas, buscar en Internet o enviar correos electrónicos. (= *el ordenador*)
2 Con este aparato se puede hablar con clientes, incluso los que están en otro país. (= *el teléfono*)
3 Es de papel. Hay muchos tipos. Recibes estas cosas por correo cuando el cartero llega. (= *las cartas*)
4 Es ropa que tienes que llevar. Todas las personas llevan lo mismo en el trabajo o en el colegio. (= *el uniforme*)
5 Es el dinero que recibes cada semana o cada mes. (= *el salario / el sueldo / la paga*)

Core reading text

The text is a memo from the management of a company to its employees, listing practical details about facilities and procedures in the office. The text is given in English translation as well as in Spanish, but with some mistranslations in the English, which form the basis of activity 2. The text covers several items of key language for the topic of communications in the workplace; students can use the *Vocabulario* on page 161 for comprehension support if needed.

The reading text is also available online as an audio file.

2 📖 🎧 The memo above has been sent to all employees within a company. Unfortunately the English translation contains five errors. Find and correct them.

Each of the five sections contains one error.

Answers:

1 ... dial zero (not five)
2 ... can be found in each office (not at reception)
3 ... on the ground floor (not first floor)
4 ... to collect phone messages (not deliveries)
5 ... only urgent calls (not non-urgent calls)

> ✏️ Guidance on using grammatical knowledge as well as context to work out the meaning of a word. This is then applied in writing activity 3.
>
> *Estrategia*

3 ✏️ 🌐 Copy and complete the sentences using the words below. Only one word will be suitable in each case, either grammatically or from a sense point of view.

Students should apply the advice in the *Estrategia* to help them work out which kind of word is missing in each case, before they make their choice from the list.

Answers:

1 enviar 2 jefe 3 mandaste
4 largo   5 rápidamente

4 🎧 *Transcript:*

1 Buenas tardes. Me llamo María Mayor, que se escribe M–A–Y–O–R. Puede llamarme después de las cinco en el 7435921.
2 Hola. Soy el Señor Hausner: H–A–U–S–N–E–R y llamo desde Alemania. ¿Puede llamarme dentro de una hora, por favor? Mi dirección de email es dieterh@aol.de.
3 Buenos días. Aquí Xanti Ansotegi: A–N–S–O–T–E–G–I. Estaré en la oficina en tres horas y media y puede llamarme entonces. El número es 9084760.

4 🎧 Listen to the three telephone messages recorded at work. Write down the following details for each one.

Students have to note, for each caller: their surname, their contact number or email address, and when to call or email back. Make it clear that they should write their answers in English. They could draw up a table or headings before they listen, and then listen once for each kind of information, or listen a few times to each message, in order to extract the exact spellings, numbers, and times.

It may be worth working on some of the time constructions with students before they listen, e.g. the difference between **después de** las cinco, **dentro de** una hora and **en** tres horas y media.

Answers:

1 Mayor / 7435921 / after 5.00
2 Hausner / dieterh@aol.de / within an hour
3 Ansotegi / 9084760 / in 3½ hours

> An explanation of how to use *quisiera* with a noun or an adjective. You could introduce the point by using illustrations of various items of office / stationery equipment with mime or a large V along with the picture to indicate if a verb is required. The point is then practised in activities 5a (nouns) and 5b (verbs). The secondary grammar point is revising possessive adjectives.
>
> *Gramática*

5a **G** Ask for the following items, using *quisiera*.

Add more items or ask students for their own suggestions.

Answers:

1 Quisiera el número de teléfono.
2 Quisiera una nueva máquina de fax.
3 Quisiera una cita.

5b **G** Say that you would like to do these things, using *quisiera* followed by the infinitive.

Add more items or ask students for their own suggestions.

Answers:

1 Quisiera dejar un mensaje.
2 Quisiera enviar un email / correo electrónico.
3 Quisiera llamar a la oficina.

6 💭 You are working for an English firm that does business with companies in Spain. How would you give the following information in Spanish?

This activity requires a range of constructions, most of which are provided in the language structure box, but you may want to do some class work with students first of all to make sure they know which tenses and which structures they will need.

Abler students could use the language structure box for help to compose and then 'leave' phone messages which include:

– stating who they are and when they are ringing
– asking a question or making a request
– asking the person to get back to them, and saying how / when.

> A note on using the relative pronoun *que* to extend written and spoken sentences. You could ask abler students to work this into their phone 'messages' (see activity 6 suggestion).
>
> *Consejo*

Plenary activity

Draw a spider diagram or a scattering of circles in which various short bits of information are written: a couple of names, some times, some days, and a few which just have ¿?. Students make up phone messages choosing any of these ingredients but they must use one ¿? i.e. make up a question or request which is the main point of the message. You could cross out the circles as they are 'used up'.

Pages 152–153

4.8 Después de los exámenes

Advantages and disadvantages of different jobs

Subject	Looking at opportunities for work and study post-16
G 1	Using imperatives (commands)
G 2	Learning about asking questions using prepositions
🔍	Finding different way to say similar things

kerboodle!
- Audio file for core reading text
- Audio file and transcript for listening activity 3
- Reading activity: *¿Qué hacer?*
- Grammar activity: Using imperatives (commands)
- Speaking worksheet
- Extension reading worksheet
- Foundation listening worksheet
- Audio file and transcript for foundation listening activity

1 🅥 💬 Work in pairs. You have five minutes to read the article and find the Spanish equivalent of the words below. Then close your book. Partner A reads out the English word and Partner B gives the Spanish equivalent. Then swap roles and see who has managed to find the most.

Answers:

obligatorio; pensar; el año próximo; consejos; ganar; formación; certificado académico; el mundo laboral; electricista; seguir; universidad

Core reading text

The article *Instituto San Jaime – ¿Qué vas a hacer el año que viene?* is from a school magazine, setting out the three options open to 15–16-year-olds once they have completed their last year of compulsory study.

The reading text is also available online as an audio file.

2 📖 🎧 Answer the following questions in English.

Activity 1 has prepared the ground with some of the vocabulary needed for this comprehension activity but students can also refer to the *Vocabulario* on page 161 for help.

Answers:

1 15–16 year olds beginning their last year of compulsory education
2 Think about future possibilities and plans for next year.
3 teachers at the school
4 earning money / having more freedom
5 They enable you to gain qualifications as well as experience of work.
6 one or two years
7 any two of: electrician, hairdresser, mechanic
8 If you have enjoyed your subjects at school and want to study more / if you want to study at university.
9 b

3 🎧 *Transcript:*

Entrevistador:	Los jóvenes de hoy tienen que tomar decisiones difíciles. Aquí en el estudio tenemos a Julia Pérez que decidió quedarse en el instituto para continuar con sus estudios en lugar de buscar trabajo. Julia, ¿fue difícil llegar a esta decisión?
Julia:	Un poco. Me gustaba el instituto pero también pensé que sería interesante encontrar un trabajo.
Entrevistador:	¿No te interesaba la idea de la formación profesional?
Julia:	No mucho. Miré la lista de cursos pero no me gustaban los trabajos.
Entrevistador:	Y ¿recomendarías el bachillerato para otros jóvenes?
Julia:	Depende. Hay algunos aspectos negativos como, por ejemplo, cuando estoy con mis amigos que trabajan siempre tienen mucho más dinero que yo. Sin embargo, también hay ventajas. Mis amigos dicen que sus trabajos son muy aburridos pero a mí me gustan mucho mis asignaturas.
Entrevistador:	Así que estás muy contenta con lo que estás haciendo.
Julia:	Pues, sí, pero me gustaría tener la oportunidad de ganar experiencia laboral. En el instituto no organizan prácticas laborales con una empresa. Por ejemplo, sería muy interesante ver el trabajo de un abogado o un día típico en la vida de un contable.
Entrevistador:	Creo que es bastante difícil llegar a ser abogado o contable.
Julia:	Bueno, yo tengo planes de ir a la universidad después de terminar mis estudios aquí en el instituto. Los universitarios tienen más posibilidades de encontrar mejores trabajos.

3 🎧 Listen to the interview with Julia and choose the correct option to complete each sentence.

Students could listen once to pick up the gist of the interview, then they should read all the questions thoroughly before listening again for the detail required. You could play the recording section by section, telling students to read the relevant question before each section of the audio.

Answers: **1** b, **2** c, **3** a, **4** b, **5** b, **6** a

> **Gramática**
> This *Gramática* introduces the difficult construction, negative imperatives. You could present a few examples using language familiar from this spread and the previous one but you will of course also need to revise present subjunctive forms with students.
> The secondary grammar point is asking questions using prepositions.

4 **G** You are giving advice to some of your friends about what not to do. Copy the sentences, changing the infinitive in brackets to the correct form of the imperative (*tú* form). Then make up more sentences giving advice to people on what not to do.

After working on the *Gramática*, you might also want to contrast positive and negative imperatives by running through the commands in activity 4 in the positive as well as the negative form.

Answers:

1 busques   2 seas
3 escuches   4 escribas

> *Estrategia*
> The advice on finding different ways to say similar things should be applied to writing activity 5. Students have practised *quisiera* on the previous spread, so this could be added to the examples of how to express what you would like to do: students may be able to come up with one or two more as well, e.g. *me gustaría, tengo ganas de*.

5 Write an email to your Spanish friend, Cristina, telling her about your plans for next year.

Students could be prompted to cover:

- the choices available to them
- their choice of action
- reasons for their choice: advantages of the option chosen and disadvantages of the options rejected
- what their parents and friends think of their plans.

They should use the language structure box to plan their answer.

> *Consejo*
> The tip advises students to learn vocabulary in small amounts, this being the most efficient way to remember new material.

Plenary activity

You could pick up on the *Consejo* by compiling with the class a vocabulary list of words to be learned from this spread, perhaps also noting next to each one whether it is a verb, noun, etc. (following up from the *Estrategia* on the previous spread, Using knowledge of grammatical categories).

Pages 154–155

4.9 Comparando empleos diferentes

Advantages and disadvantages of different jobs	
Subject	Talking about different jobs and careers
G 1	Using irregular adverbs
G 2	Revising comparative and superlative adverbs
	Checking grammar in written work
kerboodle!	• Audio file for core reading text • Audio file and transcript for listening activity 3 • Listening activity and transcript: *¿Qué trabajo es?* • Grammar activity: Using irregular adverbs • Speaking worksheet • Extension listening worksheet • Audio file and transcript for extension listening activity • Audio role play activity

Starter activity

Encourage skim reading of the text by asking some gist questions before students tackle the close reading needed for activity 1. For example:

What is the worst thing about Luisa's job, according to her? Do you think she regrets her choice?

What is the main thing that Susana likes about her apprenticeship? Do you think she misses studying her school subjects?

What does José say about his family's working life?

Core reading text

In the text, three young people describe their current job situation, the reasons for their choice and the advantages / disadvantages which are relevant to their choice of work. It contains several examples of irregular adverbs which you can use when you teach the *Gramática* on this spread.

The reading text is also available online as an audio file.

1 The people above have written about their jobs. Read the descriptions and select the correct person: Luisa (L), Susana (S) or José (J).

Encourage students to take notes, in English, on the main points from each text, before they try the questions.

You could follow up with more comprehension work: ask students to write down as table headings in English the three jobs: accountant, trainee hairdresser, farmer. Then mention various attributes of each job, and students have to note down the attribute in the appropriate column, according to what Luisa, Susana and José say about the jobs (and not according to their own opinion!). For example:

- badly paid (= farmer)
- boring at times (= accountant)
- dirty work (= farmer)
- helps you keep fit (= farmer)
- long hours (= farmer)
- meeting others like yourself (= trainee hairdresser)
- stressful (= accountant)

Context 4 Work and education

- useful training (= trainee hairdresser)
- varied (= trainee hairdresser)
- well paid (= accountant)

Answers: 1 J, 2 L, 3 J, 4 S, 5 L

2 📖 🎧 Read the three people's texts again and answer the following questions in English.

Students now need to read more closely and deductively to find the answers to two more searching questions about the texts.

Answers:

1 Susana, because she says she loves her job: it's varied, the training and practical experience of work are good, she can chat to other apprentices during the classes she attends.
2 Luisa, because she's become an accountant in spite of the fact that she was not good with numbers when she was at primary school.

3 🎧 Transcript:

a

Entrevistador:	Hola, Emilio. Todo el mundo te conoce como un torero famoso pero dinos algo de cómo empezaste a torear.
Emilio:	Bueno, todo empezó durante una fiesta en mi pueblo cuando tenía doce años. Soltaron unas vacas en la pequeña plaza de toros y yo y otros chicos tratamos de torear.
Entrevistador:	Y, ¿habías tenido experiencia tratando con vacas antes?
Emilio:	Siempre me ha gustado la vida del campo y solía trabajar un poco en una granja cerca de mi casa. Así que estaba acostumbrado a estar con animales, pero lo de ser torero, nada.

b

Entrevistador:	Entonces, ¿qué pasó más tarde?
Emilio:	Todos mis amigos me dijeron que había sido un éxito durante la fiesta del pueblo. Por eso me hice miembro de un club taurino que estaba en un pueblo vecino. Ahí aprendí a ser matador, poco a poco.
Entrevistador:	¿Es caro empezar a ser matador?
Emilio:	Al principio a veces no tenía bastante dinero para comer y pasaba todo mi tiempo viajando de un pueblo a otro tomando parte en corridas no oficiales. El problema era que tenía que pagar mis gastos y a veces no me pagaban nada.

c

Entrevistador:	¿Nunca pensabas en dejarlo y encontrar un trabajo mejor pagado?
Emilio:	Sí, muchas veces. Pero un día cuando tenía diecisiete años, gané un gran concurso, lo que me dio la oportunidad de ser matador en la feria de Badajoz.
Entrevistador:	¿Y ahora todo va bien?
Emilio:	Sí, aunque de vez en cuando recibo una herida y no puedo trabajar y eso quiere decir que no me pagan. Además, los trajes que llevo son carísimos – un traje de luces nuevo me cuesta tres mil euros.
Entrevistador:	En resumen, ¿es un trabajo que recomendarías a otros jóvenes?
Emilio:	Es un trabajo muy duro y caro, y tienes que sufrir antes de ser famoso. Pero, al fin y al cabo, para mí es el mejor trabajo del mundo.
Entrevistador:	Muchas gracias, Emilio.
Emilio:	De nada.

3 🎧 Listen to the interview with a bullfighter, Emilio Gutiérrez. Copy the table and fill in the missing information in English.

Play the recording one section at a time to allow students to deal with the questions section by section. You may wish to select some key phrases from the text to work on with students before they listen, either in a matching Spanish–English task or simply to encourage them to make an intelligent guess at the meaning of phrases which they hear you say before they have to pick them out from the longer audio.

The activity should serve to show students that they can understand key points and facts from listening even when the content includes some language that is difficult. Stress the importance of recognising tense endings and verb forms that work differently from English (e.g. *dinos* is an imperative, not a plural noun!).

Answers:

a	festival in his village
	12
	working on a farm
b	a bullfighting club in a nearby village
	He had very little money / didn't always get paid but had to cover his own expenses / didn't have enough money for meals; he spent all his time travelling around from town to town to take part in unofficial bullfights.
c	He won a big competition when he was 17.
	3000 euros
	It's hard, and you have to suffer if you want to succeed, but it is the best job in the world.

> The reminder about irregular adverbs can be presented in the context of examples from the reading texts. Luisa's text also includes *Lo peor es que* ... which you can pick up on for the secondary grammar point, comparative and superlative adverbs.
> The grammar point is practised in activity 4.
>
> **G**ramática

4 **G** Copy the following sentences and fill in the gaps with an appropriate irregular adverb from the list below.

You may wish to check students' understanding of the adverbs listed in this activity before they attempt it.

Answers:

1. mal
2. nunca
3. siempre
4. demasiado
5. poco

5 Make up a short description of a job, without mentioning the job itself. Read it out to the rest of the class to see whether they can guess what the job is.

Students can use the language structure box and the *Vocabulario* on page 161 for help with this task, and / or they can model their description on parts of the reading texts, but they should adapt and add to make the piece personal. The rest of the class may need to guess the job using English as well as Spanish.

> *Estrategia*
>
> This *Estrategia* reminds students to check the grammar in their written work, looking particularly at verb tenses and endings and at adjectival agreement. In the context of the *Gramática* on this spread, stress also that they must ask themselves whether a word is irregular – this applies mainly to verbs but also to some adverbs and others.
> This could be applied to the drafting work for activity 5 but is particularly important for the account students are asked to produce in activity 6.

6 Write an account of what would be your ideal job, giving a description of what it entails and why you would like it.

You may want to support students in this task by providing prompts to show them what points to cover, for example:

- workplace
- working hours
- pay
- training
- work colleagues.

The language structure box provides more ideas on how to construct their account. Students should follow the *Consejo* and use as wide a variety of adjectives as possible – they could make a list first. Once they have drafted their writing, they should refer to the *Estrategia* and check their text carefully to eliminate grammatical errors.

> *Consejo*
>
> Students are encouraged to use a wide range of adjectives to give their opinions, and should study the text for examples. Remind them also that they will score highly for correct use of impersonal verbs for expressing degrees of liking and interest.

Plenary activity

Work with the class to compile a questionnaire that could be used by a careers adviser working with 16-year-olds, asking them about the kind of work they would like. Encourage students to think about what question words they would use, and to come up with options for some multiple-choice questions, e.g.

¿Dónde te gustaría más trabajar?

a en una oficina
b al aire libre
c en casa

Pages 156–157

Reading and listening

Current and future jobs

- Audio files for core reading texts

Core reading text

The reading text *Prepárate para el mundo laboral* is an article giving step-by-step advice about how to prepare for the world of work.

The reading text is also available online as an audio file.

1 Read the text *Prepárate para el mundo laboral* and put these headings into the order which matches the advice given in the text.

Students need to understand that the headings do not repeat what is in the text, but reflect the general theme of each section.

Answers: **1** B, **2** D, **3** A, **4** E, **5** F, **6** C

> *Gramática*
>
> A brief reminder of how to use conjunctions and time expressions to add variety and to clarify the sequence of events. Refer to the reading text *Prepárate para el mundo laboral* and ask students to list all the expressions of time and other linking words that they can find.

2 Read the text *Enrique busca trabajo* and decide if the following statements are true (T), false (F) or not mentioned in the text (?).

Answers:

| 1 T | 2 F | 3 ? | 4 F | 5 T |
| 6 F | 7 ? | 8 F | 9 ? | 10 T |

Context 4 Work and education 105

3 Transcript:

Quisiera dejar un mensaje para Enrique Villa Blanco. Represento al ayuntamiento y hemos recibido su carta, Enrique, solicitando un trabajo como jardinero. Me alegro decirle que nos gustaría ofrecerle una entrevista este viernes a las dos de la tarde.

Para decirnos que ha recibido el mensaje y que le interesa el trabajo, por favor llámenos por teléfono o mándenos un correo electrónico. El número para llamar es 21-54-63 y pregunte por Conchita Alonso.

Por correo electrónico, se encuentra la dirección en la página web del ayuntamiento. Y una cosa, Enrique … no lleve ropa elegante, irá bien en vaqueros y camiseta … la entrevista estará en el jardín.

3 Listen to the phone message for Enrique. Answer the following questions in English.

Students listen to a phone message from Enrique's prospective employer inviting him for interview.

Answers:

1 From (someone at) the town hall.
2 Friday
3 2pm
4 Respond by phone or email.
5 21–54–63
6 Casual clothes, jeans and T-shirt are fine.

4 Transcript:

1 Parece exótico pero no lo es. Es como ser camarera, pero en el cielo. Claro que viajas a muchos países, pero normalmente vuelves en seguida y no tienes tiempo para visitar nada.
2 Es verdad que a veces el trabajo es muy peligroso porque tienes que entrar en edificios cuando hay un incendio. Pero tienes lo último de lo último en equipos para controlar el fuego y me gusta poder ayudar a la gente.
3 Creo que es un trabajo muy creativo, pero a veces también hay mucha presión porque estás preparando comida para cuarenta o cincuenta personas. Todas tienen hambre y no quieren esperar.
4 Hablo francés y español y las empresas utilizan mis servicios cuando tienen que escribir un documento formal en otro idioma o escribir a un cliente en otro país. Lo que más me gustaría sería traducir una novela.
5 Me gusta caminar y estar al aire libre así que es un trabajo que me va bien. No me importa empezar temprano por la mañana para recoger las cartas de Correos pero no me gusta ir a las casas donde hay un perro agresivo.

4 Listen to five people describing their jobs and match up each person with the correct job from the list below.

The *Vocabulario* on the page will help students to make these matches.

Answers: 1 E, 2 C, 3 G, 4 A, 5 D

Pages 158–159
Grammar practice

G Current and future jobs

Comparative and superlative adverbs

A reminder of how to form the comparative and superlative of adverbs, which students will practise in activity 1a.

1a The panel of interviewers is arguing over who to appoint for the job. Complete their arguments in the style of the example given.

Show the students how to imitate the content of the speech bubbles, with sentences about Isabel in the comparative form and sentences about Pablo in the superlative.

Answers:

1 Isabel respondió más fácilmente. Pero Pablo respondió lo más fácilmente.
2 Isabel se comportó más tímidamente. Pero Pablo se comportó lo más tímidamente.
3 Isabel pensó más profundamente. Pero Pablo pensó lo más profundamente.
4 Isabel escribió más simplemente. Pero Pablo escribió lo más simplemente.
5 Isabel contestó más seguramente. Pero Pablo contestó lo más seguramente.

1b Work in pairs. Have a competition with your partner to see how many adverbs you can each form in three minutes. Then check each other's lists to see if the adverbs have been formed correctly.

This activity could be scored: one point for each correctly spelled adverb, and an additional point for a correctly spelled adverb that your partner did not have on his / her list.

Possessive adjectives

A reminder about the purpose of possessive adjectives; students can refer to page 176 for a full listing of the forms.

2a Fill in the gaps with the correct possessive adjective.

Answers:

1 sus (*mis* would be logically possible also)
2 tus
3 nuestra
4 mis
5 vuestro
6 tu

2b Work in pairs. Partner A makes up five questions. The questions must include one of the words *tu* or *tus*. Partner B must reply in a full sentence, using either *mi* or *mis*. Then swap roles.

Make sure students understand the difference between *tú* and the possessive pronoun *tu* which they must use in the activity. The example shows how the role play should work, but you may wish to demonstrate another example before students begin, and / or display some key words from the current topic to give them ideas for questions, such as *trabajo, pago, horas de trabajo, prácticas, experiencia, ideal*.

> **Interrogatives with prepositions** *Gramática*
> A summary of word order when interrogatives are used with a preposition, to support activity 3.

3 Translate these sentences into English.
Answers:
1 What does the job involve / consist of?
2 Whose book is this?
3 To whom are you going to send this letter? (or, more realistically: Who are you going to send this letter to?)
4 By when do I have to finish the work / the job? (or, more realistically: When do I have to finish the work / the job by?)

> **Usted and ustedes** *Gramática*
> A reminder of when to use the formal *usted / ustedes* and that it requires the third person form of the verb, to support activities 4a and 4b.

4a An interviewer gives feedback to someone who has recently been for an interview. Copy the following text, replacing the pictures with the correct verb from the box below. The verbs are in the preterite, in the *usted* form.
Answers:

| a | habló | b | escuchó | c | leyó |
| d | escribió | e | pensó | f | preguntó |

4b Choose the correct form of the verb to match the person to whom the question is addressed.
Answers:
1 tienes   2 Puede   3 Eres
4 Quieres   5 fue   6 Envió

> **The relative adjective *cuyo*** *Gramática*
> A reminder of the meaning and use of *cuyo*, to support activity 5.

5 Copy the sentences and fill in the gaps with *cuyo, cuya, cuyos* or *cuyas*.
Answers:
1 cuyo   2 cuya   3 cuyas   4 cuyos

Pages 160–161

Vocabulary

V Current and future jobs

kerboodle! • MP3 files for each vocabulary list

The essential vocabulary used within Topic 2, Context 4 is presented on this vocabulary spread.

Here students can learn the key words for the topic area *Current and future jobs*. You may also want to direct students to the online audio files of these vocabulary lists, so they can hear how the words are pronounced by a native speaker.

Some words are in light grey on the vocabulary spreads in the Student Book. This indicates items that are not included in the GCSE specification vocabulary list, so students do not need to learn these items for Listening and Reading assessment. However, you may wish students to use them in Speaking and Writing Controlled Assessments.

Pages 162–165

Controlled Assessment

Refer to the section on Controlled Assessment, pages 107–112 in this Teacher's Book.

4 Context summary

kerboodle! • Interactive multiple-choice quiz

The closing page for Context 4, Work and education, provides a multiple-choice quiz which tests the key language learnt in this Context.

A longer version of this quiz is also available online as an interactive self-marking multiple-choice test.

Answers:
1 En mi colegio tenemos muchas instalaciones deportivas y hay un salón de actos impresionante. (variations acceptable: *tenemos* and *hay* are interchangeable, and each of them can go with either *instalaciones* or *un salón*)
2 The person has lost their art homework.
3 Estoy en contra de llevar uniforme porque es muy incómodo.
4 Creo que son muy **difíciles** y causan mucho estrés.
5 *Either* voy a estudiar *or* estudiaré
6 Student's own choice.
7 Student's own choice.
8 I have decided that it would be a good idea to leave school / college.
9 había
10 postman/woman (*cartero/a*)

Controlled Assessment

Controlled Assessment is probably the most convenient way of assessing students' progress. Teachers control when it is done, where and under what conditions. Students are not under immediate pressure to complete it and some of the research can be done at home.

Controlled Assessment allows centres to have more control over the content of the assessment. Teachers can choose between tasks provided by AQA or devise their own.

Centres who devise their own tasks create the opportunity for students to talk / write about topics of interest to them. The tasks are designed to be open-ended and can encompass a wide range of topics, including students' own learning experience in and out of the Spanish classroom. Making the assessment more individualised is more motivating for students.

In the Student Book we have provided examples of typical tasks for Speaking and Writing Controlled Assessment. They can be used in the classroom as practice for the Controlled Assessment part of the examination.

■ How to use the tasks

When students are ready to practise their Speaking and Writing skills within the Context they have studied, show them the tasks for that Context in the Student Book, and encourage discussion on how to approach them.

For Speaking Controlled Assessment, the specification requires that each of the points that make up the tasks must be developed. For Writing Controlled Assessment, it is the task only that needs to addressed for the purpose of the assessment. The points listed below Controlled Assessment Writing tasks in the Student Book are for guidance only therefore, but could be followed for constructing a suitable response.

As our Controlled Assessment tasks are designed to provide practice opportunity and guidance for students on how to construct suitable responses, we suggest that you go through each of the seven points listed for both Speaking and Writing, but highlight the distinction between Speaking and Writing regarding how these points should be used in the real Controlled Assessment scenario.

To access the highest marks in Controlled Assessment, students need to:

- use a good range of vocabulary
- give opinions
- use a range of time frames and / or tenses
- be accurate
- extend responses by developing ideas
- use a variety of structures
- use complex sentences
- use long sentences
- show initiative.

Ask students to study how the tasks are addressed in the Student Book and discuss how the ideas presented there are developed. Focus on just one of the points from the task under discussion as a starting point. Then ask students for four different ideas which they can incorporate into their response for this point. For example, the Controlled Assessment Writing task from Context 1, point 1 is: 'Say your age and what you look like'. The following ideas are suggested in the Student Book:

- give your age
- describe your hair and eyes
- describe your height and build
- give extra physical details (glasses / freckles, etc.).

Students should also be pointed to the Examiner's Tip, which will help them to formulate their response.

Invite students to offer further ideas and expand on those listed in the Student Book. For example, the fourth idea 'give extra physical details' could be expanded by adding the following details: How long have you worn glasses? What colour are your glasses?

Encourage students to:

- develop their ideas
- use connectives in order to have longer sentences
- give their opinion, using a variety of vocabulary and structures
- check accuracy – in this case, by looking at the use of the perfect tense in the grammar section of the Student Book.

Repeat the process for each idea and each point that make up the tasks. Have a group / class discussion exploring different ways of addressing the tasks.

■ Topic coverage of our tasks

Context 1 – Speaking	Health
Context 1 – Writing	Relationships and choices
Context 2 – Speaking	Holidays
Context 2 – Writing	Free time and the media
Context 3 – Speaking	The environment (plus an element of Context 1 – Health)
Context 3 – Writing	Home and local area (plus an element of Context 2 – Free time and the media)
Context 4 – Speaking	Current and future jobs (plus an element of Context 2 – Holidays)
Context 4 – Writing	School / college and future plans (plus an element of Context 1 – Health)

There are also two cross-Context tasks, one for Speaking and one for Writing.

Our Controlled Assessment tasks

Context 1 – Speaking	La vida sana
Context 1 – Writing	Mi familia, mis amigos y yo
Context 2 – Speaking	Las vacaciones
Context 2 – Writing	El tiempo libre
Context 3 – Speaking	El medio ambiente
Context 3 – Writing	Donde vivo
Context 4 – Speaking	Las prácticas laborales
Context 4 – Writing	Mi colegio
Cross-Context – Speaking	Mi vida
Cross-Context – Writing	¡Los jóvenes no somos así!

Please note that the Controlled Assessment tasks in the Student Book are designed as a teaching resource and not as an assessment tool. **They include levels of support and guidance which are not permissible in tasks used for assessment purposes.**

These tasks cannot, therefore, be submitted to AQA. For any tasks which you adapt from the tasks in the Student Book or which you devise for your students, the level of guidance and support must comply with the guidelines in the specification and in AQA's *Controlled Assessment Handbook*.

■ Online sample

Online you will find a sample answer for each of the tasks. They are not intended to be 'model' answers, but good answers, accompanied by a commentary that highlights what is good about them and also what could be improved upon.

The comments directly link to the assessment criteria and show students how to score well in the different criteria.

There are also further Examiner's Tips to help students tackle the tasks.

■ Speaking Controlled Assessment

Task setting – Limited Control

Although only one task will be submitted to AQA, students have to complete two Speaking tasks. The tasks should be untiered, in the form of dialogues, and different to the tasks covered for Writing Controlled Assessment.

Each Speaking task should have an unpredictable element (presented as an exclamation mark). Students, however, can (and should be) trained to predict the unpredictable! Given the context of the task, students should ask themselves: 'What can I realistically be asked at this point?' and come up with, say, four possibilities, one of which is likely to be the one that will actually be asked.

It is important to get students to practise the skill of working out what those possibilities might be.

Answers to those questions should then be prepared and incorporated in the 'plan' on the Task Planning Form.

As the 'plan' cannot exceed 40 words, it may be difficult to incorporate all four possible answers in it. Students may want to consider the use of visuals / pictures to account for the unpredictable element.

You can choose to use tasks devised by AQA or devise your own. Devising suitable tasks is not easy. In order to give students the chance to show what they can do, questions have to be open-ended so that they generate the sort of response that will get the best possible mark using the assessment criteria.

As tasks are untiered, they must be 'elastic' and therefore suitable for students of all abilities. A short and simple answer can be offered by Foundation Tier candidates and be appropriate. Similarly, a well developed answer has to be achievable by Higher Tier candidates.

Assessment in general should be an integral part of teaching and thus be interesting and motivating. You have to be aware of students' interests, lifestyles, personal experiences both at school and at home and build into the task the possibility of bringing those elements into the dialogue. Involving students personally in the dialogue will make the task taking experience more satisfying for students and probably increase their motivation to communicate and speak Spanish.

When devising tasks, you should also remember that students will not access certain marks in Range and Accuracy unless they can demonstrate the ability to refer to past, present and future events. Questions within the task should lead students to talk about their past experiences e.g. holidays, work experience, what they did last weekend, etc., as well as their intentions / hopes for the future (for example: work; holidays; what they will do next weekend, etc.).

Finally, students should be able to give their opinion on different matters and the wording of the task should lead them to do that. If the task is designed in a way that it should elicit a lot of personal information, students will have many opportunities to give their point of view.

Teachers are reminded that they can use the same tasks for two consecutive years only.

Task taking – Medium Control

All three stages below must be completed under informal supervision. This means that supervision must be sufficient to ensure that plagiarism does not take place.

The experience of task taking should replicate real-life situations. In real life, if you wanted to communicate a message to someone, you would prepare by having access to dictionaries, books and internet resources. You could also discuss with other people what you intend to say and use their advice to formulate your own message.

In practical terms, this means that class / group discussion should be encouraged in preparation for task taking but you should check that the students' responses to the task are individual. Moreover, if they think it necessary to do so, you should cross reference the work done by students who prepared for the task as a small group.

During the preparation, access to resources should not be limited.

Stage one: This is the teaching / learning stage. Students have not been given the task. Your involvement is not limited at this stage. Teachers are free to point students in the direction of suitable resources for the task and incorporate those resources in their teaching if they so wish.

Stage two: Stage two begins when students are given the task. You should discuss the task with the students. The task needs 'unpacking'. Typically, there will be 4–8 bullet points with questions in English. As students have to speak for 4–6 minutes, they are likely to be concerned about running out of things to say. The approach we have taken in the AQA GCSE Spanish course is to take one bullet point at a time and divide its content into four different ideas for developing and expanding the answer. The tasks, points and ideas presented in the Student Book are designed for students to practise this approach themselves, to implement when they are given their Controlled Assessment tasks. The working out of those four ideas for each point is a skill worth developing in the classroom as it equips students with enough material for them to carry out the task.

For example, in Context 3 Speaking:

A description of your region:

- say where you live and describe your area
- say where your home town is in relation to the nearest well-known city or where your neighbourhood is in relation to the centre or the airport
- describe the main features of your region, e.g. industrial, suburban, rural
- say which part of the country your region is in, e.g. north, south, east, west.

Each of the four points is open ended enough to allow students the opportunity to give a well developed answer. For example:

- Say where you live and describe your area. They could add whether they like living in the area, etc.
- Say where your home town is in relation to the nearest well-known city or where your neighbourhood is in relation to the centre or the airport. They could add information about the nearest city, etc.
- Describe the main features of your region, e.g. industrial, suburban, rural. They could add details about types of businesses and natural features, etc.
- Say which part of the country your region is in, e.g. north, south, east, west. They could add some information about what other areas in the country are like.

Having broken down the task into manageable questions, you can then discuss with students the kind of language they might need to use. That is not to say that you should give students ready-made phrases or structures as it would result in all students producing similar work and it would not be the students' individual responses to the task. What you should point out to students is the kind of vocabulary needed to cover a particular point. For example, helping round the house includes cooking, washing up, tidying your room, etc. You could also point out that in vocabulary lists, verbs are always given in the infinitive and that verb formation has to be considered. You could refer students to reference materials, for example: look in the grammar section for advice on how to form the perfect tense.

Having guided students through each bullet point that makes up the task, you can offer no more support.

It is then up to the students to prepare themselves for the task. They continue to have access to reference materials in and out of the classroom and can also continue to work with others for the rest of stage two. They write their 'plan' and submit it to their teacher for comment.

Stage three: The student produces the final task which is recorded and then marked by the teacher.

A task will last between 4 and 6 minutes. You should use your professional judgement in deciding whether to stop the dialogue with a particular student after 4 minutes or continue with it up to the maximum of 6 minutes.

Task marking – Medium Control

The mark scheme applies to each task. The criteria for assessment are: Communication (10 marks); Range and Accuracy of Language (10 marks); Pronunciation and Intonation (5 marks); Interaction and Fluency (5 marks). The total for a task is 30 marks.

Communication

This criterion focuses on the ability of students to:
- communicate a good amount of information
- develop answers
- express opinions and points of view.

You will have to interpret terms such as a 'good amount' and a 'reasonable amount' of information, 'regularly' and sometimes 'developed' answers. The marks awarded in the other three criteria cannot be more than one band higher than the mark awarded for Communication. The mark awarded for Communication can therefore affect the marks awarded in the other criteria. For instance, a candidate saying little but in complex Spanish delivered accurately and fluently would not score a very high mark. It is worth pointing out to candidates that it is essential to give a lot of information to gain a high mark.

Marked exemplar work is available from AQA to assist teachers in this work.

Range and Accuracy of Language

Range of Language

Candidates producing
- isolated words will score 1 or 2 marks
- short, simple sentences will score 3 or 4 marks
- generally simple sentences will score 5 or 6 marks
- complex structures and a variety of tenses will score 7 to 10 marks

Accuracy

Candidates
- who make errors that often impede communication will score 1 or 2 marks
- who make frequent errors (many of which do not impede communication) will score 3 or 4 marks
- whose Spanish is more accurate than inaccurate will score 5 or 6 marks
- who make occasional errors will score 7 or 8 marks
- whose errors usually appear only in more complex structures will score 9 or 10 marks

Both Range and Accuracy have to be taken into account to award a mark in this criterion.

Pronunciation and Intonation

What candidates have to do to score in this criterion is fairly explicit. However, what is understandable to a Modern Languages teacher is not necessarily what a Spanish native speaker who does not speak English would understand. It is the latter that matters!

Interaction and Fluency

The key ideas in this criterion are: Interaction; Initiative; Hesitancy.

A candidate who has scored well in Communication because he / she has developed answers and therefore given a good amount of information is likely to score well in this criterion too (as long as he / she is not hesitant in his / her delivery).

Initiative can be demonstrated by moving the conversation on to another area that is still relevant to the original question asked. For example: ¿Cómo es tu región?. *Es una región bonita y verde* (direct answer) *y hay mucha agricultura* (development). If the candidate then adds for instance *y pueblos bonitos con casas antiguas de piedra*, that is showing initiative. The candidate was not asked about that but chose to include it in his / her answer. It is linked to the development and relevant to the original question.

Internal standardisation of marking

Schools must standardise their marking to make sure that all candidates have been marked to the same standard. Note that AQA will also hold annual meetings for teachers to provide support in developing tasks and applying the marking criteria.

■ Writing Controlled Assessment

Task setting – Limited Control

What is required of the student is two different types of task. These two tasks will ensure that students demonstrate the ability to use language for different purposes. They will be untiered and different to the tasks covered for the Speaking Controlled Assessment.

You can choose to use tasks devised by AQA or devise your own.

There is no unpredictable element in Writing.

For advice and comments on how to devise an appropriate task, see Speaking Controlled Assessment – Task setting.

Task taking – High Control

Stage one: See Speaking Controlled Assessment: Task taking – Stage one.

Stage two: See Speaking Controlled Assessment: Task taking – Stage two.

It is the task itself which is important. If a student does not address all the bullet points, this will not automatically be reflected in their mark.

Teachers can offer students feedback on their 'plan' but this feedback can only relate to the extent to which students are meeting the requirements of the task.

Stage 3: Students produce the final version of the task and are allowed up to 60 minutes to complete each task.

- Students aiming at grades G–D should produce 200–350 words across the two tasks.
- Students aiming at grades C–A* should produce 400–600 words across the two tasks.

Students will be in the direct sight of the supervisor (exam conditions) at all times when writing up the final version.

Task marking

AQA marks the Writing part of the Controlled Assessment.

Frequently asked questions (FAQs) by candidates: Speaking

1 How many tasks do I have to complete for the speaking part of my GCSE Spanish?

There are two tasks, both of a similar kind. Your teacher will ask you the questions and listen to your answers. One of your tasks will be recorded as it may have to be submitted to AQA. Each task lasts between 4 and 6 minutes. The Speaking test counts for 30% of the whole GCSE Spanish – so, each of the two speaking tasks is worth 15%.

2 When do the tasks have to be done?

There is no specified time for the completion of the tasks. When your teacher thinks that you have been taught the language you need to complete a particular task and feels that you are ready, you will be given the task to prepare. It could be a task designed by AQA or a task designed by Spanish teachers in your school. Your teacher will decide how long you are allowed to prepare for the task (but it cannot be more than 6 hours).

3 Who will mark my work?

Your teacher will mark your work. A Moderator (i.e. an examiner) will sample the work of your school and check that it has been marked correctly. A Team Leader will check the work of the Moderator. The Principal Moderator will check the work of the Team Leader. The Chief Examiner will check the work of the Principal Moderator. This complicated but secure system ensures that candidates are given the correct mark.

4 What am I allowed to write on my plan?

You are allowed to write a maximum of 40 words on your plan. These words can be in Spanish or in English. Choose them carefully so that your plan works well as an aide-memoire. Remember that you are not allowed to use conjugated verbs (i.e. verbs with an ending other than the infinitive or the past participle) on your plan. Codes, letters or initialled words are not allowed. There is no limit to the number of visuals you can use, and you can mix visuals and words if you wish.

5 What help is allowed from the moment I am given the task to prepare?

Your teacher is allowed to discuss the task in English with you, including the kind of language you may need and how to use your preparatory work. You can have access to a dictionary, your Spanish books and internet resources. This is the stage when you will prepare your plan using the Task Planning Form. You will then give this form to your teacher who will give you feedback on how you have met the requirements of the task. When you actually perform the task, you will only have access to your plan and your teacher's comments (i.e. the Task Planning Form).

6 How can I prepare for the unpredictable element (the exclamation mark)?

Ask yourself: What question would logically follow the questions I have already answered? Practise guessing what the unpredictable bullet point might be about. You are likely to come up with two or three possibilities. Prepare answers to cover those possibilities. Practise your possible responses. When you are asked the question, focus on the meaning of the question itself to make sure you understand it and then give it your full answer.

7 How best can I practise for the test?

Treat each bullet point as a mini-task. Practise your answer to one bullet point at a time. With the use of your plan, say your answer aloud for what is illustrated by one word on your plan. Repeat the process for each word on your plan. Next, try to account for two words, then for three words, etc. Time your answer for one whole bullet point. Repeat the process for each bullet point. Always practise saying things aloud. Record yourself if possible.

8 Does it matter that my verbs are wrong as long as I can get myself understood?

Communication can break down because of poor grammatical accuracy. If that happens, you will lose marks in Communication and also in Accuracy. If you give the correct message but grammatical accuracy is poor, you will only lose marks in Accuracy. Communication is of primary importance, of course, but the quality of that communication matters too and is enhanced by grammatical accuracy.

9 How do I make sure I get the best possible marks for my answers?

You will score well in the Speaking test if:

- you say a lot that is relevant to the question
- you have a good range of vocabulary
- you can include complex structures
- you can refer to present, past and future events
- your Spanish accent is good
- you can speak fluently
- you can show initiative
- you can speak with grammatical accuracy.

10 How will my mark be affected if my Spanish accent is not very good?

You will receive a mark for Pronunciation. However, as long as your spoken Spanish is understandable, your Communication mark will not suffer.

11 What will I gain by giving long answers?

Consider the task as an opportunity for you to show off what you can do in Spanish. Offer long answers whenever possible, develop the points you are trying to make, give your opinion and justify that opinion as appropriate, etc. As a general rule, the more Spanish you speak, the more credit you will be given (provided that what you say is relevant and understandable).

12 What does speaking with fluency mean?

Fluency is your ability to speak without hesitation. Try and speak with fluency but not too fast. If you are likely to be nervous when performing the task, practise it and practise it again. Time your whole response. Make a point of slowing down if you feel that you are speaking too fast. Practise with your plan in front of you so that you know what you are going to say next and therefore do not hesitate when delivering your contribution to the dialogue.

13 What does showing initiative mean?

Showing initiative does not mean that you suddenly ask your teacher 'What about you, where did you go on holiday?' (although you could do that!). You are generally expected to answer questions. For instance, for a question like ¿Te gusta el fútbol? you would first answer it directly then try to develop your answer e.g. Sí, me gusta el fútbol. A mí me gusta también la natación.

Showing initiative means that you take the conversation elsewhere in a way that is connected to your answer and still relevant to the original question e.g. Normalmente los sábados

Controlled Assessment **111**

jugamos al fútbol, pero a veces juego al baloncesto con mi hermano y sus amigos. You were not asked about basketball. You decided to add it to your response. It is relevant, linked to what you were asked and follows your developed answer quite naturally. That is showing initiative. Use it to extend your answers and therefore show off extra knowledge of Spanish.

4 Why is it important to refer to present, past and future events?

If you are aiming at a grade C, you will need to use a variety of structures, and you may include different time frames and make reference to past and future events in your spoken language. To achieve grade A, you will be expected to use a variety of verb tenses.

5 How many bullet points are there in each task?

There are typically between five and eight bullet points. One of the bullet points will be the unpredictable element and will appear on your task as an exclamation mark. All bullet points will be written in English.

6 Will I be asked questions which are not written in the task?

That is possible. Although you will have prepared the task thoroughly and will have a lot to say, your teacher may want you to expand or give further details on particular points you have made. You must listen to your teacher's questions attentively as you will have to understand his / her questions in the first place.

7 What will happen if I run out of things to say?

If you are well prepared, you will use up all of the time with your answers to the questions on the task card, including the unpredictable question. However, if you run out of things to say, your teacher will ask you further questions, linked to the ones written on your card and will make the task last 4 minutes, i.e. the minimum amount of time.

8 What will happen if I speak for longer than the maximum time allowed?

Whatever you say after the 6 minutes have elapsed will not be taken into account when your work is marked. You will not be penalised in any way but equally you won't get any credit for it.

9 When preparing for the task, should I allow the same amount of time for each question?

There may be questions that you consider easier to deal with than others and on which you will have more to say. Give yourself an answering time to specific questions. Consider each question to be a task in itself. The whole task will probably seem to be more manageable if you do that.

20 What is the point of a plan?

It is the only support you will have in front of you when you perform the task. It is something that allows you not to have to rely on your memory in order to know what you should be saying next.

21 What happens to my Task Planning Form after the test?

Your Spanish teacher will look after it until the end of October, after which it can be destroyed.

22 How do I prepare developed answers?

You will mostly be asked open-ended questions e.g. *¿Cómo es tu barrio?* As you are rewarded for using a lot of Spanish, develop all your answers if at all possible. In this case, you would say what you do after school, what you do in the evenings, at the weekend. Add extra details such as your opinion, then you could justify that opinion, give examples of your activities in the past and explain what you would like to do in the future. The list of possible extensions to a basic answer can be very long. Give a full answer to the question but, as a general rule, don't take longer than one minute to do so.

23 Is referring to the three time frames the same as using the present, past and future tenses?

You can certainly use the tenses to refer to the three time frames. However, there are other ways which you may find easier to handle, particularly with reference to the future. You can use *me gustaría, voy a, espero* – all are followed by a verb in the infinitive.

24 How can I show a good range of vocabulary?

Vary your vocabulary as much as possible. For instance, don't repeat the same phrases to express or justify your opinion e.g. *porque*. Don't overuse *hay*. Show off the Spanish you have learnt. In your preparatory work, use all the resources at your disposal.

25 Should I keep to simple Spanish in order to ensure accuracy?

If you are not sure what range of language you may be able to cope with, start by preparing a fairly simple answer, and when you are confident that you can remember that, see what additions you can make which might increase your grade.

26 How do I know that I am using complex language?

At a fairly simple level, you can link sentences using *porque, y, pero,* etc. You can also show that you can manage structures that are different from the English equivalent, e.g. *Vivo en Madrid desde hace tres años* shows that you are aware that you should use the present tense with *desde hace* in order to say that you have been living in Madrid for three years. The equivalent English verb structure implies that the living process started in the past (I have ...) and is continuing now (-ing ending).

Another example of complexity: *Los compré en Barcelona. Los* in this case means 'them' and occurs before the verb concerned. In English, the word 'them' appears after the relevant verb.

There are countless examples of complexity you could include in your responses. Select those you can cope with and use them appropriately and accurately.

27 Why should I take great care when using a dictionary?

a Words often have more than one meaning, for example: 'the landing'. It could be a place in your house but it could also be the landing of a plane. Choose well!

b Verbs are only given in the infinitive form in the dictionary. They have to be given their correct form depending on what you want to say. For example: 'I worked' is *he trabajado*. Generally, use the infinitive form when you mean to say 'to do' / 'to work' / 'to say', etc. For example: *Voy a trabajar* = 'I am going to work'.

c Adjectives have to agree with the nouns that they describe. In the dictionary, you will find the masculine singular part e.g. *tímido* = shy, but if you want to talk about something feminine, you need to change this e.g. *Mi hermana es tímida* (the feminine form of *tímido*).

28 Should I frequently give my opinion and justify it?

Give your opinion frequently but phrase it in different ways. Using *Me gusta ... porque ...* is very repetitive and does not show that you know a lot of Spanish. Offering an opinion is a way of developing your answer to a question. There are other ways of expanding on your answer, e.g. by adding extra details, by describing, by explaining, by comparing, etc. Use as many strategies as possible to show that your knowledge of Spanish is not limited.

Frequently asked questions (FAQs) by candidates: Writing

1 How many writing tasks do I have to complete and what proportion of my Spanish GCSE is the writing test?

You have to complete two writing tasks. The tasks can be those provided by AQA, although your Spanish teachers have the option of devising their own tasks if they so wish. As in the speaking, the two tasks count for 30% of your grade (15% for each writing task).

2 How much time do I have to complete the final version of a task?

You will be given 60 minutes in one session to complete the final version of a task. It will be done under the direct supervision of your teacher. You will not be allowed to interact with others.

3 What resources will I be able to use on the day?

You can have access to a dictionary. You will also have the task itself, your plan and your teacher's feedback on your plan. These will be on the AQA Task Planning Form. That is all. You cannot use your exercise book or textbook or any drafts you may have written to help you practise.

4 What am I allowed to write on my plan?

Much the same as you are allowed in your plan for Speaking, i.e. a maximum of 40 words, no conjugated verbs or codes. You also have the option of using visuals instead of, or as well as words, in your Task Planning Form. Your teacher will comment on your plan, using the AQA Task Planning Form. Make sure you take that information on board before you write the final version.

5 How many words am I expected to write for each task?

Students aiming at grades G–D should produce 200–350 words across the two tasks, i.e. 100–175 words per task.

Students aiming at grades C–A* should produce 400–600 words across the two tasks, i.e. 200–300 words per task.

6 Can I write a draft?

You may produce a draft but this is for your use only. Your teacher cannot comment on it and you cannot have access to any draft when you write the final version. You must produce your draft under the supervision of your teacher.

7 What do I have to do to gain the best possible mark?

You will score well if:

- you communicate a lot of relevant information clearly
- you can explain ideas and points of view
- you have a good range of vocabulary
- you can include complex structures
- you can write long sentences
- you can refer to past, present and future events
- you can write with grammatical accuracy
- you organise your ideas well.

You will have noticed that there are similarities between the ways Writing and Speaking are assessed. As most of the points above are discussed in the FAQs for Speaking, you are advised to read the answers again, before you embark on your first task.

8 When will I do the tasks?

When your teacher has taught you the necessary language for you to complete a task, you will be given the task to prepare. You may be asked to do a plan using the Task Planning Form. You will get some feedback on your plan from your teacher at that point on how you have met the requirements of the task. The final version will be done after that, under the direct supervision of your teacher.

9 How many bullet points are there in each task?

Typically between five and eight. Make sure you prepare for and write about each one.

10 Who will mark my work?

Your teacher will not mark the writing part of your GCSE Spanish. Your work will be sent to an examiner from the AQA Examination Board and he / she will award you a mark for your two tasks. In order to ensure fairness, that examiner will be monitored by a Team Leader whose marking, in turn, will be monitored by the Principal Examiner who will himself / herself be monitored by the Chief Examiner. As you will have realised by now, the same measures are taken for all the components of your GCSE Spanish exam to make sure that you are given the correct mark for your work.

11 How can I act upon the advice given to me by my teacher on the AQA Task Planning Sheet?

From the general advice given on the Task Planning Sheet, you should take another look at your work and try to improve it. When you are satisfied that you have done as much as you can about your teacher's comments, you may have to amend your plan accordingly. If there is a part of the task that you think might be difficult to deal with on the day of the final version, you may want to learn the Spanish for that part.

12 My handwriting is poor. Is that a problem?

Examiners can only credit what they can actually read. If your handwriting is so poor that there is a risk of you losing marks because of it, you may want to consider the possibility of word processing your work. Discuss that possibility with your Spanish teacher before the day of the final version. If you word process the final version, you will not have access to an online spell check, translator or foreign language grammar aid.

13 Are there marks given for spelling and punctuation?

There are no marks for punctuation. Although spelling is not assessed as an individual element, it is part of Accuracy, which is assessed. Moreover, if spelling is so poor that it prevents communication from taking place, it might also affect your mark for Content.

14 What if I forgot my plan on the day of the final version?

Unfortunately, you would have to do without it!